What is Media Archaeology?

Jussi Parikka

polity

The right of Jussi Parikka to be identified as Author of this Work has been asserted in accordance with the UK Copyright, Designs and Patents Act 1988.

First published in 2012 by Polity Press
Reprinted 2012

Polity Press
65 Bridge Street
Cambridge CB2 1UR, UK

Polity Press
350 Main Street
Malden, MA 02148, USA

ISBN-13: 978-0-7456-5025-8
ISBN-13: 978-0-7456-5026-5(pb)

A catalogue record for this book is available from the British Library.

Typeset in 10.5 on 12 pt Times
by Toppan Best-set Premedia Limited
Printed and bound in Great Britain by MPG Printgroup

The publisher has used its best endeavours to ensure that the URLs for external websites referred to in this book are correct and active at the time of going to press. However, the publisher has no responsibility for the websites and can make no guarantee that a site will remain live or that the content is or will remain appropriate.

Every effort has been made to trace all copyright holders, but if any have been inadvertently overlooked the publisher will be pleased to include any necessary credits in any subsequent reprint or edition.

For further information on Polity, visit our website: www.politybooks.com

Contents

List of Images   *page* vi

Acknowledgements   vii

1   Introduction: Cartographies of the Old and the New   1
2   Media Archaeology of the Senses: Audiovisual, Affective,
    Algorithmic   19
3   Imaginary Media: Mapping Weird Objects   41
4   Media Theory and New Materialism   63
5   Mapping Noise and Accidents   90
6   Archive Dynamics: Software Culture and Digital Heritage   113
7   Practising Media Archaeology: Creative Methodologies for
    Remediation   136
Conclusions: Media Archaeology in Digital Culture   159

Notes   168
Bibliography   181
Index   197

Images

1.1 The Vintage Internet from the 2010 marketing campaign.
Maximidia Vintage Ads. Reproduced with permission from
Moma Propaganda.   4

2.1 The Maxim Captive Flying Machines from 1904
in Blackpool.   26

2.2 A foldout stereoscope, *c*.1870. Image reprinted with
permission from the Bill Douglas Centre, University
of Exeter, UK.   29

3.1 Gebhard Sengmüller's *A Parallel Image* installation (2009).
Image courtesy of Gebhard Sengmüller.   42

3.2 Illustration from Albert Robida, *Le vingtième siècle*.   50

3.3 A still from Zoe Beloff's *The Ideoplastic Materializations
of Eva C*. Reproduced with permission.   54

4.1 Machine from the Berlin Humboldt University Media-
Archaeological Fundus/Archive. Used with permission.   65

5.1 Helmholtz's sound analyser at the Lille Curiosités
Acoustiques exhibition, 2010 (Musée d'histoire naturelle
de Lille).   93

5.2 The Shannon model of communication as a diagram that
includes noise as an essential part of any communication
situation. Redrawn by Ian Bennett.   96

5.3 The volcanograph electric bomb from *Lightning Flashes
and Electric Dashes* 1877.   108

6.1 The Media-Archaeological Fundus/Archive as part of the
Berlin Humboldt University Institute for Media Studies.
Image © Lina Franke. Used with permission.   131

7.1 An image from the German theorist and artist David
Link's installation *LoveLetters_1.0*, (2009), of the early
generative-text program on the Manchester University
computer (1948). Reproduced courtesy of David Link:
www. alpha60.de/LoveLetters/2009_zkm/   138

7.2 Paul DeMarinis's *Rome to Tripoli* installation assemblage.
Image courtesy of Raitis Smits, RIXC The Centre for New
Media Culture.   142

7.3 Rosa Menkman's *The Collapse of PAL* performance.
Image courtesy of Rosa Menkman.   153

Acknowledgements

What makes books happen? A lot of great colleagues, whether in the same institution, or through other networks; several discussions on- and off-topic; things you consume through your eyes and brains, but also the gut. It takes a lot of words, and lots of deleted words; some spoken out loud, some just hidden in a file that you never opened again. A lot of things are forgotten, and some get overemphasized. And in the end, it comes down to a big list of thank-yous – at the beginning.

Mine go to people and institutions for funding, and support.

Institutionally, I want to thank the Anglia Ruskin University sabbatical fund, the Science Museum short fellowship programme, and the Alexander von Humboldt Foundation for guaranteeing me time to work on this. I enjoyed working at various institutions from Anglia Ruskin to the London Science Museum, Humboldt University Media Studies to my new job at Winchester School of Art.

Institutions consist of walls, rooms, routines, procedures, protocols, passwords, inductions and paperwork. Some of them don't have walls, and I found useful, for instance, such collections as: Gallica, Archive.org, Google Books, and the Virtual Laboratory resources on "Experimentalization of Life"' (Max Planck, Berlin).

I also gave talks in various places – an appreciative thank-you for having me talk about media archaeology goes at least to: De Montfort University, University of Bedfordshire, Wayne State University, University of Wisconsin-Milwaukee, Berlin Humboldt University, Anglia Ruskin and University of Malmö.

But what keeps institutions (and me) alive are people. I owe so much to so many. I'm not sure even where to begin so I'll start in the middle. My warmest thanks to: Wolfgang Ernst, Pasi Väliaho, Milla Tiainen, Teemu Taira, Sean Cubitt, Doug Kahn, Shintaro Miyazaki, Paul Feigelfeld, Christina Vagt, Lina Franke, Gebhard Sengmüller, Zoe Beloff, David Link, Ian Bennett, Wanda Strauven, Arne Kjell Vikhagen, Eivind Røssaak, Trond Lundemo, Garnet Hertz, Alex Galloway, Edwin Carels, Michael Dieter, David M. Berry, Robin Boast, Matthew Kirschenbaum, Seb Franklin, Jaakko Suominen, Nina Wenhart, Paul Caplan, Shannon Mattern, Brendan Howell and Tina Kendall. Also, a lot of folks on Twitter were instrumental in giving feedback or just hints and links. The comments of the several referees who read the manuscript were most useful in their feedback.

A special thank-you goes to Professor Erkki Huhtamo for the collaboration on our earlier joint project *Media Archaeology*. That project provided much inspiration, and ideas that were actualized in the book you are currently holding in your hand.

In terms of this book, I owe so much to my fantastic research assistants during this project: in Cambridge, Karolina Krawiecz, and in Berlin, Matthias Wannhoff. Further thanks go to Sebastian Döring for facilitating access to the Media Archaeological Fundus in Berlin.

Equally big thanks go also to the wonderful Polity Press team: Andrea Drugan, Lauren Mulholland and others.

But media archaeology does not take place only in archives, cellars, lecture rooms or even universities; address spaces for this book included Cambridge, London and Berlin; the Al-Hamra café as well as the Osswald, and a number of parks (of which the loveliest for me will always be Volkspark Friedrichshain).

One more set of thank-yous goes to the disco *partizanis* who dance as vibrantly as their new materialist and media theory and design flows: Ilona, Kaisa, Matleena, Pasi and, of course, Milla, whose version of Marilyn-Monroe-turned-new materialist is unique and, for me, lovely.

Chapter 5 of this book was originally published in *Media Archaeology: Approaches, Applications, Implications*, edited by Erkki Huhtamo and Jussi Parikka (Berkeley, CA: University of California Press, 2011). It is here republished in a modified form – thank you to the University of California Press for permission to use it again.

In the midst of post-riot London, September 2011

1

Introduction: Cartographies of the Old and the New

Steam punk subculture seems to be emblematic of important cultural desires circulating at the moment, in the midst of our high-technology culture. Expressed in various forms ranging from stylized nineteenth-century-inspired garments to weird inventions that mix the Victorian age with 21st-century themes, as well as a strong Do-It-Yourself (DIY) spirit, the steam punk style is much more than a quirky bunch of people who wear corsets while building mad scientific experiments such as a home-made Jacob's ladder. In a transdisciplinary spirit, the *Steampunk Magazine* describes itself as 'a journal of fashion, music, misapplied technology and chaos. And fiction'.[1] It is a bag of mixed interests and hobbyist activities, as well as curiosity for technological knowledge that does not fall in with the usual sublimated way of approaching science and technology through simple linear progress myths that see old technology as just obsolete and uninteresting.

As a spin-off from cyberpunk science fiction, steampunk (hats off to *The Difference Engine* novel from 1990, and a range of other literary products and computer games) imagines in new ways the steam-engined machine worlds of the Victorian era which marked the birth of modern technological culture, as well as the punk-influenced spirit of tinkering, *bricolage* and fascination with mad science, experimental technologies and the curiosity cabinets that such worlds offer. Indeed, steam punk occupies various worlds at the same time: combining the spirit of open source and hacker cultures that is part of the current punkish way of DIY in software and hardware cultures with a strong historical curiosity for earlier phases of intensive technologization and wide participation in actual production processes.[2] It is not interested in coming up with universalizing models for technological progress, but in experimenting with alternatives, in quirky ideas, in excavating novel paths that fall outside the mainstream.[3]

Steam punk is also a good symbol for the media-archaeological spirit of thinking the new and the old in parallel lines, and cultivating enthusiasm for media, technology and science through aesthetics, politics and other fields of critical inquiry. Even if at the risk of postmodern nostalgia (see Jameson 1989) or celebrating exactly what has been lost in the midst of increasingly closed black-box consumer mediascapes, steam punk is branded by an active tinkerer spirit. In a similar way to the steam punk DIY spirit, media archaeology has been keen to focus on the nineteenth century as a foundation stone of modernity in terms of science, technology and the birth of media capitalism. Media archaeology has been interested in excavating the past in order to understand the present and the future. Yet it is not only interested in writing historical narratives. It has always been quite theoretically informed, open to recent cultural theoretical discussions and borrows as happily from film studies and media arts as it does from the historical set of methodologies. Media archaeology has never been only a pure academic endeavour, but, from its early phases in the 1980s and 1990s, has also been a field in which media artists have been able to use themes, ideas and inspiration from past media too in order to investigate what the newness in 'new media' means.

This book is called *What is Media Archaeology?* and it sets out to elaborate the potentials of the media-archaeological method in digital culture research. As such, it is not an archaeology *of* digital culture. We *do* need many more critical archaeologies of post-World War II cultures of computing; software and design; the institutionalization and commercialization of software production as well as open source; the military-industrial complex behind the emergence of network culture; the formations of creative labour and work inherently connected to new forms of production; alternative media that emerged from open source as well as hacktivists engaging in hardware hacking and circuit bending – but this book does not exclusively focus on such topics. (On archaeologies of software, see Alt 2011; Wardrip-Fruin 2011; Manovich 2001). Instead, it offers an insight into *how to think media archaeologically* in contemporary culture, and maps the various theories, methods and ideas that give us guidance on how to do that. Media archaeology is introduced as a way to investigate the new media cultures through insights from past new media, often with an emphasis on the forgotten, the quirky, the non-obvious apparatuses, practices and inventions. In addition, as argued in this book, it is also a way to analyse the regimes of memory and creative practices in media culture – both theoretical and artistic. Media archaeology sees media cultures as sedimented and layered, a fold of time and materiality where the past might be suddenly discovered anew, and the new technologies grow obsolete increasingly fast.

It is easy to see how media archaeology fits into a wider cultural situation where vintage is considered better than the new, Super-8 and 8-bit sounds are objects of not only nostalgia but also revival and retrocultures seem to be as natural a part of the digital-culture landscape as high-definition screen technology and super-fast broadband. Death of media is mourned: the discontinuation of production of the Technics 1200 vinyl turntable (1972–2010), or the Sony Walkman (1978–2010); lost formats from magnetic tapes to floppy disks of various sizes have their own preservation enthusiasts; abandonware like games from the early 1990s is living a zombie life on the Internet; and media consumption practices are becoming retro too – for instance, the recently emerged vinyl listening clubs in London where the whole of the vinyl record is played non-interrupted in a nearly religiously meditative retro-fashion.[4] Partly this can be explained by the personal attachment that the current young consuming middle-class (now in their 30s–40s) who were the first generation to grow up in the midst of personal computers and gaming, handheld devices, Walkmans and other 1970s and 1980s electronics, have to such popular culture of their youth. Donkey Kong, Pac Man and Tetris still have a special place in several hearts (and hands) and some of the reuses and communities – for example, around cassettes – has found a new life with the Internet and on smartphones and i-Pads (see Cramer 2010; Suominen 2008). Tetris-inspired furniture Tat-ris, by the designer Gaenkoh, captures some of the affective nostalgia, as do music rewirings through the circuit-bending activities of the Modified Toy Orchestra (www. modifiedtoyorchestra.com), in which you are not sure whether you are dealing with the old or the new in music technologies.

That *new media remediates old media* (Bolter and Grusin 1999) seems an intuitive way to understand this cultural situation in which notions of old and new at times become indistinct. New media might be here and slowly changing our user habits, but old media never left us. They are continuously remediated, resurfacing, finding new uses, contexts, adaptations. In the midst of talk of 'dead media' by such writers as Bruce Sterling, it was clear that a lot of dead media were actually zombie-media: living deads, that found an afterlife in new contexts, new hands, new screens and machines. In the globalized information cultures so often described in terms of speeding up and temporalities surpassing those of our human perceptional possibilities, a fascination also with the past seems to be emerging.

Image 1.1 The Vintage Internet from the 2010 marketing campaign. Maximidia Vintage Ads. Reproduced by permission of MOMA Propaganda.

So perhaps this is a book of zombies, of the living dead of media culture, which specifically touches on media archaeology as a theory and methodology of digital media culture. This book offers both an outline of the crucial debates within media archaeology and cognate disciplines of academic and media artistic interest and some new directions in which to develop media archaeology as a set of theories, methods and ways to understand the mediatization of cultures of memory as well as the dynamics of old and new media. It offers insights into new media and old media in parallel lines and extends into discussions concerning the various – at times contradictory and competing – strands of media-archaeological investigations. Where do you start when you begin thinking media archaeologically? Do you start with past media, like a 'proper' historian? Or from our own current world of media devices, software, platforms, networks, social media, plasma screens and such, like a 'proper' analyst of digital culture would? The proposition of this book is that you start in the middle – from the entanglement of past and present, and accept the complexity this decision brings with it to any analysis of modern media culture. In this context, this is a book on the pasts and futures, the past-futures and future-pasts, as well as parallel sidelines of media archaeology. It maps the key contexts from which this brand of media theory and methodology emerged, but also argues that it needs continuously to renew itself in relation to emerging questions concerning digital culture, memory and technical media.

Media archaeology – multiple backgrounds

Media archaeology has stemmed from various directions. These include inspiration offered by the studies in archaeologies of power and knowledge of Michel Foucault (1926–84), the early excavations into the rubbles of modernity by Walter Benjamin (1892–1940), New Film History in the 1980s, as well as the various studies that, since the 1990s, have sought to understand digital and software cultures with the help of the past, a layered 'unconscious' of technical media culture. Yet, we need to be prepared to refresh media archaeology itself. So far, outside the collection *Media Archaeology* (Huhtamo and Parikka 2011), even summaries of theoretical work and mapping of crucial debates have been missing (however, forthcoming is Strauven 2012). But in addition to such an important task of mapping its multiple histories, we also need to develop it as a methodology for critical media studies as well as think through its ties with archival institutions. One of the crucial themes, as we will see later in the book, is to outline the centrality of the archive for media studies as has been done for philosophy and cultural theory (see, for instance, Derrida 1996; Didi-Huberman and Ebeling 2007).

However, we need to identify some key points from media-archaeological research – themes that have offered centres of gravity for such sets of theories and methods. Articulated by a range of theorists such as Erkki Huhtamo, Siegfried Zielinski, Thomas Elsaesser, Friedrich Kittler, Anne Friedberg, Tom Gunning, Lev Manovich and Laurent Mannoni, as well as several even earlier writers such as Walter Benjamin, Siegfried Giedion (1888–1968), Aby Warburg (1866–1929), Marshall McLuhan (1911–80) and others, the archaeological rumblings in media pasts and presents in parallel lines have been branded by multiplicity.

Traditionally, two theorists have stood out: Michel Foucault and Friedrich A. Kittler. Foucault's contribution to the archaeology of knowledge and culture was to emphasize it as a methodology for excavating *conditions of existence*. Archaeology here means digging into the background reasons why a certain object, statement, discourse or, for instance in our case, media apparatus or use habit is able to be born and be picked up and sustain itself in a cultural situation. Kittler builds on Foucault's ideas and has demanded a more media technological understanding of such archaeological work: such conditions of existence not only are discursive, or institutional, but relate to media networks, as well as scientific discoveries. Kittler wanted to look at technical media in the way Foucault was reading archives of books and written documents. What if we start to read media technology in the same way that Foucault exposed cultural practices and discourses to an analysis of how they were born and made possible in certain settings? Of course, such archaeological questions are closely related to what Foucault later started to call 'genealogy'. Here, the emphasis was more on questions of 'descent' and critique of origins as found in historical analysis of his time, and it spurred a lot of research that was keen to look for neglected genealogies and minor traits of history: histories of women, perversions, madness and so forth – counter-histories. In this manner, a lot of media-archaeologically tuned research has been in writing counter-histories to the mainstream media history, and looking for an alternative way to understand how we came to the media cultural situation of our current digital world. It is for media archaeologists as it was for Foucault: all archaeological excavations into the past are meant to elaborate our current situation.

Foucault and Kittler are just two examples of theorists who have had a crucial impact on media archaeology theory. Any attempt to impose unity on the canon of media-archaeological works, of course, risks dismissing the heterogeneity at the core of this enterprise, but even with that threat in mind one could claim that it has been successful in certain important areas. Key themes and contexts have included: (1) modernity, (2) cinema, (3) histories of the present, and (4) alternative histories.[5] Elaborating these briefly below gives a tentative insight into what media archaeology *has been*. The subsequent chapters address these themes in more detail, and also gradually point towards questions of what media archaeology *is becoming*.

(1) Modernity

Modernity itself as a process of technological, social and economic (capitalism) components has proved to be a key 'turning point' in various media-archaeological theories. These range from the German cultural theorist Walter Benjamin's early twentieth-century investigations into new forms of sensation emerging from modern urban settings and media technologies such as cinema, photography and the telephone (2008) to such key studies of more recent media theory as Anne Friedberg's (1993) *Window Shopping*, which investigated new media technologies, gender and consumerism from the perspective of the lively debates on the postmodern. Various studies raised the questions of what it means to be modern, and how new scientific and technological innovations contribute to the changing cultural landscape and even our basic ways of being in the world: seeing, hearing, thinking and feeling.

The nineteenth and early twentieth centuries especially have become the key excavation grounds for such analyses, which aim to establish the centrality of modernity for the grounding of contemporary media experiences and industries. Modernity can hence be seen as an era that is part of an emergence of a new sense of history as well, with such institutionalized forms as museums offering a new presence for the past (and faraway places as in anthropological colonialism, or alternative life worlds as in animal and natural history collections), and new technological, urban environments acting as conduits for altering structures of perception, experience of temporality and memory, as well as new types of rationalization in the midst of emerging forms of capitalism and bureaucracy. In addition to Benjamin and Friedberg, key studies include – just to mention a few examples – Jonathan Crary's (1990, 1999) writings about observation and attention as modern 'techniques of the subject'. From an earlier perspective, in the midst of such changes, one can mention *Panorama of the 19th Century* (1977 [1938]) by Dolf Sternberger (1907–89) and *Mechanization Takes Command* (1948) by Siegfried Giedion.

The latter addressed the birth of mechanical culture from labour to slaughterhouses, kitchen appliances to bathing and, in the words of Paul DeMarinis (2010: 211), 'is a sourcebook of problems, solutions, and the solutions that became problems'. In addition to these, one can point to art historical studies such as the cultural historical outlining of new forms of visuality by Aby Warburg's *Atlas-Mnemosyne* project and, in general, his investigations into configurations of the image (see Michaud 2007). Sternberger, Giedion and Warburg are some good examples of early contemporary theorists of modernity and the emerging technological media culture.

Indeed, what has to be noted is that already then we can discover how early art and cultural historians such as Jacob Burckhardt influenced Warburg, and how these early fields of 'image science' had, through a canon of art historical writers such as Erwin Panofsky (1892–1968), an influence on the historical discourses concerning art and media in the 1980s and 1990s. Hence, it is no wonder that writers such as Lev Manovich (2001) have argued for a historical connection between early avant-garde (paying special attention to 1920s Soviet filmmakers) and contemporary digital aesthetics. Forms of montage, as well as principles from the 1920s New Vision movement of artists such as Moholy-Nagy (1895–1946), Rodchenko (1891–1956) and Vertov (1896–1954), can be found implicitly at the core of computer imaging and art practices. In another context, for such key theorists as Friedrich Kittler, not only modernity but also modernism as a techno-artistic articulation of historical development, acts as a key figure through which, one could say, we were given the vocabulary of our technical media culture. Such a presence of modernity/modernism was evident in Kittler's 'archaeology of the present' that also accounts for 'data storage, transmission, and calculation in technological media' (Kittler 1990: 369).

(2) Cinema

As a key technology of modernity, cinema has been at the core of media-archaeological theories. The idea of 'archaeology' of the medium appeared already in the title of *Archaeology of the Cinema* (1965) by C. W. Ceram (1915–72). Ceram was known for his various writings on archaeology (in the original sense of the discipline and term) but also for his past with the propaganda troops in Hitler's Germany. Ceram's leap from archaeological discipline to cinema archaeology followed, however, a method was that still very linear and, despite mapping pre-cinematic technologies, was very keen to focus on the birth of the 'proper' cinematic form from 1895 onwards.

Much of the modern theorization started off from the New Film History wave of film studies from the 1970s and, especially, the 1980s. It established new perspectives on early cinema and the development of related screen and viewing technologies and practices from: (1) archival work and discovery of new films and material (often mentioned is the by-now classic 34th International Federation of Film Archives – FIAF, www.fiafnet.org – conference in Brighton in 1978 where a significant number of films from 1900 to 1906 were screened for an audience of film scholars); and (2) the cinema theories concerning spectatorship, power and gender (such as Mulvey 1975 and the psychoanalytically loaded theories concerning the apparatus of cinema and ideology of Jean-Louis Baudry, Jean-Louis Comolli and Christian Metz). These two strands – theory and new historical work – were, from early on, closely connected too. A lot of research on early cinema, and its distinct role as a specific form of sensation, emerged especially through the work of Tom Gunning and the idea of 'attraction'. In 'The Cinema of Attractions: Early Film, its Spectator and the Avant-Garde' (first version in 1986), Gunning outlined this concept of early cinema and its key components in the non-narrative, exhibitionist quality of the image that drew on 'cinematic manipulation' such as close-ups, slow motion, reverse motion, substitution and multiple exposure, as Gunning (1990: 57–8) outlines. Gunning and related perspectives drew directly from new archival material and established the idea that we should also take pre-cinematic apparatuses and contexts seriously. These were not only a 'warm-up' for the main act of cinema, but deserve attention in their own right. (For critique of Gunning, see, e.g., Musser 2006a and 2006b).

Hence, scholars started to talk about cinema and television – the prime media industries and aesthetics of the twentieth century – only as *entr'actes*, not the final act, in a wider field of visual and mediascapes (Zielinski 1999). A lot of emphasis was placed on mapping the multiplicity of technologies of producing and viewing images, and projects from camera obscuras to magic lanterns and the real burst of visual culture from the eighteenth and nineteenth centuries – with phantasmagorias, panoramas, daguerreotypes, thaumatropes, anorthoscopes, phenakistoscopes, praxinoscopes, mutoscopes and stereoscopes. Suddenly, in the light of such massive historical studies as Laurent Mannoni's *The Great Art of Light and Shadow* (2000), which bore the subtitle *Archaeology of the Cinema*, the better-known key inventions such as cinema and photography became merely one stream of innovation.

In this context of research, film scholars turned to emphasizing such cinematic technologies not only as 'primitive' forms of what was to come – the classic Hollywood form for film fiction that seemed to be the norm at least until the 1970s emergence of 'New Hollywood' – but as alternative practices of cinematic experience, mediascape and industry. The notion of the spectator widely debated in the 1970s, and later theories concerning the apparatus and its role in the fields of power and ideology, became historicized. Simultaneously modes of sensation and perception became embedded in an analytical view that encompassed multiple, non-linear histories. Instead of in terms of a rupture, cinema was to be analysed through the various *others* of mainstream cinema form that were constantly suppressed in teleological perspectives (Gaudreault 2006: 87; Zielinski 1999).

As Thomas Elsaesser (2004) points out, the media-archaeological spirit at the core of New Film History feeds into a further set of toolboxes for digital culture research whereby the current debates concerning convergence and the digital can actually be complexified themselves with the increasing understanding of early and pre-cinematic visual cultures. In Elsaesser's insightful contextualization of 'New Film History as Media Archaeology', the turn to the digital becomes itself an epistemological switch, which can be used to investigate ruptures and continuities, intermedial relations and parallel histories. Through the lenses of the digital, we start to see old media anew as well. Similarly, the multiple worlds of visual culture of the nineteenth century, with its 'vaudeville, panoramas, dioramas, stereoscopic home entertainment, Hale's tours and world fairs', as Elsaesser (2004: 80) lists them, are a further good reminder of the dangers of homogenization – such as the myth of convergence as the sole driving force of media evolution – and point towards the various ways in which connections and ruptures emerge, and how some characteristics, such as 'attraction' as a mode of sensation, work across media from early cinema to our culture of computer games, revitalized interest in 3D, and other spectacles.

(3) Histories of the present

In the midst of the emphasis on the audiovisual and the (pre- and post-)cinematic, and the methodological emphasis on alternative paths and transdisciplinary regimes of knowledge, media-archaeological research adopted the idea – familiar from Foucault – that archaeology is always, implicitly or explicitly, about the present: what is our present moment in its objects, discourses and practices, and how did it come to be perceived as reality? The hype surrounding the 'newness' of the digital culture of the 1980s and 1990s was contextualized in many ways that complexified the way new media were seen as 'new'.

Hence, instead of the myth of linear progress, studies such as Carolyn Marvin's (1988) pointed out that old technologies had also once been new – and investigated the telegraph, the telephone, and electricity and light as media phenomena that were embedded in the aura of newness in the nineteenth century, and how they were part of a wider rearticulation of social ties, expert knowledge and professionality, and new high-tech spectacles integrated as part of everyday life. Newness is always a very relative concept, and a focus on technical qualities such as 'speed, capacity, and performance' (Marvin 1988: 4) is secondary to the social issues through which technical efficiencies are mobilized as negotiations between audiences: experts and amateurs, insiders and outsiders, users and non-users (1988: 4). One is, indeed, allowed to conceive of new media and new technologies already in the nineteenth century, or even earlier, as a more recent title suggests: *New Media, 1740–1915* (Gitelman and Pingree 2003).

The relativity of the new is taken as a starting point in works by perhaps the two most influential media archaeologists. Arriving at the concept from slightly different directions, Erkki Huhtamo's and Siegfried Zielinski's works are emblematic of the formation of the research field, and both have been important in rethinking the temporal structures of newness and opening up, through a variety of historical apparatuses, the question of *what the new is* and how we should incorporate historical knowledge into thinking about current and future media.

Huhtamo's work has centred mostly on the idea of *topoi* (plural of *topos*): topics of media culture that are recurring, cyclical phenomena and discourses that circulate. Arriving at media-archaeological theory from cultural historical training and the 1980s critique of positivist and chronological historical writing, Huhtamo (1997: 221) maps media archaeology as part of the understanding of history as a 'multi-layered construction' which, in media-related work, had been developed early on by Gunning, Zielinski, Marvin, Avital Ronell, Susan J. Douglas, Lynn Spigel, Cecilia Ticchi, William Boddy and others. Borrowing the key concept of *topoi* from a curious direction – namely, from the 1948 historical study *Europäische Literatur und lateinisches Mittelalter* by classicist Ernst Robert Curtius (1886–1956), Huhtamo develops his own brand of media archaeology through the idea of *commonplaces* – the aforementioned motifs that are recurring – whether as more general cultural phenomena like the discourse concerning immersive environments which was not unique to the 1990s virtual reality boom, or in more tactical uses, as in marketing.

Thinking cyclically has been one media-archaeological strategy for critiquing the hegemony of the new. Siegfried Zielinski (1999) connects the compulsory newness to what he calls the *psychopathia medialis* of our current capitalist condition. His solution is to promote heterogeneity of arts and media environments through the concept of variantology. Zielinski's development of media archaeology as research into the deep time of media – modes of hearing, seeing and sensing in general – is another way of developing an alternative temporality that moves away from a hegemonic linearity that demands that we should see time and history as straight lines that work towards improvement and something better. In such linear perspectives, the past is only a lost present. Instead, Zielinski promotes a more paleontological time for media: a time of development that 'does not follow a divine plan', and he insists that 'the history of the media is not the product of predictable and necessary advance from primitive to the complex apparatus' (Zielinski 2006a: 7).

We can see how such ideas concerning dynamic, complex history cultures of media are at the core of how we should think in terms of current media environments as well – this is evident from the involvement of such figures as Huhtamo and Zielinski among a number of others in arts institutions and festivals in which media-archaeological work, and the ethos of creativity have been directly channelled into creative practice. In the words of Zielinski (2006a: 11), 'The goal is to uncover dynamic moments in the media-archaeological record that abound and revel in heterogeneity and, in this way, to enter into a relationship of tension with the various present-day moments, relativize them, and render them more decisive.'

Several artists have engaged in similar ways of thinking as well. Paul DeMarinis, Zoe Beloff, Bernie Lubell, Masaki Fujihata, Catherine Richards, Gebhard Sengmüller, Julien Maire and David Link have been among the creative practitioners who have taken a keen interest in looking at how to do media archaeology – and to rewiring temporality – with practical, artistic means. In addition to such earlier pioneers, learning about and meeting other artists and practitioners – such as Garnet Hertz, Shintaro Miyazaki, Sarah Angliss, Aleksander Kolkowski, Rosa Menkman, Brendan Howell, Martin Howse, Elizabeth Skadden and, for example, the artist-curators Kristoffer Gansing and Linda Hilfling who were the organizers of the Art of the Overhead Project event series – influenced this book and the way in which media archaeology is being articulated here.

(4) Alternative histories

What should have become clear by now is that, while media archaeology writes histories of the present, it is also looking for *alternative* presents and pasts – and futures. Within the context of new theories and histories of cinema, one of the key driving ideas that feeds into media archaeology is something that Elsaesser (2004: 81) attributes to Noël Burch: the idea of 'it could have been otherwise'. What the meticulous assessment of film and cinema produced were not only film histories, but histories of audiovisual culture in which film, understood in the mainstream sense, was only one possible end result from the various strands, streams and ideas that formed the (audio)visual culture of, for instance, the mid and late nineteenth century. This reminds of Foucault's genealogical method of questioning simple origins and teleological and pre-determined ways of understanding (media) cultural change.

The media-archaeological perspectives meant looking at the pre-cinematic technologies and practices as one resource for rethinking our current visual and media field. This includes meticulous research into non-mainstream technological and mediatic apparatuses, and increasingly opening up contemporary technologies through new kinds of genealogies – an important task especially since the 1980s' and 1990s' hype around the supposed newness of digital technologies, which presented themselves in various policy, marketing and public discourses as inevitable improvements and novelties. The discourses of 1990s' new informational capitalism were in a way challenged by a range of genealogies of high-tech media in which the new was tied to the old in terms of discourses of newness, convergence, interaction, immersion, virtuality, materiality, etc. (See, for example, Manovich 2001; Grau 2003; Lyons and Plunkett 2007; Huhtamo 1997 and 2012; Rabinovitz and Geil 2004.) Media archaeology stepped in to challenge the strategic amnesia of digital culture.

In this sense, it was more in the spirit of Foucault's genealogical theories, instead of his archaeology of knowledge, where inspiration was sought. New cultural histories (see Burke 2004) were shifting their interest to writing about representations, constructions, practices and histories of the previously neglected subjects (women, children, gays, the body, etc.), and Foucault's genealogy was one theoretical articulation of how to think historically but avoid the idea that there are such things as simple origins. Instead, writes Foucault (1998: 374), it is a matter of preserving the heterogeneity in history and

identify[ing] the accidents, the minute deviations – or conversely, the complete reversals – the errors, the false appraisals, and the faulty calculations that gave birth to those things which continue to exist or have value for us; it is to discover that truth or being lies not at the root of what we know and what we are but the exteriority of accidents.

Indeed, media-archaeological research embodied an interest in and a need for new ways of understanding media cultures outside the mainstream. It also expanded media studies outside analyses of entertainment media. Hence, another key trend in terms of alternative histories was the horizontal widening of media-historical research – something that Elsaesser has summed up as an interest in the perverse S/M-histories of cinema and media – not necessarily sexual perversions but *epistemological perversions*: a non-mainstream approach to media cultural innovations and applications. To paraphrase Elsaesser (2006: 17), S/M perversions of film and media history include science and medicine, surveillance and the military, sensory-motor coordination, and GMS and MMS in reference to the mobile communication cultures that expand how cinema and the visual are taking new forms.[6] Indeed, what characterizes such a take is the bravely transdisciplinary nature of the methodology in which the alternative histories for media cultures are sought somewhere on the fuzzy borders of art/science/technology.

Media archaeology – act two

The themes that are outlined above are not exhaustive in any way, and the amount of work that is in spirit, even if not always explicitly in name, media-archaeological is vast.[7] Hence, I tried to show only some ideas that are running through the body of work and the context from which this book stems. Having said that, it is the intention of this book on media archaeology not only to offer an overview of the 'has-beens' and past themes but to articulate how we are able to use – and reuse, remix, reshuffle – media-archaeological methods and theories, as well as the research ethos, as something that is still an exciting and fresh way to tackle past and present media cultures in parallel lines. We need a 'second act' for grounding our new theories and practical ideas about media archaeology.

What this book develops are insights into how arts and technology can work in relation to cultural theory – and articulate history, practice and theory in a fruitful mash-up. In a similar sense to how media art histories have been interested in institutions, practices and ideas that articulate practical laboratories, whether for artistic or technological creation – there is a long history of science, technology and art collaborations which is the focus of, for instance, media art histories conferences and publications (www.mediaarthistory.org/) – I propose as acute a need for *concept labs*, where we twist, experiment and open up concepts, as in circuit bending. Similarly, we can ask what in addition to such labs are the key places where media archaeology takes place? One obvious answer is the archive – one key institutional 'site' of memory with an intertwined history with modernity and the birth of the state apparatus, but which now is increasingly being rearticulated less as a *place* of history, memory and power, and more as a dynamic and temporal network, a software environment, and a social platform for memory – but also for remixing. The archive is becoming a key concept for understanding digital media culture, and its practices are worthy of investigation in the context of media archaeology as well. This means bringing media archaeology into proximity with the archive as a key site of digital software culture, as well as – through that agenda – bringing media studies ideas into proximity with key non-academic institutions involved in cultural heritage in the digital age.[8] As such, this has affinities with the recent interest in *digital humanities*.

Hence, I approach media archaeology historically but also as a travelling theory, mobile concepts and shifting institutional affiliations. Borrowing loosely from Mieke Bal (2002), this refers to how media archaeology has historically resided in between academic departments (media studies, media arts, film studies, history) and arts institutions and practices. It has never really found one institutional home, and even if it is important to avoid romanticizing nomadism, this still is something that also can be turned to an advantage in the sense of promoting dynamics of concept creation and knowledge exchange. Media archaeology is a travelling discipline, based on a mobile set of concepts. Jumping aboard the travels of media archaeology, this book is cartographic: it maps media archaeology, and, by doing so, also creates one possible way to understand the place of media archaeology, history and media theory in contemporary digital culture – and to understand digital culture media archaeologically.

This cartographic task aims to think anew the place of time and history in our digital culture. This does not mean returning to such accounts that argue memory as a human capacity for remembering, retrieval or trauma, but focusing on a media-technologically informed understanding of the networks in which memory becomes partly an issue of technical media – a theme underlined by German media theorists such as Wolfgang Ernst and, to an extent, Friedrich Kittler. Indeed, it is increasingly the non-visual that media archaeologists are turning their focus on – whether through archaeologies of the technological present in, for example, opening up the layers of consumer software and hardware and, for example, the electromagnetic spectrum surrounding our WiFi, Bluetooth, UMTS, EDGE, HSPA, GSM and GPS traffic,[9] or repurposing dead media with a DIY spirit and methods[10] and using media archaeology as an artistic methodology and hence transporting it from investigation of texts to material culture as well.

Structure

This book is divided into seven chapters in which I elaborate new directions and ideas in relation to the existing media-archaeological body of theory and research as well as practice. The chapters have been chosen to illuminate key fields of media-archaeological research from film to software, from genealogies of imaginary media to material media theory. In addition, chapters on archive and creative practice are included to address how media archaeology relates to the cultural heritage institutions in their archival work, and to creative practice, where the past becomes a resource for fresh ideas.

The order of the chapters loosely follows the way media archaeology has evolved. The earlier chapters are about those research directions which have been more clearly articulated and written about during the past years: for instance, film-studies-oriented media archaeology, imaginary media and German media theory. The later chapters address slightly more neglected topics, such as media theory of the archive and media archaeology as an artistic method. It is, of course, an exaggeration to say media-archaeological art has not been written about, but the chapter takes a new perspective and illuminates recent, more software-oriented, art as well. In the conclusions, the politics of the materiality and temporality of media archaeology is elaborated.

The next chapter, chapter 2, is dedicated to some of the film-studies contexts from which media archaeology has emerged. Discussing New Film History, the debates of media archaeology in film studies since the 1980s and the more recent turn towards non-visual and more affect- and multimodal-based ideas concerning media histories, the chapter entails both a historical and a theoretical understanding of how to think media pasts intertwined with contemporary media cultures of, for example, gaming. Hence, it already points towards the regime of algorithmic, digital culture as important for a wider media-archaeological mapping. Here the idea of the cultural and historical nature of senses is investigated. One of the key concepts emerging from the chapter is 'epistemic rupture' as a methodology for media archaeology, as suggested by Thomas Elsaesser.

The third chapter is called 'Imaginary media: mapping weird objects' and taps into the discourse of imagined media. Imaginary-media research has been an integral part of the media-archaeological discourse, and is emblematic of the drive to find important ideas and contexts outside actually existing technologies. It also expands towards regimes of the supernatural and other worlds significant from a cultural historical perspective, while promoting an argument for a very material reading of imaginary media in technical modernity.

The fourth chapter continues this materialist drive. It introduces important German influences on media archaeology, not least Friedrich A. Kittler whose works since the 1980s have had a significant impact in both the Germanic and Anglo-American media theoretical circles. His brand of 'media materialism' can also be connected to a range of other thinkers such as Bernhard Siegert, Claus Pias, Cornelia Vissman, Wolfgang Hagen and also Wolfgang Ernst, Professor of Media Studies at Humboldt University, who has specifically insisted on calling his continuation of Foucault's ideas 'media archaeology'.

In chapter 5, we focus on noise and provide an alternative reading of media history. The chapter offers a case study of how media archaeology can work with empirical material, and elaborates in practice the idea of offering alternative viewpoints to media history. How might communication media look from the point of view of non-communication, disturbance and noise? As a media-archaeological excavation of what was left out and what has been considered the anomalous, in archaeologies of the network society and digital culture we need to look at the underbelly of communication. This takes us to mapping non-communication, spam, noise, interference and disconnection as crucial ways to understand the politics and tactics of technical media cultures from telegraphy to the Internet.

A lot of media-archaeological writings rely on the archive – but it has been quite an undertheorized theme for media archaeologists. Hence, chapter 6 is a mapping of how we need to rethink this crucial philosophical and practical context as part of software cultures. This takes us to remarking the proximity of some media-archaeological theories, such as Ernst's, to software studies – for example Wendy Hui Kyong Chun's (2011b) work, as well as Matthew G. Kirschenbaum's (2008) theories – and elaborating what it means that our regimes of memory are embedded in dynamic, changing and processual software platforms.

Chapter 7 taps into creative practice and how media archaeology has been used as an artistic methodology. As part of the investigation of how we can mobilize these theories into media cultural design as well, the chapter looks at important theoretical ideas and practical projects as well as drawing on some interviews with key current artists who build on old media technological innovations and cultures.

The concluding chapter is, besides, a summary, a further short elaboration on the methodology of media archaeology as a transdisciplinary take on digital culture. As such, it is introduced as analysis of the contemporary, the transhistorical, the non-linear and nomadic – hence, media archaeology is not 'only' a historical venture into media cultures but also asks the fundamental question: what do we *do* with media theory?

As this book is meant to work as both an introduction to and a continuation in media-archaeological theory and practice debates in contemporary theory, each chapter ends with a short paragraph summary that rounds up the themes discussed. The summary serves a pedagogical function, but also as a catapult towards further discussions and readings, hoping to spark off a media-archaeological interest in excavation of the everyday culture of digitality. It also points to some relevant articles, books or collections of articles, or Internet links, that take the interested reader and student to deepening insights and ideas. A recommended companion reading is the volume *Media Archaeology: Approaches, Applications, Implications* (Huhtamo and Parikka 2011).

The basic question of media archaeology could be seen simply, and in a manner indicated by Foucault, to be: what are the conditions of existence of this thing, of that statement, of these discourses and the multiple media(ted) practices with which we live? Such questions are political, aesthetic, economic, technological, scientific and more – and we should refuse attempts to leave out any of the aspects.

2

Media Archaeology of the Senses: Audiovisual, Affective, Algorithmic

A major inspiration for media-archaeological research has come from film theory and New Film History. As a parallel to new historicism (and the so-called 'new cultural histories') in the history disciplines since the 1980s, the New Film History methodology of bringing cinema history into proximity with theory was itself a key way to develop historically *and* conceptually rich ways to understand and broaden the centrality of the cinematic as a focal structuration of modern worlds of experience, memory, aesthetics and politics. Such agendas are evident in the works of a range of film theorists who can be considered closely affiliated with media-archaeological research, from Thomas Elsaesser to Tom Gunning, Anne Friedberg to emerging scholars such as Wanda Strauven and Michael Wedel. Indeed, as Strauven (2012) demonstrates referring to recent years of research, the questions of 'what', 'when' and 'where' cinema is/was become constitutive ways of thinking about the continuous temporal, institutional, spatial and experiential displacements of the cinematic. Cinema has continuously changed form over its history, and similarly we can apply this idea to other media technologies. Not only does media change our worlds – its worlds are also continuously changing. Furthermore, these questions that stemmed from research into early cinema actually provided excellent motivation for asking the same of other media technologies too.

What follows is an argument that, in addition to the emphasis on early media archaeology in cinematic and film studies contexts, has also included the potential to develop into a rich multisensorial and intermedial research methodology. In New Film History, this was evident in the keen interest, for instance, in sound and early film (see, for example, Abel and Altman 2001; cf. Kittler 1999, and Levin 2003 for archaeology of visual sound; see also Strauven 2012). I will track some of the themes that connect to that mode of thinking the cinematic with theory and history in parallel lines, and consider how we can develop media history from the point of view of such concepts as experience and event (cf. Elsaesser 2004: 109). This means investigating the subject (the spectator, the viewer, the user, the gamer) of media culture in historical ways. This approach also feeds into an understanding of the historical and complex forms of sensation – that we access our media not only with our eyes, but with our hands (Strauven 2011), ears and, more widely, the affective registers of the body. Even if we start with some themes related to New Film History, this chapter, however, is not only an explication of that position.

The key idea of the chapter is that media archaeology is a good methodology for an analysis of how our senses are always articulated in media contexts: modes of sensation themselves can be seen as historically structured. The German writer Walter Benjamin was an early pioneer of such ways of thinking already before World War II. The past and media history act as interventions and new kinds of openings to understand the current emerging media landscapes. It sounds so banal that it is slightly painful to say it aloud, but one learns through the past – not in the sense of universal truths about how media evolution unfolds but in seeing the media pasts as reservoirs, toolboxes for design and thought. One of Marshall McLuhan's frequently quoted ideas was that we approach the present through a rearview-mirror perspective, which already includes in itself the idea of the past as an archive of future directions.[1] Indeed, if we take media theory in general as a crucial aide that helps us to conceptualize and critically manoeuvre through the immense impact media technologies have on our cognitive and affective capacities, we should constantly try to stay up-to-date with the difficult questions present media environments pose.

In this sense, we are increasingly forced to take into account how new modes of haptic interfaces in the age of touch-screens and much-more-than-visual interfacing reorganize sensory capacities, react to skin and touch, register movement as well as voice (Kinect, *PlayStation®Move*) not only allowing us to watch but also looking back (face recognition, movement capture technologies); and how distributed environments demand that we conceptualize the relation between senses and media in new ways.[2] Indeed, with augmented reality, RFID (radio frequency identification) and ubiquitous media, the interface disappears as a separate entity, and is swallowed up as part of the world of things. Software culture presents a new challenge in understanding the contemporary media sphere and its histories, and the way in which our cognitive and perceptive capacities are being trained anew in the midst of 'smart environments' that measure, react to and survey us (see Hayles 2008: 27–8). Media change forces us to think about not only the future, but the past too, in fresh ways.

Methodological guidelines: theory and history intertwined

From photography to the cinematic, the visual has persisted for a long time as the key reference point as a technology of modernity. Not only singular technological apparatuses but also the discourses concerning reproduction and the function of imaging practices from entertainment to science were frequently debated prior, and in addition, to Benjamin's much-quoted 'The Work of Art in the Age of its Technological Reproducibility' from the 1930s. What Benjamin (2008: 21) outlines is how reproduction itself, as a process – not only one specific technology of reproduction – had by around 1900 'captured a place of its own among the artistic processes'. Indeed, as part of the emergence of the 'sciences of the image' (*Bildwissenschaften*), the new presence of the image in the everyday as reproduced had raised much interest among art historians such as Wölfflin (1864–1945) and later Panofsky and scientists such as Robert Koch (1843–1910) who, as early as 1881 in his 'Zur Untersuchung von pathogenen Organismen', had written how 'the photographic picture of a microscopic object can under certain circumstances be more important than [the object] itself,' (quoted in Bredekamp 2003: 420).

The technical image and its function as a seeing/visualizing but also reproductive medium had huge epistemological implications. With such new media, we started to think the world in new ways, the cinema itself acting as 'an anthropology of modernity' (Väliaho 2010: 9). In media-archaeologically tuned art, this is exemplified in perhaps even Jean-Luc Godard's *Histoire(s) du Cinéma* (1988–98) and certainly in Gustav Deutsch's *Film ist* (1998) – a screen art piece that, by (re)using archival material, sums up so well cinema as a technology of scientific modernity, from measuring time and movement in terms of, for example, physiologies of human and animal bodies, to radar screens as real-time mapping of bodies in movement; from science and the military to new forms of public entertainment and a culture industry of thrills and emotions.

In this epistemological sense, the emphasis on (moving) audio-visual culture has turned into a media-archaeological method as well. Elsaesser (2008) turns cinema studies methodologies into a media-archaeological guideline that takes such media changes as digitization not as ends of cinema per se: digitization might mark a change from the optico-chemical material grounding of *film* to the algorithmic (digital image and cinema), but it is more important as an *epistemological rupture* that has implications for how we see the whole spectrum of media technologies. Less a technology and more like a complex dispositif and tool-for-thought, the cultural episteme is in this manner seen through the prisms of media technology. Hence, such 'ruptures' are 'more like a zero degree that allows one to reflect upon one's present understanding of both film history and cinema theory.' (Elsaesser 2008: 232).[3] In other words, digitality and digital culture become a 'heuristic device' or a focus for thinking through multimedia environments and media history in new ways. For Elsaesser, cinema is a tool to reconsider the already-mentioned S/M perversions of cinema history, and in a related manner we can acknowledge its usefulness for the media-archaeological set of concepts and methods. Elsaesser uses it in this sense to point towards the interconnections of moving images in relation to pre-cinematic practices, the phonograph, radio waves and electromagnetic fields, new scientific theories such as Einstein's, technologies of aviation, calculating machines and computing history, and the wider contexts of rationalization, measuring and mechanization – acknowledging that much of the media-archaeological interest of knowledge is geared towards what could be modestly called 'what is missing or has been suppressed and left out in our genealogical chart' (Elsaesser 2008: 233) of media apparatuses and their contexts.

Thoroughly embedded in the senses, Elsaesser's archaeological theory of mediatic modernity has implicitly at its core the genealogical idea of Foucault (and Friedrich Nietzsche (1844–1900)) that we think through the body. It is an inscription surface on which to map out the work of emergence, *descent* and other forces of a genealogical kind: 'descent attaches itself to the body. It inscribes itself in the nervous system, in temperament, in the digestive apparatus; it appears in faulty respiration, in improper diets, in the debilitated and prostrate bodies of those whose ancestors committed errors' (Foucault 1998: 375). Cultural theory has investigated the body as an object of modern biopolitical governance: as gendered, ethnic, lived agency. And media theory can similarly proceed through the idea that the body is already from the start deeply mediatic in the forms of perception, sensation and other capacities that it has been afforded with.

Whereas there is nothing new in the turn towards the body, the way it is intertwined with a complex historical account of embodiment, the senses and their media technological conditions is what distinguishes media archaeology as a useful methodology. In Elsaesser's account, this leads to a theory/history interest in the senses and forces us to question the primacy of the eye. Such excavations start from and question the idea of 'ruptures' in our epistemological framework (Elsaesser 2008: 239): is the digital a completely new phase of sensation? Are we moving beyond the primacy of the eye and seeing? The understanding of the senses becomes reshuffled when we realize how the digital is itself beyond the 'threshold of the visible' (2008: 239), non-sensuous and mathematical.

Furthermore, media archaeology enables a temporalization of theory itself. Media archaeology reads media history and media theory hand in hand. Again, for Elsaesser and Hagener (2010) in their *Film Theory: An Introduction Through the Senses*, this becomes a method for incorporating the wider sense regimes of touch, nerves/brain and hearing as part of film theory. For us, we can further emphasize this as one way in which media archaeology can develop a cultural analytical methodology of media history: media archaeology as an investigation into the apparatuses as events and experiences, or, in other words, theoretically rethought genealogies that are able to 'put in crisis habitual classifications and categories, such as text, work, or author' (Elsaesser 2004: 89, see also 109) – and, we could add, genre, apparatus, technology, media and the past as distinct from the present or future.

Attractions and intermedial relations

My point is that some of the origins of media archaeology in New Film History are able to offer the foundations for research into touch-, haptic- and distributed cognition- or affect-based notions important for recent years of media theory and design. Yet, instead of simply assuming that any change from an optical mode of perception to a haptical one coincides with the emergence of digital culture as a new form of aesthetics, we can attempt to find more complex, multitemporal ways of understanding technological change in relation to modes of sensation. Indeed, the whole debate from the 1980s surrounding the cinema of attractions can be seen as one emblematic step in that direction where early cinema and pre-cinema were not merely investigated as one particular undercurrent of cinema and the regime of the eye, but as a logic of sensation and aesthetics in their own right. True, the debates since then have revolved significantly around the differences between narration and showing, or *monstration* (as a concept that André Gaudreault introduced) – or, in other words, representation and presentation (Strauven 2006: 14–15). The focus is on those modes of presenting that rely on an *astonished* embodiment in which the spectator becomes less immersed in the narrative than in the spectacular image-situation. Or, to put it more accurately (Gunning 1995), it is less the immersion in the psychological narrative sense that the aesthetics of the nineteenth century promoted, than a fascination with the technological apparatus that was able to depict movement moving. In this sense it fitted in with the wider processes of urbanization and the birth of media culture as analysed by Siegfried Kracauer (1889–1966) and Benjamin before World War II.

Hence, the focus is on the sensing, multisensorial body that is lured by sights and sounds. Gunning's work, and more widely the theories that emerged from the post-Brighton[4] context, brought not only a new visibility for early cinema but significantly introduced 'attraction' as a concept to an emerging generation of media theorists interested in such new media spectacles as big screens like the IMAX, the new digital screen technologies and virtual reality, and the tactility of video games and electronic media. As part of this context, we should mention the special-effects cinema phase, from the 1980s and 1990s, that welcomed a range of big-budget action blockbusters in the midst of what was soon discussed more widely as the emergence of 'attention economy' as a central feature of late capitalism (see Elsaesser 2006: 207–9). Indeed, spectacle was perceived as one key vehicle through which to investigate the embodied sensory worlds of the spectator, in order to foreground how cinematic effects modulate our sensory worlds (Bukatman 1998: 79).

Yet the lure of the concept of attraction has itself to be put under careful scrutiny as has been done by a range of scholars who have pointed towards the complex political economy surrounding early film, offering counter-evidence to Gunning's claims (see Elsaesser 2006: 210). It is in the context of these warnings that a careful development of the conceptual ties with media history can elaborate neglected paths and new ideas concerning media cultures.

Alongside the debate about its accuracy as a way to understand early cinema, the concept of attraction can be seen as a catalyst for a range of perspectives. One of them concerns how the aesthetics of attraction in screen and moving images captures the senses; hence, numerous cinematic examples are often mentioned in this context, including the so-called 'rube films' – Edison Manufacturing Company's Uncle-Josh's adventures (e.g. *Uncle Josh at the Moving Picture Show* from 1902) are among the most famous, even if preceded by *The Countryman's First Sight of the Animated Pictures* (1901) by the British Robert Paul (1869–1943). Other early examples are also relevant, such as the early Lumière brothers' trains not only arriving on stations but threatening the viewers (even if historians have found scarce evidence of such panic reactions), or *Electrocuting an Elephant* (1903; cf. Strauven 2011: 156–7). Besides being part of the new screen media of the past, attractions can be seen emerging as part of the new entertainment worlds designed to capture the variety of bodily sensations in a manner that was paradoxically pre-modern in how it attached itself to the skin and the gut. In the words of Gunning (1995: 122), the concept of attraction was able to describe the relation between reality and mediated illusions:

> This vertiginous experience of the frailty of our knowledge of the world before the power of visual illusion produced that mixture of pleasure and anxiety which the purveyors of popular art had labelled sensations and thrills and on which they founded a new aesthetic of attractions. The on-rushing train did not simply produce the negative experience of fear but the particularly modern entertainment form of the thrill, embodied elsewhere in the recently appearing attractions of the amusement parks (such as the roller coaster), which combined sensations of acceleration and falling with a security guaranteed by modern industrial technology. One Coney Island attraction, the Leap Frog railway, literalized the thrill of The Arrival of a Train. Two electric cars containing as many as forty people were set towards each other at a great speed on a collision course. Just before impact one car was lifted up on curved rails and skimmed over the top of the other.

What is illustrated in such perceptions concerning the early forms of technological reproduction and mass-produced 'thrill' as an affective form of capitalist entertainment industry is the relation between different media – and the expansion of media technological effects into such environments in which thrills and affective states are able to be reproduced their attraction. Hence, attraction is not restricted only to a particular screen event, but to a complex intermedial phase, which ties in earlier entertainment practices, the emerging screen media of cinematography, social situations, new modes of the capitalist leisure industry, and the affects of the body not reducible to the eye. This is a point Huhtamo (2004) also makes, pointing out that the aesthetics and the social nature of the attraction stem from the eighteenth- and nineteenth-century popular culture of a variety of performance shows.

Anne Friedberg's (1993) *Window Shopping* was a nod towards such an 'extended version' of cinematic analysis which aimed to 'widen the historical focus in accounts of the emergence of cinema' (1993: 3) through a transversal use of concepts that cut across media lines.

Image 2.1 The Maxim Captive Flying Machines from 1904 in Blackpool, originally part of the culture of speed and entertainment for the gut, and now still present but embedded as part of corporate-sponsored spectacles whose aura has, however, radically diminished because of other modes of technical spectacle in digital culture. Wikimedia Commons, John Phillips235

The notions of 'mobilized' and 'virtual' as used by Friedberg were exactly such cross-cutting tools that looked at the parallel practices of displaying (shopping), cinema (as a training of the body and senses in terms of immobility / moving images) and tourism as a practice of cognitive mastering of the outside world. Drawing a theoretical parallel from the experience of postmodernism, but situating that as part of the emergence of moving-image cultures attaches a new flavour to the theory / media history parallelism, which provides a new embodiment for practices of vision. Indeed, it is less the screen per se than the designed environments and practices which convey 'spatial and temporal mobility' (1993: 12): arcades, department stores and exhibition halls. Yet Friedberg is very much embedded in a Lacanian vocabulary, which still relies on those architectures of vision in which the notion of 'gaze' is seen as a primary. Gaze becomes gendered, mobilized, moving, and a concept with which to investigate intermedial relations (if we allow, for the sake of argument, expansion of the notion of a medium to, for example, shop display windows, which is one of the exciting implications of Friedberg's work) – yet it still remains as part of the constellation of looking.

More specifically, Friedberg offers an 'architecturalized' analysis of cinematic modern subjectivity – a subjectivity that we also know to an extent from 'postmodern' philosophies such as that of Luce Irigaray. Proceeding from Foucault's idea of the panopticon (further adopted from Jeremy Bentham (1748–1832)) as a model for organizing the visual relations of watching in institutions such as the factory, the asylum and the hospital, Friedberg's analysis of modernity as a mobilization of the gaze in such constellations as the panorama and the diorama continues this into media-technological contexts. For Friedberg (1993: 22), the panorama, as it emerged after 1792,[5] provided 'virtual spatial and temporal mobility, bringing the country to the town dweller, transporting the past to the present'. The large canvas of the panorama was hence part of the emerging urban experience, or illusion industry, which featured in the growing cities London and Paris, but differed from another urban experience, the diorama, in which the viewer became a frozen spectator of the show.

Yet a significant feature for Friedberg was that the gaze was embedded in the virtual – the image which functioned through the more 'immobile, passive' (1993: 28) position of a virtual reality before the 1990s digital hype. Indeed, what is noteworthy in Friedberg's methodology is that it not only historicizes media technologies into a long perspective but historicizes cultural theory and philosophy as well – and especially *media*-historicizes them. Irigaray, Baudry and DeCerteau, with their accounts of the eye, vision and disembodiment, become for Friedberg (1993: 33) part of the story of how to understand modern subjectification that is to be grasped through media-technological modernity and those media-technological practices that take place in urban settings. Perhaps not as provocative as Kittler (1999: xxxix), with his claim that our 'Media determine our situation' and are already inside our heads, inside our capacities of understanding and writing, our theoretical concepts, memories and such, yet these perspectives of a media-archaeological kind elaborate the wider intermedial fields in which the human body is trained as part of the modernization process. For Zielinski, the cinematic (and televisual) is replaced with a more transversal concept of 'audiovisions' that rejects attachment to one particular technology and looks for connections across them. Methodologically this involves a cultural historical movement in which 'the audiovisual overlaps with other specialist discourses and partial praxes of society, such as architecture, transport, science and technology, organisation of work and time, traditional plebeian and bourgeois culture, or the avant-garde' (Zielinski 1999: 19).

Yet Friedberg and a lot of other earlier writers on the archaeologies of subjectivity in media environments start from the horizon of visuality and cinema, which automatically loads their academic concepts in a specific way. Instead, if we were to start genealogies of contemporary media differently, we might begin perhaps with gaming (tactility, the skin and gesture), immersive or algorithmic media (evasive to the phenomenologically sensing human body), from mobility, kinaesthesia and synaesthesia (for early examples of such considerations in human–computer interface design, see Sutherland 1965 and 1968) as a crucial feature of the media experience (Strauven 2011), or from the conceptualization of the primacy of sensation embedded not primarily in the gaze, but in the wider synaesthetic and physiological layer of *affect*.

Let's address games first. An increasing amount of scholarship has argued for a more game-focused perspective to media histories, in which Dulac and Gaudreault's (2006) work in extending attraction to gamelike toys of the pre-cinematic era has been one catalyst. In such media as phenakistoscopes, narrativity did not exist in a linear form: the loop structures of simple gestures guaranteed only an 'eternal return of the same', but so that it functioned as a preinteractive attraction (2006: 230–3). Mapping pre-digital practices of interaction is useful in highlighting how tactility featured as part of such toys that were not only pre-phases of cinema – as Huhtamo (2005) points out, the multiple gambling machines as well as such hand-cranked visual machines as mutoscopes, gave the control to the viewer 'able to adjust the cranking speed, and interrupt the session at any point to observe a particularly interesting frame (perhaps a half-naked lady)' (Huhtamo 2005: 9).[6]

Such machines engaged in a synaesthesia of the body non-reducible to the eye and vision. The nineteenth-century fascination with the hand as the primary tool and model for machines of the human being (Kapp 1877) was more practically developed in the leisure machines that complemented the new mechanical work environments in factories and offices (Huhtamo 2005). Such motifs have been reworked in digital contexts by media-archaeological artists such as Zoe Beloff (2002: 288), who expresses her interest in magic lanterns, Zoetropes and hand-cranked projectors as 'a secret history of Quicktime movies, producing images that are tiny, unstable and, most importantly, interactive. They remind us that interactivity, far from being a new phenomenon, was integral to the production of the nineteenth-century moving image.' These perspectives allow us a wider understanding

Image 2.2 A foldout stereoscope, *c.*1870, emblematic of the hands-on viewing culture of the nineteenth century. Reprinted with permission from the Bill Douglas Centre, University of Exeter, UK.

of the supposed novelty of interactivity, and, subsequently, how our bodies are activated and moulded by media technologies.

The physiological body: affect and thickness of the attraction

We started the chapter with an outline of how media archaeology has developed as a historical methodology for understanding media change in cinematic modernity. Now, we are gradually turning towards an emphasis on affect, which offers another perspective on media culture research, moves our discussion a bit farther from New Film History, and resonates with recent debates in media theory concerning embodiment. What kind of implications for media archaeology does it carry?

The interest in affect has been a key theme during the past years in media and cultural studies. It has provided a way to think both outside the primacy of the eye and the gaze – as witnessed in various accounts concerning media and experience –and differently from the emphasis on meaning and representation promoted in some other cultural studies approaches. Drawing on a range of clinical studies, including Daniel Stern's and Silvan Tomkins's, media scholars such as Richard Grusin (2010) have turned to affect as a way to think of media outside representation and as a process of material mediation that attaches to the body outside the cortex as well, so to speak (see also Protevi 2009). This means addressing those layers of media where affect is not conflated with feelings or emotions, but is the material stuff of multisensorial, kinaesthetic (moving), pre-conscious capacities and thresholds.[7] Media are about affects in addition to communication studies effects. Such studies in affect have shown a special interest in the pre-object realms of sensation, which for Mark B. N. Hansen (2006: 71) constitute a dimension that actually bootstraps, grounds the phenomenological body and its capacities. For Hansen, it is the tactile, the skin, and more specifically the infratactile as a primordial sense, through which differentiation of senses works. Whereas eye–hand coupling (Strauven 2011) has been essential in the development of computer interfaces for everyday life, Hansen (2006: 81) extends his idea especially to virtual environments which reshuffle experiential coordinates and questions the primacy of the visual as well.

Hansen flags up a whole tradition concerning thinking through the body, embodiment and its sensations through an inherent, not just accidental, relation with technicity. From the anthropological theories of André Leroi-Gourhan (1911–86) to Gilbert Simondon (1924–89), this tradition offers a thoroughly layered view of the development of modes of sensation always articulated through the outside world, so to speak – replacing the internal–external divide with a view towards processes of individuation through which our sensation is always on the border of those two seemingly separated worlds.[8] So actually the outside is not the outside, but a fold which affects our capacities of sensation, perception, affection.

Indeed, whereas the ideas and projects in media arts have helped to catalyse some important insights concerning affect as part of how we should understand media, we can at the same time appreciate how an understanding of the messy materialities of affective regimes stems largely from nineteenth-century physiology, experimental psychology and a variety of scientific and experimental measurements in which the capacities of perception were embedded in the deep layers of the body.[9] In other words, there is a media-archaeological side to the notion of affect as well. Meticulous research in experimental psychology with new laboratory settings and special machine instruments such as the *tachistoscope*, as well as the methods for recording movement in time developed by such pioneers of scientific 'cinema' as Étienne-Jules Marey (1830–1904), were made to map the thresholds of the sensory and affective capacities of the animal being and what can be said to constitute the grounding for understanding cinematic perception embedded in the affective body (Väliaho 2010: 53–63).[10] The cinematic has one of its beginnings in the scientific measurement of time and motion of animal bodies, and this can be elaborated as the biopolitics of mediatic bodies: the way the governing of the living body is at the centre of political measures in modernity. This also means that the 'history of processes of perception' (Cubitt 2004: 66) – the more accepted field of media analysis – finds a shared ground with biopolitics.

So, in other words, what media theory calls the 'technics of the body' – that our bodily capacities have always been technologically conditioned – can also be discovered through a media-archaeological investigation into processes of perception where we find both: (a) an interest in the wider affective body (where affect is understood as the pre-conscious, physiological); and (b) the body's attachment to developments in visual and other media technologies. It is important to continuously underline that affect should not be directly reduced to emotion, but instead refers to the embodied, visceral, pre-conscious, but also relational, tuning of bodies of various kinds.

As a supplement to the academic discourses that arose around spectatorship and the attraction, art historian Jonathan Crary's account takes the 'technicity of sensation' to such a level that the knowledge concerning sensation cannot be detached from the technical assemblages in which it takes place. Epistemology and aesthetics are then both conditioned by media culture. What he names 'the observer' is, as a form of subjectivity, a result of the various institutional relations that include both social and technological contexts, and more specifically optical devices that are the object of analysis 'not for the models of representation they imply, but as sites of both knowledge and power that operate directly on the body of the individual' (Crary 1990: 7).

Yet what Crary establishes in his analysis of the historical conditions of the spectacle (in reference to Guy Debord (1931–94), and not so much explicitly to the notion of attraction) is a problematization of the relations between senses. Crary (1990: 19) argues that, whereas touch and haptics had been so valued in terms of 'classical theories of vision in the seventeenth and eighteenth centuries', a more complex differentiation of the senses and 'unloosening of the eye from the network of referentiality incarnated in tactility and its subjective relation to perceived space' (1990: 19) takes place in relation to 'new objects of vision', as well as an understanding of the observer not only as a consumer but as an object for scientific empirical study. While the eager consumer, spectator of media entertainment, is attentive to the events of the screen, the scientists and the marketing professionals have been as keen to track the behaviour and affective responses of that viewer on their screens. Can we find the early traces of affective marketing and neuromarketing already in such ideas of attention in the nineteenth century?

Mapping the displacement of the model of the camera obscura which, according to Crary, subsisted as a key model in physical optics and as a concrete technical, cultural apparatus (1990: 29), he is able to elaborate how the discursive 'unloosening of the eye' takes place in a wider understanding of the body in its *thickness*. Whether his emphasis on camera obscura is always loyal to the wealth of empirical material can be debated, but Crary's provocative argument is worth close consideration. Methodologically, 'it's a question of an observer who also takes shape in other, grayer practices and discourses, and whose immense legacy will be all the industries of the image and the spectacle in the twentieth century' (1990: 150). Indeed, what Crary seems to be after is an emblematic example of his media-technologi- cal rethinking of Foucault's and Deleuze's concepts. This is also close to what Elsaesser maps as the media-archaeological methodology of extending cinematic histories into the S/M perversions, and mapping the emergence of attraction/spectacle from the sciences of sensation of the nineteenth century. What could be called the 'cinematisation of the eye and of perception' (Zielinski 1999: 48) was taking place in an extensive field from actual entertainment toys and practices to emerging capitalist commodification, and on to science labs and research such as Hermann von Helmholtz's writings (for instance, 1867) concerning vision and tone.

While the camera obscura worked as part of a wider regime of a metaphysics of interiority that mapped the observer/individual as a 'nominally free sovereign individual and a privatized subject con- fined in a quasi-domestic space, cut off from a public exterior world' (Crary 1990: 39), the emergence of the new form of subjectivity as corporeal matches closely with theoretical themes concerning the ontological proximity of the interior to the exterior. Crary offers a historical investigation into the multiple modalities of sensation that can be approached as a historical condition – an archaeology – as well. Instead of focusing merely on vision as the key modality for modernity, he maps the modalities of the body through the historical relations between vision, hearing, touch and so forth, and the further context of how such capacities of the body are articulated in the late nineteenth and early twentieth centuries through new 'machine vision and techniques for the simulation of continuous movement' – all 'central elements in an incipient reshaping of mass culture' (Crary 1999: 5). However, in this perspective, the modern mass (media) culture does not start with the representational image or the gaze as focused on an object of representation, but in the processes of attention, movement and the wider sensations of the body which do touch the eye as much as the gut. Indeed, 'psychological regression' seemed to be a constant theme not only in clinical research but as an essential part of the entertainment industry that established a hidden continuation from earlier forms of popular culture to the burgeoning cinematic attractions:

> Beginning in the late 1880s, also, fairgrounds and related spaces included new kinaesthetic experiences such as ferris wheels, roller coasters, slides, and loop-the-loops. Within these 'controlled' circumstances the inciting of dynamogenic bodily sensations, for example on a merry-go-round, was a fragmentary and mechanical recuperation of carnival energies. Needless to say, during the next decade and a half, it was on this same social terrain of the fairground that another kinematic form of visual fascination implanted itself. Cinema would radically displace survivals of premodern forms like the circus, but would also powerfully constitute itself as a related 'enclave' for different modes of regression and phantasy. (Crary 1999: 238)

In short, if the notion of attraction has been a key vehicle that emerged from archival research, fed into film studies discourse and acted as a conceptual reshifting of interests towards a historicized spectator of affects, shocks and jolts of modernity, then a further drive has exported the notion of attraction from the screen to the wider kinaesthetic pleasures of the gut.[11] Hence, theoretical concepts and archival research can be seen working in a circuit that has expanded an interest in the epistemological conditions for the experience and knowledge of the body in media attractions and spectacle. Furthermore, as research has shown (see, e.g., Wilson 2004; Crary 1990, 1999), the physiological should not merely be reduced to a metaphor: for example, the gut, and its relation to, among other things, proprioception (kinaesthetics), might actually be taken into a fresh focus for a media archaeology of embodiment.

After senses: software culture

For media archaeology, epistemic thresholds can be used as heuristic devices. Elsaesser synthesized this realization as one of the lessons coming out of New Film History that, in combination with Foucault's archaeological and genealogical writings, provides guidelines on how to think new media through the old – and vice versa. In this sense, this example of investigating modes of sensation in modernity has been a key theme in (audio)visually oriented studies of media cultures – not least because of Gunning's and others' work in relation to the concept of attraction. Media technologies have, in differing ways, been elaborated as a condition of the modern mode of perception. In addition, the notion of attraction and related debates have provided one key context for approaching digital culture as well: both the emergence of cinema, and now the emergence of the digital, are embedded in a wider culture of affective, multimodal and intensive experiences spurred by the new medium. Yet, as we saw, a range of work also elaborated the logic of the cinematic in relation to other intermedial and architectural formations of modernity. Writings by, for example, Crary have been importantly situating the birth of the spectacle in the physiological – in terms of pointing out both that the visual has, since the nineteenth century, been understood as only part of the thickness of the body, and that this more fleshy, more nervous, more visceral notion of media and sensation provides an important epistemological condition for understanding contemporary media culture.[12] Crary is, of course, not alone in such an emphasis, and, for example, Kittler (2010) has been adamant in his claim that in order to understand the discourse network of technical media culture, we need to see such technologies as cinema as *psychotechnics* (more on that concept in chapter 4). Interestingly, Kittler claims that Crary is not radical enough and too focused on the human body: instead of a focus on bodies and histories of senses of the human being, Kittler claims, understanding technical media is a matter of materiality and not only of physiology. Geometrical optics was indeed replaced, but by something that is no longer focused on the human perceiver, and in which light does not always bend only 'on human bodies and eyes' (Kittler 2010: 148).

What does this cryptic statement mean? Instead of only physiology, Kittler is interested in mathematics and physics as the basis for a quantification of how modern sciences measured stimulation of the human senses. Sensations that form the 'attraction' can be measured as quantities, and that quantification forms the basis for a technologization of the sensorium through technical media, and later digital media. According to Kittler, we need to dig deeper into the scientific background and scientific theories from which media technologies are made and which then form conditions for perception for us too. Kittler's interest in the Fourier transform of the mathematician

Jean-Baptiste Joseph de Fourier (1768–1839) is a good example of this drive to find the mathematical roots for the logic of dissecting and codifying cultural techniques – such as music – into the modifiable world of software. Such scientific techniques form the ground for translating the analogue (continuous wave functions, such as sounds) into the discrete (for instance, the digital). Kittler is interested in genealogies of the image and sensation from a perspective of technical media, and, to be rigorous, it needs to start from quantification of stimuli and reaction in animal bodies, and hence leads to physics and mathematics more than to psychology. Indeed, starting from the cinematic escorts us to genealogies of the media condition that starting from the haptic and gamelike would not, and similarly starting from the algorithmic is bound to open up a new regime of investigation that reorders the way we understand senses, sensation and the mediatic entwined in modernity.

In Elsaesser's vocabulary for media-archaeological method, this relates to how we are, with the digital, at the 'very threshold of the visible' (Elsaesser 2008: 239), which does not refer only to digital cinema and, for example, its new forms of distribution in the network era, but to how the idea of the cinema as a machine of the visible – as Comolli once phrased it – is disappearing. The image is turning to quantifiable bits, algorithms, and is part of software culture. What we see (and hear) is conditioned by a whole layer of what itself seems to escape sensation: the mathematics of software (cf. Chun 2004, 2011b: 15–54). If several media archaeologists have been arguing that one cannot understand modern media culture, the cinematic, attractions and such without turning to how it is conditioned in relation to the physiological body, this new understanding of the software image seems to be arguing that we cannot understand spectacle and attraction without understanding it mathematically. The earlier-mentioned technological non-conscious then not only is about human bodies, but involves a complex knowledge of the computational premises of contemporary media culture.

When it boils down to technical contexts and mathematics, Kittler (2001) argues for a perspective into the pixel-centred image that, despite its phenomenological qualities (i.e. how we perceive the image as image), is basically very different from other modes of visuality, and certainly from optics. Computer graphics is a two-dimensional coordinate space of pixel-neighbourhoods, where every pixel is a mixture of intensities of red, green and blue – the RGB colour model of three primary colours. Techniques of image manipulation work then on a different level of pixel manipulation from chemical-based images: easy-to-use in contemporary Photoshop-culture for creation of objects for amateur use (modifying before uploading to Facebook), or for object-creation before selling in the mini-economy of Second Life, or when creating professional images for commercial use in a manner that Manovich (2001: 302–3) argues is a return to pre-cinematic animation practices and painting the image. But painting is in this case quite a bad metaphor, as we have moved farther away from the gesturality of the painter, the hand and the use of colours on canvas. Instead, we are in a culture of coding and encoding colour intensities in a gridded pixel space, conditioned at a variety of levels, from the image production software to capacities of screens, and in-between a whole plethora of protocols for compression and transmission. This is codec culture.

Furthermore, images are functions in the mathematical realm, made visible for us humans with such historical techniques as raytracing and radiosity – light, the basic 'substance' of optics and media cultural phenomena for a long 'deep time' of visual culture is itself something that becomes a special case of calculus (in the case of raytracing, differential calculus of light rays between objects; in radiosity calculations, integral calculus, according to Kittler 2001: 42). The image comes out as a mixture of the pixels in the raster (my current resolution is 1280×800) – starting from the point 0,0 at the top left corner – a space that is a space not only of visibility but of trackability (you are able to identify any minute point in an image with precision), and hence connected to themes of surveillance. Sean Cubitt has shown how this paradigm of surveillance society (from spatial mapping) and database economy (from Excel sheets to database management) is inherent in such grids, and how the genealogy extends from the early experiments with photography by Henry Fox-Talbot (1800–77) to experiments with wireless image transmission and scanning of images across distances, to LCD screens and on to the ecological-material implications of the gases used in plasma screens.[13]

Media archaeology starts suddenly to sound like software (and hardware) studies, as well as opening up a new relation to the nineteenth-century media culture. Basically such approaches, even if not always explicitly branding themselves as media archaeology, are suggesting that we need to be media-specific: we need to understand the particularities of each mode of transmission, processing and storage in our culture to have a real grasp of what media is doing to us. However, the descent of, for instance, digital cultural devices might actually start much earlier than the actual devices were built – for instance in earlier physics and mathematics. And yet it is not *only* about the media technologies. As part of larger themes concerning quantification, standardization and money, the question of the numerical mathematical basis of media culture can be tracked in various ways. Similarly to how Crary mapped the relation of attention to new regimes of work and capitalist consumption of media cultural objects, we can observe the relations between standardization across regimes of signs – from money to images / media-cultural objects, affects now for the first time being packaged by such inventor-entrepreneurs as Thomas A. Edison (1847–1931) into consumer products ready to be sold as distinct events and units (see Crary 1999: 31–2). We can see this idealization of bodies (Kittler 2001) into more manageable units as one crucial feature that ties in image technologies with typewriters as modern standardization of letters and writing, the calculating machines of Charles Babbage (1791–1871) as well as Turing machines, and a range of other entertainment and office equipment as part of the same episteme concerning creating a commodity form (Gere 2002: 17:40). Instead of merely linear histories of media, we see intertwined parallels and links emerging; the universal machine, as the 1930s idea of British mathematician Alan Turing (1912–54) was called, was able to be programmed to imitate logically any existing machine, and can be seen to correspond, for example, to ideas concerning universality of exchange values, argued by Karl Marx (1818–83) and others to be one pillar on which capitalist economy formed; Crary had suggested a parallel link between photography and money, that – to quote – were creating 'totalising systems for binding and unifying all subjects within a single global network of valuation and desire' (quoted in Gere 2002: 33); similarly the automation of labour processes with, for example, automated looms such as Jacquard's, and the subsequent automation of intellectual processes with Babbage's Difference Engine and plans for the Analytic Engine, had close links with increased demands for 'dealing with ever-greater amounts of information' (2002: 25). Circulation of goods and money, as well as information (telegraphy played a key part in this development in the nineteenth century), became crucial for the new formation of intermedial links as the backbone of capitalism (2002: 32).[14]

In terms of an archaeology of image technologies and their relation to software cultures since World War II, this ever-widening interpretation of media presents new challenges and opportunities for research. Computing machines of the steam period, network technologies and systems already existing in the age of the so-called 'Victorian Internet' (a term coined by Tom Standage (1999) to refer to the telegraph system of the late nineteenth century) have made it into the cartographies of media theorists interested in long-term continuities and ruptures, but the past fifty years of emergence of software and hardware cultures is something that is still waiting for more thorough work. The way Gunning's concept of attraction made early cinematic cultures the reference point for understanding new digital technological attractions can perhaps be expanded to what Crary already hinted at: namely, archaeologies of the spectacle. This could provide a link to the emergence of software-embedded post-Fordist cultures, and also to how such processes and practices can be incorporated into a wider network of media relations.

What defines our contemporary culture is that media are calculated and processed in algorithms. Computing and media merge. This both changes the way we see past media cultures and demands that new kinds of archaeologies and histories of its own emergence be written. In other words, Casey Alt's (2011) question of how and when 'computation became media' captures the full breadth of the turn towards algorithmic cultures – and how our archaeologies of 'code' need to become sufficiently specific to look at concrete practices, ontologies and epistemologies, as, for instance, in object-oriented programming, from the Spacewar! game on PDP1 computers (1962) to Alan Kay's programming environment Smalltalk (1972) – the first time computation and data for visual media cultures became understood through environments of software objects interfaced in topological relations with each other. An increasing amount of interest is then focused not on sensations that the human sensorium registers from media, but on relations between software objects, processes, hardware, networks and more.

Archaeological excavation seems to turn towards a two-fold mission then. From the 1980s roots in New Film History and the emphasis on mapping the link between the visual, the media industries of attractions, and the subsequent work on the cinematic, the new software culture archaeologies demand:

(1)   genealogies in which media are always formed in intermedial relations, and as conditions for sensation (that much we knew already from earlier film theories that emphasized, for instance, synaesthesia as part of the modern cinematic experience – see Strauven (2009); and

(2)   archaeologies of media in the more technical sense; digging under the screen in order to reveal the conditions of the present as embedded in the workings of the machine – software, hardware, networks. Such theorists as Kittler place as much emphasis on scientific disciplines, such as physics. Software objects of our everyday life are hence layered in multiple ways; they have histories but also are layered in the technological

sense of conditioning the way they attract, and act as conduits of power, governance, economy and relations between humans and non-humans. This double bind, a two-fold understanding of archaeology, will be elaborated throughout this book.

We will deepen such media archaeologies of the material and the digital in later chapters, and next turn to imaginary media research as one special way of doing media studies. This relates to how media archaeology can also take as its objects media and technology that did not exist, as well as imagining new histories of the suppressed, neglected and forgotten voices of media history, to find the perversions in media history, the stories and ideas that do not always fit in with our rationalized and standardized image of media-historical progress. In addition, the next chapter aims to think outside the normal categories of what are perceived as 'media' and to expand the notion of the 'medium' in surprising directions.

Summary

Media archaeology has close affinities with New Film History and, more widely, the rethinking of cinematic cultures from the point of view of the early cinema, as well as the pre-cinematic. Such perspectives have, since the 1980s, been brought to bear on the emergence of digital media culture as well, and they have been used to highlight such conceptual approaches to media as attraction, tactility, affect and other material, and even physiological, ways of understanding the effects of modern visual culture. Media archaeology originating from film studies turns increasingly to look at the new media-cultural contexts, as a perspective for writing media histories anew. Such aspects as software or, for example, human–computer interfacing in real-time computer cultures demand new vocabularies that do not see changes completely as historical ruptures but as epistemological possibilities for discovering new material aspects from our digital cultural past.

Further readings

Elsaesser, Thomas (2004) 'The New Film History as Media Archaeology' *CINéMAS*, 14(2–3), 71–117.
Elsaesser, Thomas (2008) 'Afterword: Digital Cinema and the Apparatus: Archaeologies, Epistemologies, Ontologies' in *Cinema and Technology*.

Cultures, Theories, Practices, ed. Bruce Bennett, Marc Furstenau and Adrian Mackenzie (Basingstoke: Palgrave Macmillan), 226–40.

Huhtamo, Erkki and Parikka, Jussi, eds. (2011) *Media Archaeology. Approaches, Applications, Implications* (Berkeley, CA: University of California Press).

Strauven, Wanda, ed. (2008) *The Cinema of Attractions Reloaded* (Amsterdam: Amsterdam University Press).

Strauven, Wanda (2012, forthcoming) 'Media Archaeology: Where Film History, Media Art and New Media (Can) Meet' in *Preserving and Exhibiting Media Art: Challenges and Perspectives*, ed. Julia Noordegraaf, Cosetta Saba, Barbara Le Maître and Vinzenz Hediger (Amsterdam: Amsterdam University Press).

3

Imaginary Media: Mapping Weird Objects

Walking around Gebhard Sengmüller's *A Parallel Image*, part of the Transmediale 2010 art exhibition, was a kind of a media-archaeological exercise in itself. The visitor was confronted with a weird, messy, luminous device of wires and screens that suggested more accurately unsuccessful, wild dreams of technology than anything that we hope our media to be: functional, nicely packaged, most often in some rectangular (plastic) form, whether we are talking of televisions, screens in general, computers, mobiles or, for example, stereo-systems. *A Parallel Image* had a direct affiliation with a media-archaeological strand of thinking/doing old media – new media in parallel lines but also of imagining possible pasts and futures outside linear media history. It investigated imaginary media and the discursive framings of televisual technology history – but it did this in a very material fashion. It imagined through alternative design.

Sengmüller constructed a transmission device for visual data that does not break the visual field into discrete elements that are then sent over to the receiving end serially, but employs a very messy (one has to say) method of parallel image transmission: every pixel element is sent in parallel 'directly' to the receiver via some 2,500 cables, using ideas rather like those of Paul DeMarinis in his *The Messenger* installation (1998), which reworked parallel transmission for the telegraph system. Hence, *A Parallel Image* detaches from the universally adopted ideas that were formulated early on by Frenchman Maurice Leblanc (1857–1923) in 1880: that images are to be broken into lines before transmission and that light is then to be translated into electric signals, and at the receiving end, the receiver's function is the translation of electric currents into an image. Developed further with the

Image 3.1 Gebhard Sengmüller's *A Parallel Image* installation (2009). © Gebhard Sengmüller

invention of the Nipkow disc, and decades later in early experiments by John Logie Baird (1888–1946) in 1926, the idea of serial image signal transmission has remained a standard way to transmit images in which the breaking down of the images into rows and the time synchronization are the key elements through which we receive moving images over distances.[1]

Instead of following this mainstream idea, Sengmüller describes his idea – of practical uselessness but of media-archaeological interest – as

> an apparatus that links every pixel on the 'camera side' with every pixel on the 'monitor' side in the technically simplest way possible. Taking this idea to its logical conclusion, this leads to an absurd system that connects a grid of 2,500 photoconductors on the sender side with 2,500 small light bulbs on the receiver side, pixel by pixel, using a total of 2,500 copper wires. In addition, there are wires that supply each of these 'image transmission – micro units' with electricity.[2]

As you can guess from the amount of elements, the device resembles more an early mainframe computer or telephone switching centre in size. The spirit of the work is emblematic of the curiosity cabinet style of media-archaeological artwork, perhaps in a similar way to Sengmüller's early *VinylVideo* (1998) work which recorded analogue TV signals on LP record format, creating different technological solutions that stretch between past media reimagined and new media outside the commercial sphere, but also in various other ways:

(1)   It exemplifies some ideas of imaginary media – media non-existent, fabulated, or at one point deemed impractical for any serious mass-production, or just at some point vanished and dead (Zielinski 2006b: 30); the piece offers a 'what if' view to media culture, and engages with alternative histories as a resource for understanding the assumptions concerning media techno-logical innovations. Why do certain designs, technological solutions and assumptions concerning media use habits persist, and others vanish? What if the contemporary media culture is not a Leibnizian best of all possible worlds, and what if, on the other hand, it is not as unique in its novelty as is rhetorically claimed in marketing and other discourses whose job is merely to steer media-cultural objects into a homogenized *psychopathia media-lis* as claimed by Siegfried Zielinski (2006a:8) in *Audiovisions* and *Deep Time of the Media*?

(2)   Yet the piece is not only discursive excavation, but engages in a work of planning, building, realizing a spatially present machinic installation; it sets media-archaeological ideas into action – a bit like the early 1990s reconstruction of Charles Babbage's Difference Engine no. 2 which, due to lack of funding, remained as plans and diagrams until then. Such a trend is increasingly visible not only in nationally significant projects that strategi-cally (re)produce histories of computing, such as the Babbage reconstruction at the London Science Museum, but also in the experimental sense of engaging with technical media culture and what we are going to discuss below and especially in the chapter on media-archaeological art methods. In other words, media critique is not only about saying things, it is about design and materiality – *doing* critique in an alternative fashion, against the grain, so to speak (see Lovink 2003: 11). Through such mate-rial existence, the media-archaeological work puts the spectator/user/viewer into a new relation with the imaginary, and hence forces us to engage creatively with the presence of media – new and old, imagined and real.

This chapter investigates imaginary media research, how it extends to conceptualizing the impossible, the unviable pieces of alternative media history, communication in spheres usually left out of official media histories, variantologies of media, but also, nearer the end of the chapter, offering a glimpse of what might be a slightly more material definition of 'imaginary media'. In other words, imaginary media is something you do not always find in basic media studies textbooks: media that are the stuff of dreams as well as nightmares, at times existing only in the minds of inventors or science-fiction writers. Pasts can also be (re)imagined as in steampunk fiction. Ideas for imaginary media come from various directions, and in this chapter I try to extend the idea of the 'imaginary' outside its psychoanalytic connotations. Instead, the imaginary of technology is something that moves from artistic creations to scientific contexts, even if such are often discursively described in discourses of the paranormal.

Archives of the impossible

The role of imaginary media research within the media-archaeological field is rather difficult to decipher. This is not because there would be any doubt about whether they have an intimate relation – it's more because the relation is so close that the themes get quite easily conflated. Hence, one might say that most of imaginary media research has been media-archaeologically driven, but that media archaeology cannot be reduced to imaginary media research. Furthermore, what was once imaginary might have become part of reality later. In the words of the writer and journalist Henry Adams (1838–1918), as a contemporary of the modern world of invention circa 1900 which, in its pace of innovation, exceeded imagination and the human senses and found only some precedents in world history:

> Impossibilities no longer stood in the way. One's life had fattened on impossibilities. Before the boy was six years old, he had seen four impossibilities made actual – the ocean-steamer, the railway, the electric telegraph, and the Daguerreotype; nor could he ever learn which of the four had most hurried others to come. He had seen the coal-output of the United States grow from nothing to three hundred million tons or more. (Adams 1918/2000: chapter 34)

This was a world of science as occult and supersensuality, and things just slightly earlier deemed imaginary, such as X-rays, electromagnetic waves and electricity, became real. Such 'galleries of machines' forced people to see the inventions as major thresholds for perception and the sense of temporality in machine culture (Tomas 2004). Hence, imagining futures in writing and audiovisually has been a crucial way of framing the futures of, for example, computing, as in the BBC1 short clip on *Tomorrow's World* introducing the home computer terminal in 1967: extrapolating a future where the computer acts as an online calendar, bank account interface and educator for kids, with an easy-to-use typewriter-modelled input interface (www.bbc.co.uk/ archive/, accessed 23 Nov. 2011). With hindsight, imagination does not always seem that imaginary or impossible.

Imaginary media are not media of prediction, but there seems to be a very systematic relation between invention, imagination and the birth of scientifically based modern media culture that is not always discussed only in scientific terms.[3] Similarly, imaginary media and media archaeology are often interested in the forgotten which now seems like new – a good example could be the 'theatrophone' from late nineteenth-century France: a mode of delivering news and entertainment through the telephone (Mareschal 1892). In the UK, an equivalent service was the 'Electrophone', from the 1890s till the 1920s, and in Hungary, the Telefon Hirmondo.[4] Such modes of using the telephone disappeared, and were superseded by broadcasting, and hence, from the current perspective, seem peculiar and imaginary.

In this sense, I shall continue in this chapter to discuss how the notion of media imagined relates to rethinking media histories, how to complexify the notions of 'actual' and 'imagined' media and what kind of work has been done under this rubric, but also how the latter term affords much beyond its normal use in the Lacanian psychoanalytic sense. Indeed, as we will discuss below, the notion of media-not-quite-real relates to a wider theme in modern media: media are increasingly not object-based. Instead, as non-solids, they escape direct perception, as in the case of electromagnetic fields, so crucial for the birth of broadcasting and current mobile culture. Perhaps imaginary media research is a shorthand for discussing such novel realms of media, and media outside the normal checklist of what we intuitively see as media (and listed as part of media studies undergraduate courses)? This chapter is hence about celebrating weirdness in media culture and its non-linear pasts, and using that weirdness as a methodological guideline for further investigations concerning our normalized assumptions about more docile bodies of mainstream media (to adopt Foucault's (1995) idea into a media context).

Eric Kluitenberg, who in 2004 organized a significant media-archaeological symposium and festival in Amsterdam at the Debalie Centre, on imaginary media, offers extensive and important notes on the concept itself. Kluitenberg (2011) attaches the concept to a wider social field of production of desire, and to the role media that are imagined play in contextualizing *actual* media. Suggesting that imaginary media are important not only as exercises of imagination but as entry-points to the wider unconscious surrounding the technological culture, the notion becomes a way to look at how technological assemblages are embedded in hopes, desires and imaginaries of mediation. As such, it shares some methodological premises of the cultural studies in media research, such as Raymond Williams's (1974/2003) work that sought to analyse how technical possibilities take effect only in wider social fields. Hence, imaginary media are not, to paraphrase Kluitenberg, 'only' imaginary:

> More often than not, the expectations contained in such imaginaries far exceed that what actual media machines are actually capable of doing. However, the actual media machines are themselves afflicted with impossible desires that are ascribed to or projected on to them, by their designers as well as in their perception by the public. The transition between imaginary and actual media machines, in terms of their signification, can be almost seamless. Thus the imaginaries of imaginary media tend to weave in and out of the purely imagined and the actually realized media machineries. Because impossible desires can never be fully realized or satisfied, imaginary media exceed the domain of apparatuses (realized media machines) and their 'histories'. They articulate a highly complex field of signification and determination that tends to blur the boundaries between technological imaginaries and actual technological development. (Kluitenberg 2011: 48)

If we were to follow a Lacanian view of imaginary media – that it is based in lack, and the impossibility of desire as the basis for impossible media – we might want to analyse how such machines and machinations are vital in producing seeming unities and rationalities as models for subjectivity in media cultures. For Lacan (1901–81), the imaginary is one key stage in creating the unified subject out of the primary fragmented flows that, for example, the newborn infant embodies. The imaginary acts as a necessary illusion, so to speak, which maintains our subject–object relations. The imaginary brings coherence where there might be none, and this might be a good way to analyse the dream worlds promised by contemporary media-technological discourses, whether in terms of their role in social relations (being always connected, across distances and times, as in so many mobile media discourses) or as a source of endless 'gratification' (the *joy-stick* nature of media, instant-delivery of dream content in a post-broadcast culture of on-demand). As Kluitenberg (2006b: 11–12) argues, imaginary media can be seen to have close links with ideals of community and connection, and this works through a similar logic to that of the myth: a naturalization that offers ideological support to values, ideals and aspirations in communication society.

I, however, argue that imaginary media can be developed from a non-Lacanian perspective as well. Closer to such historical methodologies as media archaeology, we can map the relation to Foucault's archaeology and how his expansion of the notion of the archive from a mere spatial place of documentation to encompass discursive rules and conditions for what can be said is a good way to develop imaginary media methodology. After all, the question of imaginary media is: what *can* be imagined, and under what historical, social and political conditions? What are the conditions for the media imaginaries of the modern mind and contemporary culture, and, on the other hand, how do imaginaries condition the way we see actual technologies?

Media archaeologists interested in the imaginary are as interested in the actual as they are in the impossible. As Kluitenberg (2011) outlines, but taking a different stance from him and his detachment of imaginary media archaeologies from Foucault, we can find several necessary clues to archives of the impossible in Foucault (2002). *The Archaeology of Knowledge* and Foucault's other works offered methods of investigating conditions of knowledge outside the traditional frameworks concerning truth and fiction, and hence offered a more transversal, transdisciplinary, insight into what kinds of thoughts, practices, discourses are sustained, and what are discarded as non-sense. Hence, occupying a space outside the normal disciplines of, for example, history, psychology and sociology, such analysis of conditions of knowledge looks at how objects of knowledge are always temporarily stabilized in discursive practices that give them the status of knowledge. Object do not precede their discourse; discourses constitute them as epistemological objects of knowledge, and hence 'make possible the appearance of objects during a given period of time' (Foucault 2002: 36). This is the passage, so to speak, from things to objects (2002: 52) that are always regulated systematically in relations through which they start to become part of officialized, stabilized and often scientific knowledge, and it is through cultural practices that such discursive relations are sustained.

Hence, even if Kluitenberg (2011) reminds us that media archaeology has been fetishizing the apparatus in the various investigations of, for example, pre-cinematic technologies, and that Foucault himself was not interested in the object behind the discourse, I believe that this seeming contradiction is a misunderstanding of the ways in which Foucauldian archaeology can be mobilized. The materiality of the archive is part of regulated, discursive serialization that puts objects and statements into inseparable proximity. Yet, archaeological analysis is able to map things that do not seem to have a material presence, but that are for Foucault (2002: 116) always bound up with an institution that is not necessarily spatio-temporally localizable. Deleuze (2006: 43) referred to Foucault's methodology of archaeology as the audiovisual archive because it articulates how the sayable and the visible are expressed and made possible. The archive is completely mediatic, completely real, even if it does not necessarily deal with actually existing things.

Such a notion of the archive is first and foremost interested in the blunt fact that *something is* as an object of knowledge (Foucault 2002: 124). This something is recorded, kept, maintained, inserted into a series as a symptom and is part of a wider network of knowledge about a medical condition, or, in our case, as media technologies participate in creating regimes of knowledge across arts and sciences. Media too are epistemological machines. For Foucault and his notion of the archive and the archaeological, key points are, as paraphrased from *Archaeology of Knowledge* (2002: 155–6):

1)   Archaeology is monumental, i.e. it does not look at what is behind a discourse, and does not try to interpret by referring to something outside the discourse. It is focused on the fact that something is – a monument.
2)   Archaeology focuses on the specificity of the discourse, and not on establishing a continuity and transition.
3)   Archaeology works outside disciplines and normal boundaries of knowledge, such as *oeuvres*.
4)   Archaeology and its conception of the archives do not point to origins, secret or obvious, but are interested in rewriting practices and 'systematic description of a discourse-object' (Foucault 2002: 156).

The reason for this rehearsal of Foucault's ideas from his early work is that it enables us both to think imaginary media as part of technical media culture and to link them up with discourses concerning institutions (even fabulated) of invention, as well as with the expansion of a media-cultural interest from actual to the imagined, or non-present, media. As we will see later (chapter 6), this is also instrumental to some developments which restore the centrality of the archive for media studies (Ernst 2000, 2011).

Such an archaeological approach to the imaginary acknowledges that there are differing regimes of knowledge. What we now perceive as media imagined might have featured as part of a wider metaphysical worldview and system of ideas and objects in various relations to what is now seen as scientific knowledge, as with natural magic (and human-made artificial magic), from Giambattista Della Porta (1535–1615) to the extensive networks of Jesuits such as Athanasius Kircher (1602–80).

For Kluitenberg (2011), imaginary media afford an analysis of communication with divinities, as with the medieval *Horologium Sapientiae* ('Wisdom's Watch upon the Hour', 1339) of Heinrich Suso (*c*.1300–66) in which the calculational regularity of the clock synchronizes a relation with God; and of communication with spirits, as during the nineteenth-century conflation of technical media with the practices of mediums' communication with the dead, extending even to Thomas A. Edison's interest in machines that reach to the afterlife (Sconce 2000; see 'Mr Edison's "Life Units": Hundred Trillion in Human Body May Scatter After Death – Machine to Register Them', *New York Times*, 23 Jan.1921),[5] but also to such imaginary media as time-machines (such a beloved theme of modern science fiction), teleporter machines (as in *Star Trek*) and much more. The media-archaeological artist Paul DeMarinis (2010: 204) described his *Torch Song* performance from 2002 as an assemblage of 'a variety of archaic and "impossible" audio media, including real-time shortwave radio transmissions, Edison cylinder recordings, flame loudspeakers and manometric flame oscilloscopes to conduct a radiophonic séance with the voices of dead dictators'. To such examples one can add Peter Blegvad's (2006) audiovisual musings on the topic, in which imaginary media have no fixed time–space coordinates, nor do they have to be physically present to the senses, yet they can be described through the consistency of the discursive object, which in this case is imaginary. As Kluitenberg underlines, even in such a case, the task remains that of involving the imaginary media in methods of situated knowledge, and pinpointing such imaginations 'in a specific historical and discursive setting, to uncover the network of material practices in which these imaginaries are embedded' (2011: 55).

Variantology and imaginary pasts and futures

In the midst of a number of different weird examples, how do we then make the field of imaginary media seem more consistent? One of the key proponents of this approach – or what he has also called not only archaeology of media but, more provocatively, *an-archaeology* of media – is the Berlin-situated professor Siegfried Zielinski, who aims to offer methodological and ethical guidelines for the development of

Image 3.2 Albert Robida's novel *Le vingtième siècle* (1883) imagines a future to come – a future embedded in fantastic media devices that infiltrate everyday life: technologies of telecommunication, imaginary vehicles, new screen media, surveillance and peeping, as well as marketing and branding that infiltrate every corner of the urban space – including air space.

such a research programme. Indeed, what his variantology of media offers is exactly a multiplication of our understanding of what counts as media, and hence it aims to provide insights into how imaginary media can be seen as a useful, albeit radical, concept for media studies and media practices.

In terms of specifically imaginary media, Zielinski offers us this division:

(1) untimely media and machines which are outside their own time – 'realized in technical and media practice either centuries before or centuries after being invented';

(2) conceptual media and machines that were outside the possibilities of the actual world – media sketched, modelled and diagrammatized but never really born;

(3) impossible media and machines whose 'initial design or sketch makes clear that they cannot actually be built, and whose implied meanings nonetheless have an impact on the factual world of media' (2006b: 30).

For all of the above, we can offer examples from the vast variantologies that Zielinski himself writes and edits,[6] or look at the 'moon
media apparatuses', such as the spectrophone, the parlamonium and
the oneiroscope that Walter Benjamin introduced in his short radio
play *Lichtenberg* in the 1930s.[7] We won't run out of weird inventions
and mad ideas in the history of art and science. Imaginary media seem
to reside in the *theological* – such as the various inventions of Jesuit
father Athanasius Kircher (1601/2–80) – and delusions of paranoid
schizophrenics from *c*.1900, between the drawing boards of *mathema-
ticians* and the imaginations of *science-fiction writers*. For Zielinski,
the connection to the notion of variantology serves an important
function as a concept and methodology of media studies that in a
Foucauldian manner steers clear of 'firsts' and resists the aforementioned *psychopathia medialis* that tries to normalize, to make docile,
our (understanding of) media. With 'media', and especially digital
media, becoming the primary fantasy object of the new capitalist
economy's wet dreams since the 1990s, Zielinski's important goal
seems to be to resist such an economically driven, narrow appropriation of media technologies.

With the idea of 'variantology', Zielinski flags the need to use media-
archaeological methods as part of an excavation of practices of invention. In *Deep Time of the Media* he starts out by outlining variantology
in relation to ideas of the deep time of the earth – an abandoning of the
linear time of progress – and, with the help of palaeontologist Stephen
Jay Gould metamorphosed into a media theorist, the discourses (as in
'images, metaphors, and iconography') used to confirm the existence
of progress from higher to lower as an evolutionary ladder are to be
replaced with a palaeontology-turned-media-archaeology:

> Instead of looking for obligatory trends, master media, or imperative
> vanishing points, one should be able to discover individual variations.
> Possibly, one will discover fractures or turning points in historical
> master plans that provide useful ideas for navigating the labyrinth of
> what is currently firmly established. In the longer term, the body of
> individual anarchaeological studies should form a *variantology* of the
> media. (Zielinski 2006a: 7)

As a celebration of experimentality and heterogeneity, Zielinski's
call is at the heart of imaginary media – or, in a more active sense,
imagining media and its histories so that they can return the possibility of imagining alternative futures. While trying to carve out the
especially critical and innovative aspects of variantology that expand
the possibilities both of thinking of media 'outside the box', so to
speak, and also of thinking of time in novel, more complex ways, I

will point out some contradictions inside Zielinski's theoretical–methodological writing. While at the same time insisting, in a rather fruitful way that connects him to, for example, Siegfried Giedion's 'anonymous history', that technology is deeply inhuman (Zielinski 2006a: 6), the methodology turns soon to a celebration of heroes and putting 'people and their works' in the methodological focus. With case studies ranging from Empedocles to Giovanni Battista della Porta (1535–1615), Robert Fludd (1574–1637), Athanasius Kircher, Johann Wilhelm Ritter (1776–1810) and Aleksej Gastev (1882–1939), Zielinski is able to point to a wider geographical field of hubs of invention that offers important clues to thinking about the geopolitics of media archaeology (which, just to mention as a sidestep, has for a long time neglected, for example, most Asian regions and their media cultural histories, as well as, for example, the Arabic world, in addition to South America, Africa, and Australian indigenous people[8]). However, even if geopolitically progressive, gender-wise what is offered is indeed a history of *male* heroes in which the quick reference to 'heroines' is not followed up. A sympathetic reading would say that such heroes are entry points to understanding wider media strategies of invention, experimentation and excavating ever deeper, always more obscure ideas and pre-personal forces in a Deleuzian approach to how to understand the relation between hearing and seeing. But, at the same time, a sceptical critic would claim that the defence offered by Zielinski of being a 'romantic' (2006a: 34) is inadequate in terms of providing a sound methodological base from which to look for inspiration.

Hence, it is interesting to read Zielinski in relation to Zoe Beloff's media archaeology, which is executed more in screen and installation-based art projects than in writings. Despite this difference in the media used, Beloff engages in what seems to be a similar call for imaginary media, or media reimagined with the use of archival material and past media as a storehouse – something that Beloff (2002: 287) has described in terms of (in a Benjaminian-sounding phrase) '"the dream life of technology" (not what technology is or was, but what people believed or desired it to be)'. Not only a discursive excavation, this task is a reimagining of the past and the future in order to restore what she refers to as 'a multiplicity of cinematic apparatus' – develops through that archive of multiplicity 'new languages of vision' (2002: 287) in the age of what we call 'new media'. A good example of this is her database-panoramic CD-ROM work *Beyond* (1997), which itself was an elaboration of the parallels between the infant imperfections of incipient media such as Quicktime and the similarly fragmented early cinematic cultures from which they drew inspiration – elaborating an archaeological logic symptomatic of modernity (Shaviro 1998). Hence, in *Beyond* and in her later works, the imperfectness, clumsiness and clunkyness (Beloff 2006: 215) are part and parcel of a rejection of seamlessness, and bring to the fore the material assemblages in which media take place – apparatuses, but ones that are embedded in wider networks of desires and dreams. In this way, imaginary media become anti-Lacanian, in that the imaginary is not the smooth unity that keeps together our dreamworlds. It actually breaks them apart, not perhaps by way of deconstruction but by exaggeration (Beloff 2006: 232).

Yet, where Beloff shows her acute sense of the critical archaeology of 'technology, bodies and psyches' as 'fantastic hybrids' (2006: 236) that characterize modernity is in the work subsequent to *Beyond* and *Where Where There There Where*. After these projects, she tackles archaeologies of the female body intertwined with emergence of modern media technologies, as well as institutions of mental health, and psychoanalysis. Her *Charming Augustine* 3D 16-mm film addresses the media history of female hysteria and its relation to the emergence of cinema through the case of the patient Augustine at the famous La Salpêtrière clinic in Paris in the 1870s, and how the female hysterical body – in her case surrounded by an aura of pre-cinematic stardom of significant theatricality – provides a motive for Beloff to investigate the link between cinema and mind, but also the capturing and showcasing of the female body as an object of investigation. A similar link between technology and hallucination is taken from another medical history case: *The Influencing Machine of Miss Natalija A.* (an installation from 2000), recalls the case study taken up by Victor Tausk (1879–1919) in 1919 of a young female who claims to have been influenced across distance, from Berlin, by electrical forces. The installation displays a stereoscopic diagram on which the user/viewer not only can see the various images that thematically touch on the case study, but becomes surrounded herself by voices, visions and other electromagnetic traces from the 1920s and 1930s: German home movies, medical and technical films, soundbites, etc.[9] The user/viewer also becomes embedded in weird, penetrating 'influencing machines' from the past media era, which provided the early symptoms of the affect economy, and of political influencing as mobilized by Nazi Germany soon after this case. In such projects – media imagined, communicating with the dead, or supernaturally influencing the mind – Beloff stays more aware of the gender implications in which modern media became articulated: the supposedly passive female body was conceived as a perfect medium for receiving messages.[10]

Image 3.3 A still from Zoe Beloff's *The Ideoplastic of Materialization of Eva C.* © Zoe Beloff

Hence, in terms of mapping these differing examples of how to address imaginary media and dreams of past and future, Zielinski's variantology succeeds in providing a basis for an elaboration of non-standardized experimental practices that turns into a guideline for media critique; by mapping past worlds of practice and imagination, one is able to highlight alternatives for contemporary and future media worlds. But it is in Beloff's art where similar ideas are worked into a more gender-aware context of creative practice that entangles histories of bodies with histories of technology. What one finds with Zielinski is a poetics of imaginary media and archaeology (2006a: 258) that also affords politically important medium-specific criticism, as shown above, but this poetics, this dreaming with imaginary media is what enables Beloff's work to highlight the blind spots in Zielinski and offer a complementary approach.

Zielinski's methodology leads to more aberrant paths in the worlds of art, technology and science – the palaeontologies of those practices that create media worlds in which we imagine; but Beloff's differently focused approach to modern media fantasies can, as we will see next, forward us to an understanding of a new aspect in imaginary media research. To quote Beloff's idea, technologies are themselves embedded in mental constructs, or constructed in a wider set of desires and dreams, but 'at the same time they define the boundaries of our thoughts' (Beloff 2002: 291). This boundary setting is what further-more can be defined as connected to a less poetic interpretation of imaginary media. In a similar way to how Kittler uses the hallucinated ideas of paranoid schizophrenics to draw up a material media theory, we can perhaps establish a more material definition of imaginary media. Explicating that materiality of the imaginary is my contribu-tion to the discussions concerning 'imaginary media'.

Non-human media

Beloff's work includes an extensive interest in ghosts as well as the netherworlds of communication with dead people through the medi-umship of, usually, the female body. Much of the research that can be labelled as part of 'imaginary media' has focused on the theme of death, ghosts and psychical communication, especially in the nine-teenth and early twentieth centuries, and, for example, communication with other worlds such as those of aliens. Jeffrey Sconce's *Haunted Media* is in this sense a wonderful condensation of the underbelly of the supposedly scientifically rational modernity, and an investi-gation of the 'fantastic' that accompanies screen, broadcasting and telecommunications media. In what he describes as a cultural history of these haunted media, or the sense of presence that haunts media technologies of modernity, Sconce maps something methodologically similar to Huhtamo's *topoi* analysis of recurring cultural narratives and genres when he identifies three key 'recurring fictions', as he calls them: (1) disembodiment and leaving the body; (2) teleportation, or the electronic elsewhere: and (3) 'anthropomorphization of media technology' (Sconce 2000: 8–9). He insists that these are not straight-forwardly 'deep structures' or 'founding mythemes of the media age' (2000: 10) but have to be closely interpreted as entry points to the historically specific discourses of which they speak. Yet, through such an investigation into how the new technologies of telegraphy and broadcasting were embedded in a larger discursive network which tackled psychical powers, gender relations and assumptions concern-ing new technologies, Sconce is able to show meticulous genealogies of digital culture as well. Indeed, as we know from the contempo-rary media sphere which seems to be haunted by such non-human actors as worms and viruses as semi-living agents of destruction, it is no wonder that the imaginary of the nineteenth century and, for example, the broadcasting era since the 1910s and 1920s envisioned the dead, the absent and the alien on the wires, or on the oceanic waves of wireless transmission.

The phenomenon of electricity had represented a spectacle long before the famous, cruel cinematic exhibition of the electrocution of Topsy the elephant in 1903 (*Electrocuting the Elephant*, Edison Company, 1903): Jean-Antoine Nollet (1700–70) carried out an experiment with wired Royal Guards (1748) and later wired monks to illustrate conduction of electricity through bodies, which was exemplary of what was later followed by Galvani's twitching frogs' legs, and then by the even more spectacular stunts with electricity of his nephew Giovanni Aldini (1762–1834) – wiring dead criminal bodies, and amputated limbs – and repeated by Nikola Tesla lighting lamps with a current that passed through the assisting person, Mr Clemens (Mark Twain).[11] Such end-of-the-nineteenth-century showmanship as Tesla's already reached other worlds in his early reports, from 1899, of receiving unexplained signals from Mars, backed up by other similar reports during the early decades of the twentieth century.

While receiving 'ghost' voices was part of broadcasting technology and radio waves, these were also continuously transformed discursively into speculations about aliens, the dead or some other uncanny form of communication that haunted scientific media (to use another term for technical media); this was a parallel phenomenon to Tausk's already-mentioned Influencing Machine case from the 1920s, which can be read as indexical to the considerations of power and new media technologies, even if conveyed through the language of neurosis and psychosis (Sconce 2011). What, however, is translated through the language of psychosis is, one could argue, the attempt to grasp the completely new sensory realms that came about with new media technology. In short, what seems imaginary, what was hallucinated and can be tracked methodologically through medical histories, case studies of madmen, fiction literature, and stories of fantastic other-worldly communication, is actually indexical of the fact that technical media was non-human media too.

Indeed, as Jeffrey Sconce highlights regarding Kittler's reading of the famous schizo-memoirs of D. P. Schreber (1842–1911) from the early twentieth century, these delusional narratives are the double of the emerging technologies of the recording and telecommunications networks. Schreber (1903/1955) was convinced that there were celestial scribes who wrote down every single one of his thoughts and actions, like meticulous monks. For theorists such as Kittler this is less of a referral to an individual pathological condition and more an index of the paranoid delusions particular to the age of technical media that record (almost) everything, just like the phonograph already proved to do. Hence, imaginary 'media' of rays affecting the nerves, hallucinations and delusions are, in Kittler's analysis, a way of understanding the link to the new psychoanalytic understanding of the body *circa* 1900, as well as emblematic of the discourse network of 1900 in which neurophysiology and new forms of technical media which produce and store only fragmented bits (Schreber 1903/1955: 172) are the new means of understanding the psyche (Kittler 1990: 290–9; see also Sconce 2011).

New media have constantly been imagined as media of mind control. The delusional side is only the paranoid schizophrenic hyperbole of what happens with technical media that do not translate easily into everyday language and understanding. Schreber imagines (or lives in) a world of complete transliteration of his inner thoughts that represents a media system in which Schreber, as Sconce (2011: 77) writes,

> proposed a model of 'nerve' that presented its own paradoxical relationship to transitional understandings of energetic transmission and telecommunicative circulation. The *Memoirs* frequently present 'nerve' as an articulated network, evoking the familiar image of the nervous system as conductive tendrils of electrical transmission. In this regard, Schreber regarded the physical body's nerve tissue as both a storage center (containing a person's memories and soul) and a metaphysical aerial sensitive to vibratory influence ('I receive light and sound sensations which are projected direct on to my inner nervous system by the rays, for their reception the external organs of seeing and hearing are not necessary').

For Kittler (1999), this ability to record outside meaning – recording that does not record only meaningful language but all the noises of the body, all the quirks, slips, hesitations, sighs, grunts – is the ability furnished by the technical media of photography and, in the regime of voices, the phonograph. Technical media such as the phonograph records the Real, not the Symbolic, or even the Imaginary, as Kittler translates the Lacanian ideas of the tripartite structure of the psyche as part of media history. The persistent interest in the bodies of psychotics, or ghosts, is actually about technical media showing how they work as inscription-machines with the human body being merely a relay point for a wider discourse network, as Kittler argues. In such a material version, then, the weird bodies of modernity – insane and otherworldly – are less hallucinations than part of the material logic of discourse networks.

In a way, with modification one could apply a methodological lesson from Slavoj Žižek (1992: 104–5) when he is analysing horror films: remove the horror element, such as the birds from the Hitchcock film *The Birds*, and what are revealed are the social relations and, in Žižek's psychoanalytic formula, the Oedipal relations. Applied to imaginary media, try the same: remove the imaginary, remove the supposedly fantastic or otherworldly, and see what is revealed: a world of social relations, networks of communication, and new worlds of media technologies which *are* non-human in the deep scientific sense of reaching out to the non-phenomenological worlds of electricity, electromagnetic fields and, a bit later for example, quantum mechanics. In such theorizations, however, we do not need the Oedipal.

This link between scientifically constructed new media and the more phantasmatic discourses and practices of psychic research was a crucial context in which new media emerged in the nineteenth century (Sconce 2000; see also Enns 2008). The US and the UK had their respective societies – founded in the 1880s – the American Society for Psychical Research and the Society for Psychical Research, whereby spiritualists shared ideas with natural scientists. Indeed, what is important to note is that the discourses of and interest in the paranormal were not that easily separable from the new sciences of electromagnetism, or the new technologies of telegraphy and other forms of long-distance communication. As John Durham Peters (1999: 14) writes, 'Though one might be amused at extreme forms of the enthusiasm to connect mediumless communication to deep metaphysical interests, early radio history is inseparable from daring imaginings about the flight of souls, voices without bodies, and instantaneous presence at a distance. Dreams of bodiless contact were a crucial condition not only of popular discourse but of technical invention as well.' This was evinced through such figures as William Crookes (1832–1919), both the inventor of the cathode-ray tube and a believer in communication directly between brains (1892: 176). A range of the early media pioneers thought that the new technologies present such radical changes to our worldview that they demanded a whole new coordinate system for the so far seemingly solid and stable world. In 1892, in 'Some Possibilities of Electricity', Crookes wrote:

> Whether vibrations of the ether, longer than those which affect us as light, may not be constantly at work around us, we have, until lately, never seriously inquired. But the researches of Lodge in England and of Hertz in Germany give us an almost infinite range of ethereal vibrations or electrical rays, from wave-lengths of thousands of miles down to a few feet. Here is unfolded to us a new and astonishing world – one which it is hard to conceive should contain no possibilities of transmitting and receiving intelligence.

Electrical vibrations pierce walls and travel through solids, Crookes writes educating the wider public about the new medium. In addition, he outlines, implicitly, the post-phenomenological world into which people were entering; we are continuously surrounded by 'ethereal vibrations', which were – by the already- mentioned Henry Adams (1918/2000) – described as the new world in which one 'wrapped [one]self in vibrations and rays', a world which, according to him, was 'supersensual occult; incapable of expression in horse-power'. These were the first signs of the transition from the world of industrial technology and production by muscle power and manipulation of matter to 'immaterial labour' and the 'cognitive capitalism' of communication, signal processing and invisible rays that connected not only lunatics but everyday people tuned into radio shows, television sit-coms and, later, mobile communications of social media culture.

In other words, the *fin de siècle* expressed itself as a rapid change in terms not only of inventions, but of the whole new world that it brought about:

> In these seven years man had translated himself into a new universe which had no common scale of measurement with the old. He had entered a supersensual world, in which he could measure nothing except by chance collisions of movements imperceptible to his senses, perhaps even imperceptible to his instruments, but perceptible to each other, and so to some known ray at the end of the scale. (Adams 1918/2000: xxv)

All of the discourse surrounding imaginary media of ghosts, visions, supersensuality and new technologies points to the new worlds that had lost the past scales of measurement – not only of the old world, but of human perception. Hence, in terms of imaginary media, the new world of science and technology *was* the imaginary that was often most easily affiliated with the dead, with ethereal communication between brains, and with understanding the new through such metaphoric transitions. Yet the metaphors whereby phonographs and recording of sound brought back the dead and media could also mean female mediums were a point of transition towards the forthcoming radio era and part of the wider material network of the passage to technical media. Ghosts were a recurring theme, at least after the Robertson phantasmagoria shows of the late eighteenth century. All this begs the question whether imaginary media are to large extent shorthand for new media and its non-human scales?

For such German writers as the mysticist Carl du Prel (1839–99), the occultist was rather similar to McLuhan's later description of artists: an early warning system that, through art, signalled what was to come. Du Prel saw the occultist as someone whom the 'technician of the future' can learn from, and draw upon (du Prel 1899: 19). Du

Prel's *Die Magie als Naturwissenschaft* ('Magic as a Natural Science') from 1899 was a critique of natural sciences executed through an empiricist argument that various new phenomena called the grounding notions of science such as causality into question, and it exposed unexplained gaps in the scientific worldview (Du Prel 1899: 7).[12] Naturally, the later spiritualist and other supernatural discourses concerning media technology had predecessors in the work of Franz Anton Mesmer (1734–1815) and the wider contexts of mesmerism and animal magnetism, also acknowledged by du Prel, but the connections to media technologies such as telegraphy and, for example, the new visual technologies of X-rays were much starker with the *fin-de-siècle* movements. As precursors to both the birth of broadcasting itself in the 1920s (Andriopoulos 2002, 2005) and such later case studies as Tausk's conceptualization of the Influencing Machine, studies such as du Prel's become interesting if we follow the Žižek guideline: remove the fantastic, the supernatural, the imaginary, and what remains? The world of telecommunications, of electromagnetic fields, vibrations as the grounding ontology of the world, and phantasms of future screen technologies – all those things that are actually too quick, too small, too fluid to be 'things' in the normal material vocabulary (see Bennett 2010: viii) but are still what defines the material ontology of modern technical media culture.

Indeed, as Andriopoulos (2002) outlines, these developments of the imaginary and the high-tech go hand in hand, and these imaginary media devices between brains, or even links to the worlds of the deceased, are a necessary double to the new worlds of communication. Theories concerning the origins of media that were voiced in Germany in the nineteenth century, primarily Ernst Kapp's (1877) thesis concerning 'organ projection' as the primary model for technology, were developed by du Prel and others in a direction which tried to take into account the non-visible spheres of nerves, brains and communication across distances. Again, we can emphasize the material interpretations for such imaginary media; modern media as well as transportation were bringing about a new arrangement of time and spatiality (Kern 2003), and such 'media materialists' as Kittler (1999) have continuously emphasized the double bind between ghosts and technical media where, by making 'speech immortal' (Scientific American, 17 November 1877, 304), the voices of the dead also become immortal, zombies. Fragments of people in terms of voices and images were having an afterlife now through storage media such as the phonograph: 'A strip of indented paper travels through a little machine, the sounds of the latter are magnified, and our great grandchildren or posterity centuries hence hear us as plainly as if we were present' (ibid.; on the haunted nature of voice, see Dolar 2006). Talking about media zombies, in his fiction novel *Locus Solus* (1914) Raymond Roussel (1914/2008: 59) conjures further, more imaginary media in the fabulation of Danton's revitalized head, which works as a phonograph, uttering the voice of the dead man through powers of animal magnetism.

John Durham Peters makes a convincing case extending Kittler's idea in order to underline the dreams of communication embedded in technical discourse networks, which through the most advanced technologies of the time kept alive archaic visions of angelic communication. Furthermore, Kittler argued that the ghostliness of media was an index of how communication had itself fled from the human body. In the same way that transportation – and especially transportation of messages – was no longer tied to human speeds, but travelled with the help of steam and electricity, the words of visual and auditory signs were also not tied to the phenomenology of our sense-capacities (Peters 1999: 140).

In this sense, we can understand later imaginary media reworkings of ghosts and aliens as archaeologies of the conditions of technical media. Hence, one could see a range of recent media artistic work that scans the electromagnetic sphere for the invisible but completely real world of such vibrations as the new impersonal regime of cognition that extends from the parapsychological to the high-tech. Examples include: the aptly named GhostLab; the Spectrotopia exhibition in 2008; Micro Research Lab's Detection Workshops that combine the ideas of Electronic Voice Phenomena (EVP) with technical investigations of surrounding signal worlds; and Zoe Beloff's, Edwin Carels's and Gebhard Sengmüller's projects, which rethink media histories and technologies through imaginaries that engage in non-linear time.

Summary

One can decipher different strands of imaginary media research, and much of it is well summed up in Kluitenberg's (2006a) edited collection *Book of Imaginary Media* (see also Kluitenberg 2011). Imaginary media research has to a large extent focused on:

1) media imagined, non-existent, but worthy of exploration in terms of how it can reinvigorate current media cultural design and debates; a kind of a reservoir of weird ideas that might provide blueprints for future media design;

2) the dreamworlds surrounding media and technology, and the way they get invested with weird desires and social constructions (Beloff's media-archaeological art being one of the best examples of this).

In addition, as I want to argue:

3) imaginary media as shorthand for what can be addressed as the non-human side of technical media; the fact that technical media are media of non-solid, non-phenomenological worlds (electromagnetic fields, high-level mathematics, speeds beyond human comprehension), and because of that ephemeral nature they are often described in the language of the fabulous, the spectacular.

Hence, imaginary media are tightly interlinked with non-human technical media, especially since the early nineteenth century, and this materialist notion of imaginary media also differs from Zielinski's more poetic vision. This chapter tried to point towards how imaginary media research can extend in new directions, to think the 'imaginary' as less Lacanian (providing dreamworlds of unified imaginary bodies) but as an affordance for the new – to think media anew, and in weird places, in weird bodies.

Further readings

Kluitenberg, Eric, ed. (2006) *Book of Imaginary Media. Excavating the Dream of the Ultimate Communication Medium* (Amsterdam and Rotterdam: Debalie and NAi Publishers).
Peters, John Durham (1999) *Speaking Into the Air. A History of the Idea of Communication* (Chicago and London: University of Chicago Press).
Sconce, Jeffrey (2000) *Haunted Media. Electronic Presence from Telegraphy to Television* (Durham and London: Duke University Press)
Zielinski, Siegfried (2006a) *Deep Time of the Media. Toward an Archaeology of Hearing and Seeing by Technical Means*, trans. Gloria Custance (Cambridge, MA: The MIT Press).

4

Media Theory and New Materialism

We finished the previous chapter with a call for a more material way of understanding imaginary media: how the various phantasmatic expressions such as ghosts and other supernaturals are actually super-phenomenological – supersensual, as Henry Adams described them; they expand outside the normal human ways of sensation. This has been an important theme in media studies in general: in addition to mapping the social, political and historical contexts of emergence of new forms of human communication, whether we are looking at remediations of blogs in relation to earlier modes of writing technologies, techniques of communication over distance from the telegraph to the Facebook era, or the visions of human communities from the suburban television families of the 1950s to the online cultures of peer-to-peer, there are important non-human elements which are integral to what constitutes the modern scientific world. This chapter continues the theme of materiality by explicating, through German media theory (a slightly unsuccessful term that suggests too much national spirit), also often called materialist media theory, or even hardware theory, how media-archaeological research has elaborated the material ontologies of and challenges to the storage, distribution and processing of communication events. In this chapter, I will look more carefully at such writers as Friedrich Kittler, Bernhard Siegert, Claus Pias and Wolfgang Ernst, among others. But German media theory is, of course, not the only one to address materiality, and nearer the end we will connect some of the threads to recent developments in Anglo-American media studies. As such, the key themes that stand out from this chapter are things and materiality, as well as medium-specificity.

Hard(ware) theory

Media archaeology has been always fascinated with objects, apparatuses, and remnants of past media cultures – monuments from past media ages. Even to an excessive amount, it has shown a curiosity-cabinet kind of awe of quirky devices and pre-cinematic toys as the alternatives to a mainstream media history. Marshall McLuhan was one of the early media theorists interested in expanding the notion of 'media' in a variety of ways in which different spatial and temporal constellations, from architecture to clocks, could be seen and conceived as 'media'. One of the reasons for this was that he was very much embedded in a similar situation to the one we are in now, concerning a media cultural change: having to rethink many of the institutional but also aesthetic contexts of seemingly familiar media technologies such as cinema (expanded cinema discussions in the 1970s), as well as books and writing (one of McLuhan's favourite topics, due to his background as a literature scholar) which meant moving away from the Gutenberg-era book-object to much more decentralized, distributed and mobile forms – what we now talk about as 'e-books'. Hence, the material basis of media technologies – and books are only one example – is changing, for which historical perspectives might give not only comforting back-up ('nothing is as permanent as change') but also ideas to push the change forward: how to rethink familiar media technologies in new material constellations and in ways that lead to new modes of using, consuming and institutionalizing media.

The emphasis in media archaeology has been on nineteenth-century devices that seemed to gesture not only a way towards the birth of cinema, but also to the possibilities for differing routes. As outlined in chapter 2, such devices signalled relations more tactile, more personal and otherwise different with regard to the body than occurred with the later birth of the mass-audience full-length fiction film. In other words, 'hardware matters' (Christie 2007), and investigations into the material hardware characteristics of media technologies matter as much – in terms of how they can demonstrate the different ways in which toys, instruments and tools were incorporated into practices of use and the visual culture of the nineteenth century. Emphasizing hardware matters in the midst of the increasing invisibility of consumer objects in digital culture is an important political task for media-archaeological research; this invisibility was already part of the birth of the cinematic apparatus, but is increasingly part of the structuring of media technology in the age of easy-to-use machines and digital rights management software and platforms. And similarly, hardware, toys and automata from the past can be used in different ways to illustrate, for example, how, through objects, we can interpret the birth of the automated factory system, as with Jessica Riskin's (2003) reading of the Vaucanson Duck as the key figure in Enlightenment thought and technology. Indeed, to an extent, one could say that it's not only the curiosity cabinets and such-like that have been a focus of rethinking media and archives through models of heterogeneous order and amazement (see, for example, Stafford and Terpak 2001), but also that media history itself can become such a curiosity cabinet – for better or for worse, as the danger lies in being drawn into writing about 'curiosities' for their own sake, instead of asking the simple and critical question 'why': why is this particular technology important, and what is the argument behind this research into this curiosity of media history?

Things matter in terms of their politics and how they participate in the constitution of our world. Media hardware can be understood to be important from a variety of perspectives, from design to aesthetics,

Image 4.1 Media archaeology has focused on a range of objects and apparatuses, often proto-cinematic ones but, increasingly, other forms of technical media such as recording and sound reproduction. In addition to social contexts and, for instance, design, media-archaeological theories are interested in going 'under the hood' to investigate the material diagrammatics and technologies of how culture is being mediatically stored and transmitted.
© Sebastian Döring

politics and critical cultural studies. The idea of 'hardware media theory' has been most often connected to the writings of Friedrich Kittler, and the circle of scholars influenced by his post-Foucauldian thoughts concerning media history. He is one of the leading figures of the so-called 'German media theory school' – which is far from a unified school, and more often perceived as such a unity from Anglo-American perspectives in a similar way to how a lot of French philosophy after the 1960s was labelled under the vague category of 'French theory', or 'French poststructuralism'. Of course, in addition to Kittler, there are various other writers – many of them still untranslated into English – who have their own approach to thinking about art, materiality, science and media history (see, for instance, Hagen 2005; Pias 2002; Siegert 2003; Zielinski 2006a; for a critique of Kittler and an alternative cultural historical approach to media art and modernity, see Daniels 2002). In other words, the label 'German' is a sort of misinterpretation, and even relating Kittler's work to a 'Berlin-school of media theory' would neglect a lot of institutional and academic detail. Kittler definitely is not, and never was, the only media theorist in town. Yet, despite continuing inaccuracies in terms of such generalizations as 'German media theory', it is clear that Kittler's writings, which stemmed from his background in literature studies had a huge influence in terms of how international – and especially Anglo-American – media theory considers systems of writing, storage and communication as material networks. As a historical constellation, German media theory, especially in its mix of enthusiasm for close-reading of technological systems and high theory, can be understood as a critical reaction to the Marxist analyses of media by the Frankfurt school, and, on an international scale, as a desire to differentiate from British cultural studies – a point that Geoffrey Winthrop-Young (2006: 88; 2011) articulates well.

Winthrop-Young identifies Kittler alongside, for example, Jochen Hörisch as part of the poststructuralist generation of scholars interested in Foucault, Derrida and Lacan that initially emerged outside any official schools in Germany (Winthrop-Young 2005: 34). Later there was talk of the Kassel school of media theory in which Kittler and others were influential, as well as, since the 1990s, the Berlin (Humboldt University) school of media theory, identified as very materially driven. The generation that turned poststructuralist philosophy into media theory soon carved out an original and radical niche in the disciplinary field. In addition, this intervention in media studies included a strong emphasis on the importance of the scientific and the technological. The German-language use of *wissenschaften* ('sciences'), in their terminology for cultural and media *sciences* as well is where some of the Kittler-influenced media theory distances itself from cultural *studies* that 'know higher mathematics only from hearsay' (quoted in Winthrop-Young and Wutz 1999: xiv). Such provocations serve to frame the difference between the science- and technology- oriented sciences of culture and the studying of human actions and structures of meaning, which offer a different way of seeing the constructed nature of the cultural world. For Kittler and his like, it is mathematics and engineering that concretely construct worlds through modern technology. As provocations, such critiques of cultural studies, the Frankfurt school and other alternative approaches are often, however, crude generalizations (cf. Winthrop-Young 2011). And yet the ideas are not only about provocations, of course: Kittler can be described as the 'first renegade Germanist to teach computer programming' (Winthrop-Young 2011: 74), and the Berlin Humboldt University Institute for Media Studies is one of the few places that have offered such undergraduate courses as 'Mathematics for Media Studies'.

This division between the special case of Germany and 'the old Europe' (as Kittler might want to have it) and the Anglo-American cultural and media studies feeds into a specific way of understanding media archaeology. To be fair, and to point it out sooner rather than later: Kittler himself has never said he is a media archaeologist, and, more recently, he has announced his difference from the explicitly media-archaeological theory of another Berlin Humboldt University-situated professor, Wolfgang Ernst (Armitage 2006: 32–3). In a short passage in an interview, Kittler discusses briefly the importance of such 'non-linear media history', with which he agrees, but underlines that Ernst's work does not stem from his own. In the interview Kittler continues to talk about the need to think history outside narratives and in terms of what he calls 'the recursive', which clearly has resonances with media-archaeological methods – even that of Huhtamo's (1997, 2011) cyclical and recurring *topoi*. Kittler mentions the Sirens as one such example of recursive history 'where the same issue is taken up again and again at regular intervals but with different connotations and results' (Armitage 2006: 33): from seductive Greek sea nymphs to monsters of early Christianity, from mermaids of the Middle Ages to the nineteenth-century technical use of the term in the form we understand it, i.e. as a signalling device with a loud sound, subsequently playing a key part in the mapping of the thresholds of hearing as well as the development of radio (2006: 33).

But let's step back a bit, and introduce the key points of Kittler's theories about why he has, in the first place, been named as one of the most influential media-archaeological writers, without himself wanting to be labelled as such. After that, we shall return to how he has afforded and been followed by a range of other thinkers whose media-theoretical and historical writings are of the highest relevance to media archaeology too, and give us insights into materialities of media history. Such ideas resonate with a wider trend in cultural theory called 'new materialism', as well as some other new fields in Anglo-American media studies (software studies, platform studies, media forensics).

Kittler's concept 'discourse networks', from the translation of the same name (originally *Aufschreibesysteme 1800/1900*), was itself an important step towards applying Foucault's methodological positions to media. The two key things that Kittler was able to do and to offer humanities and media studies were: (1) to look at 'old media' such as literature as media systems for transmitting, linking and institutionalizing information (with a nod towards Harold Innis); and (2) to offer insights into how power works in the age of technical media. Indeed, it is through his emphasis on the importance of the technical as a system of inscription, in the manner Foucault talked about, which related to both archaeological (conditions of knowledge) and genealogical (history is inscribed in various bodies, or materials) theories, that the link to media archaeology was born.

The notion of 'discourse networks' and the whole *magnum opus* that was translated in 1990 into English introduced a way to read literature as media, and technical media as a new regime of posthuman sensation and agency. Media, from books to cinema to computers, were not reducible either to content or to sociological conditions, but had to include considerations that took into account how media technologies afford specific forms of perception and modes of memory as well as social relations. By marking radical epistemic breaks *circa* 1800 and 1900, Kittler was not trying to make a historical claim that a clear break in how our technologies and we, 'so-called-humans', change in intimate connection takes place in these specific years, but to map out the epistemic conditions for media. He wanted to produce a mix of Foucauldean archaeology of conditions of knowledge, McLuhan-inspired interest in how media form our sensory and cognitive abilities, and a vision of media history that stems less from social history than from communication physics (for a wonderful elaboration of Kittler's basic ideas, see Winthrop-Young 2011). In other words, as Kittler explicates later in his *Optical Media* lectures (from the late 1990s), it is the engineering communication theory of Claude Shannon (1916–2001) from the 1940s that provides the template for teaching how media work. In other words, not meaning, not representation, not any imaginary of media that is conditioned by the social, but the act of communication in its physical distributing and effective channelling of signals stands at the core of media, claims Kittler. Communication can hence be methodologically understood through the elements of the Shannon model of: data source, sender, signal, receiver, addressee(see image 5.2). In other words, the process of coding, signal processing and decoding becomes of higher importance in this model, in which Kittler (2010: 44, cf. 1990: 370) underlines that, 'in contrast to traditional philosophy and literary studies, Shannon's model does not ask about the being for whom the message connotes or denotes meaning, but rather it ignores connotation and denotation altogether in order to clarify the internal mechanism of communication instead'. As a sidenote, this focus on science and engineering does not prevent Kittler from using fiction literature – for example Thomas Pynchon's – to illuminate his ideas. That is one of the peculiarities of his style of writing.

Discourse Networks 1800/1900 was itself an opening to a world of understanding the 'so-called human being' – a world in which the paranoid schizophrenic Judge Schreber (see chapter 3) acts as a good symbol of technical media, and where pioneering use of the typewriter by Friedrich Nietzche (1844–1900) is indexical of the transformation into a new regime of language and the self. Despite his technological enthusiasm, Kittler is not afraid to use fiction literature and stories – quite often quirky, forgotten ones – to support his analyses into the new regimes of articulation where subjectivity is renegotiated in the complex network of new sciences of sensation and the brain, the new media technologies of moving images (cinema), recording (gramophone and phonograph) and writing (typewriter), and the new arts of such technical media. Hence, the notion of 'network' in the translation, which does not follow directly from the original title *Aufschreibesystem* ('system of inscription'), is apposite: despite often being accused of being a technological determinist in the same way as McLuhan, Kittler's work is more nuanced in its methodological way of tieing arts, sciences and technology into a co-constitutive interaction. Technology does not just determine arts, science does not just determine technology, and art is not only creation and contemplation of beauty. They all work in a co-determining network of historical relations where aesthetics is also tightly interwoven with science and technology (cf. Siegert 2008) – although, to be frank, it is mostly science and technology that are emphasized in the last instance. Literature and fiction are more like ways of self-inscription of the media technologies of the age, and a methodological tool for approaching the effects of the hard core of science and technology.

At the end of *Discourse Networks 1800/1900*, Kittler (1990: 369) offers a definition of the concept: 'The term discourse network, as God revealed it to the paranoid cognition of Senate President Schreber, can also designate the network of technologies and institutions that allow a given culture to select, store and process relevant data.' Hence, it is in this link between institutions and technologies that various kinds of agents, signals and processes appear and are posited in systematic relations. Kittler's materialism is thus more than just substance-based, so to speak. He is adamant about a claim that stems from a poststructuralist background (Winthrop-Young and Wutz 1999: xx): we do not speak language, but language speaks us, and we have to participate in such systems of language, which are not of our own making. But language in the age of technical media is not just natural language: it is the new technological and physical regimes introduced by media, such as the typewriter, and later computer software languages, which should methodologically be seen in a similar way – they impose new regimes of sensation and use to which we have to accommodate ourselves in order to be functioning subjects. We are secondary to such systems. Besides agency, this has to do with power. Power is no longer circulated and reproduced solely through spatial places and institutions – such as the clinic or the prison, as Foucault analysed – or practices of language, but takes place in the switches and relays, software and hardware, protocols and circuits of which our technical media systems are made.

Archaeologies of the material body

Kittler is an important posthuman thinker in how he outlines through careful media-archaeologically tuned analysis the way technical media includes a new agency of the machine. This becomes evident especially when he talks about computer media, and the programmability of media as well as of humans. His approach to poetry of the Romantic period is in a way anachronistic in terms of its method, when he claims that the structuration of the message by such writers as Goethe is actually about *programming* the nation into certain kinds of social and family structures (Winthrop-Young and Wutz 1999: xxi). In the analysis of the discourse network of 1800, the family unit becomes a way of transposing the body in its movement and sound – the movement of the hand in the writing technology of handwriting as an organic flow, and the Mother's Voice as an integral part of the pedagogical discourse which was, in a way, almost transposing the voice of Nature to the learner – as part of the nation-state system that was educating its pupils into writing. *Bildung* ('education'), as the key word of the Goethe era (and then the emerging Humboldtian university system) is actually programming through teaching the media technology of writing by hand (Kittler 1990: 83–6). So, in other words, even before technical media came along, we had techniques of media – the ways in which we had to learn to use media such as writing and literature, and how that process of learning constituted subjects in the sense that post-structuralism talked about the production of subjects:

> The discourse network of 1800 functioned without phonographs, gramophones, or cinematographs. Only books could provide serial storage of serial data. They had been reproducible since Gutenberg, but they became material for understanding and fantasy when alphabetization had become ingrained. Books had previously been reproducible masses of letters; now they reproduced themselves. The scholarly republican heap of books in Faust's study become a psychedelic drug for everyone. (Kittler 1990: 117)

Even such seemingly non-technical regimes of 'media' as handwriting, or for that matter fine arts (Kittler 2010), are technological because they involve techniques of regulating the body and teaching it certain patterns and institutional relations, but also because they engage more with effects and affects of the body rather than producing meanings.

To emphasize, Kittler is not attributing this state of mathematical, non-human media only to digital or technical media. He outlines, for example, the history of analogue practices such as painting as innately mathematical, at least since the development of the linear perspective, evident especially in the art of Filippo Brunelleschi (1377–1446) and inherent in the geometric ways of modelling the world adopted by Leon Battista Alberti (1404–72) – the so-called 'Alberti's window' – which pixelated the world before the raster screen, and offered windows as the worldview before Windows® by Microsoft (Kittler 2010: 54–62; cf. Friedberg 2006). In addition, the hallucinatory aspects of media do not escape Kittler who, as well as seeing Romantic literature as the LSD of that era talks of the Counter-Reformation in the seventeenth century as based on the specific use of visual media to oppose the rationalizing media technology of the Reformation's Gutenberg printing. Counter-Reformation and, for example, the Jesuit order were based, argues Kittler, on the aim 'to overwhelm the five senses' which combined the spiritual order with 'sensual hallucination.' (Kittler 2010: 78; on the history of special effects from the Vatican to the twentieth century, see Klein 2003).

Despite some of the links to debates in new materialism, and being able to offer vocabularies for the materiality of media, Kittler's work has been thoroughly embedded in a Lacanian understanding of this link between the body, the psyche and media. Especially in the early work of *Discourse Networks 1800/1900* and *Gramophone, Film, Typewriter*, Kittler articulates the birth of technical media in terms of the Lacanian triad of psychic spheres: The Real, the Imaginary and the Symbolic – with each corresponding to one key technology of media. So the by-now almost classic phrase (which has spurred the accusations of Kittler being a media determinist), 'media determine our situation, which – in spite or because of it – deserves a description' (Kittler 1999: xxxix), is partly at least to be read from a Lacanian-inspired position. Kittler is interested in how historically changing media constellations, the episteme of media cultures so to speak, activate and modulate our thoughts, sensations, perceptions, memories and, indeed, the way we hallucinate or even go mad. The formula *Lacan + media technology* was the methodology through which, in the early 1980s and 1990s, Kittler tried to connect the psyche to its outside, especially media technology. Nietzsche was one of Kittler's key references early on. The letter from February 1882 stated the principle of all media: 'Our writing tools are also working on our thoughts' (quoted in Kittler 1999: 200). The specific nature of the discrete, spatialized sign is where writing, for Nietzsche, started – along with the whole regime of discrete media as a new era of writing technologies, and technologies of thought in parallel lines.

So the typewriter, originally designed for the blind to assist in their writing, is the Symbolic: a finite and predefined set of signs open to variations from that set. For film, it is the Imaginary that is the primary regime in terms of its psychic and senso-motorial form: it offers a mirror image of the body, writes Kittler. And finally, the Real is revealed most acutely through the recording technologies of sound, which is the medium of coughs, sighs, whispers, stutterings and, in general, what we term 'noise' – the unwanted of communication, which, however, always creeps in as the noisiness of our body, or the material communication channel which produces its own 'waste' (Kittler 1999: 15–16). And yet Kittler moves onwards from this material and mediatic reading of Lacan. Instead of continuing towards the discourse of the Oedipal as the horizon for psychoanalytic explanations, as usual, Kittler is interested in how the actual explanations and theories of Freud and Lacan should be historicized in terms of media technological changes. As we saw earlier, in the previous chapter, he does this to mental illnesses too – so it is only logical to include the theories of mind, psyche and the senso-motorial self in this method of explanation. Kittler's archaeology and genealogy of the body as the inscription system is not so much interested in food and morals as was Nietzche, or prisons and the power of medical institutions as was Foucault, but uses the same method to look at inscriptions on the body by media.

The recent years of cultural theory have been talking of 'cognitive capitalism' and affective labour as new regimes of capitalism in which our ways of thinking, communicating and socializing have become key motors for value creation, and hence under new forms of control. Theorists such as Paolo Virno, Maurizio Lazzarato, Franco 'Bifo' Berardi, Tiziana Terranova and others, based on earlier writings by Deleuze, Guattari and other influential thinkers, have claimed that this regime is a new kind of occupying of the psyche – something that Bernard Stiegler (2010) has extended to demands for a new political economy that takes into account psychotechnologies and 'noopolitics'. Despite the interesting connections between such thinkers as Kittler and Stiegler, and the latter's interest in the capitalization of the memory through technologies and their links to capital accumulation and value-creation processes based on capitalist logic, the German media-theoretical stance – and especially Kittler – only implicitly hints at an archaeology of this 'cognitive capitalism'. To simplify: what is often missing from recent political and philosophical analyses in these fields is the medium-specificity and accuracy German media theory does well; although, at the same time, one can say that it is not often that one finds strong articulation of politics in the context of the techno-epistemological research of such media theory. However, the various, complex and often meticulously written analyses of the intertwining of the psychic with the technological also afford ways to think the modern *psychotechnics* as a crucial form of power. In other words, if Michel Foucault's work afforded, on the one hand, extension of archaeological and genealogical methods into media contexts, his writings on biopower and biopolitics have been extended into an analysis of politics of the contemporary media sphere – but we can see that Kittler has already contributed as much to this through an analysis of the technics of the psyche.

As a term, 'psychotechnics' originates from Hugo Münsterberg (1863–1916), the early twentieth-century film theorist pioneer, and the view of cinema as a technology for directly tapping into the unconsciousness of the viewer – modulating the affects, perceptions and psyche of the cinema-goer confronted with technically moving images (Kittler 2010: 175). Cinema is a laboratory of sorts for manipulation of states of mind and brain with the help of methods such as 'close-ups, flashbacks, flashforwards, and reverse shots' (2010: 175) as well as, more broadly, techniques of time-reversal. Such examples are perfect for Kittler as this enables him to argue for the intimate link between media technologies and the psychology and physiology of the so-called 'human' being. No wonder, as Münsterberg himself was educated in the context of experimental psychology, and hence continued, in media-technological terms, what significant European scientists of the nineteenth century such as Gustav Fechner (1801–87), Hermann von Helmholtz (1821–94) and Wilhelm Wundt (1832–1920) and, in the US, William James (1842–1910) were conceptualizing in writing and in laboratories. In experimental psychology, and in new laboratory settings, an empirically measured human being was born, in contrast to the transcendental subjectivity suggested by Kantian philosophy since the eighteenth century.

The nineteenth-century practices in experimental sciences are in this sense crucial to the way Kittler understands the archaeology of technical media. What such perspectives flag is that we can connect our analyses of digital culture to pre-digital developments. Contemporary media are media of scientific knowledge and products of meticulous works from mathematics to physics labs, as well as experimental psychology settings. As we suggested earlier about Crary concerning a complex methodology of science–technology–arts for media analysis, Kittler also provides similar methods. In short, the place of such seemingly fundamental human qualities as language, communication, feeling and creativity was actually, more or less, in the link between their physiological and neurological basis and how that was mapped in emerging brain sciences, experimental laboratory practices and other measures which made the human body a new object of investigation. What Sigmund Freud (1856–1939) achieved in psychoanalysis and his books but concretely linked to the same discourse networks, i.e. moving from consciousness to the unconscious and subconscious as the fundamental motor of our everyday, also happened through the sciences and media: 'Prior to consciousness, then, there are sensory and motor, acoustical, and optic language centers linked by nerve paths just as the working parts of a typewriter are connected by levers and rods' (Kittler 1990: 251).

Technological media are media of nerves and the unconscious, and the pioneers of such research become media theorists *avant la lettre* (and *avant le McLuhan*). Fechner (interested in the psychophysics of sense perception), Helmholtz (through his various research into acoustics and the perceptional thresholds of the human body), Wundt's similar researches into the nerve basis of our 'being in the world', and other notable physiologists and experimentalists investigated what used to be called 'arts', but for Kittler are now media.

Indeed, it is very emblematic of the Berlin orientation of cultural and media analytics that the Humboldt University's Centre for Cultural Techniques – which one is tempted to see almost as a counterpart to the Birmingham School of Cultural Studies – is called the *Hermann von Helmholtz Centre*. Naturally, this is not the only institutional base where such historical and cultural research into the meticulous conditioning, governing and regulation of sensory data was conducted. Take, for example, the research of such historians of science as Henning Schmidgen, in which the work of Helmholtz and others takes a central place in understanding the building of the culture of technicality. As Schmidgen (2002) shows, Helmholtz was a key figure in starting the mapping of the body as a system of nerves whose reaction times – i.e. how quickly the body conveys the signal through nerves to the brain to process – could be accurately measured, and how this interest in the physiology later extended into more psychological measurements too.

An interest in time, in quickness and slowness at the basis of sensation, was at the core of this phase and the grounding of how we have lived in technical media culture since the nineteenth century (and not least because the apparatuses that were used constitute in themselves proto-mediatic devices for a cyborgian past of sorts). Such suggestions of 'time critical perspectives' emerging in media archaeology (Volmar 2009) point towards the fact that we need to understand the materiality of technical media through temporality. Hence, questions such as how many vibrations a second the tuning fork of a phono-autograph registers (Schmidgen 2002: 144), how quickly humans and animals can react to stimuli, how we synchronize multiple stimuli to different senses, how media themselves as a sensation system of sorts synchronize and synthesize, for example, discrete registered states into continuous movements, as with film, are at the centre of media archaeologies of temporality.

For Kittler, the emergence of such posthuman agency as cinema as nervous systems in their own right, and the link between nineteenth-century sciences and media, are summed up in his account of technical media through Münsterberg:

> everyday reality itself, from the workplace to leisure time, has long been a lab in its own right. Since the motor and sensory activities of so-called-Man (hearing, speaking, reading, writing) have been measured under all conceivable extreme conditions, their ergonomic revolution is only a matter of course. The second industrial revolution enters the knowledge base. Psychotechnology relays psychology and media technology under the pretext that each psychic apparatus is also a technological one, and vice versa. (Kittler 1999: 160)

Such technologies for mapping the body's possibilities and thresholds are themselves the point of entry for new regimes of drilling, training and media pedagogy. We find this emphasis on training of the senses as part of modernity in Walter Benjamin, analysed by Crary (1990: 112) in relation to the phenakistoscope, and emphasized continuously by Kittler in relation to war (1999: 140; see also Winthrop-Young 2011: 132–3).

Kittler (1999: 27) writes about Eliza Doolittle (the literary character in the play *Pygmalion* (1912) by G. B Shaw (1856–1950)) as a perfect example of the subject of drilling in the discourse network of 1900, where the possibilities of capturing and reversing (spoken) sounds prepare the way for rehearsing their improvement; similarly, what Kittler's perspective affords is a whole new way of looking at the materiality of the body as part of media networks that extend to work (Taylorism and, for example, the 1920s ideas of Frank Gilbreth (1868–1924)), to the military (as the obvious regime of drilling, but also of high-tech media used for logistics, control and communication in the battlefield) and, of course, in the more everyday sense of media, to how we are trained to use and interact with media devices. This is naturally present in the culture of user manuals for hardware and software, as well as, for example, Acceptable Use Policies in online networks. Also the broader questions of design can be connected to this: the earlier work in human–computer interface design and related computing fields since pioneers – such as Douglas Engelbart, Ivan Sutherland, J. C. R. Licklider, Alan Kay and others, working in key institutional sites like the Xerox Palo Alto Labs, MIT, University of Utah and other places – opened up computing as a medium for lay human beings: not only for number-crunching, but for symbol and graphic object manipulation, and hence meant for eyes (graphic user interface screens) and hands (the keyboard, mouse), and encompassing complete ecologies of objects and processes (see Alt 2011; see also Gere 2002).[1]

Psychotechnology as a tool for understanding the archaeology of contemporary software media culture is employed by Claus Pias in his extensive work on computer games. Pias maps the ways of mobilizing the body as part of regimes of control and order: analysing the way our gestures and movement were ordered in the work management context by Frank Gilbreth in the early part of the twentieth century, reading through the conservative writer Ernst Jünger (1895–1998) the extensions of management of work into management of bodies in war, especially by World War II, and then through post-war HCI design the regimes of psychotechnologies of computer culture which prepared the action-perception patterns of humans to be ready for and attentive to how we should be interacting with the new screen technologies that emerged and later conquered our desktops through software such as games. As Pias (2002, 2011) shows, the history of such seemingly innocent consumer software as games is entangled in histories of science and war, and the management of bodies – a theme that directly stems from the impulse given to media studies and media-archaeological research by Kittler.

In this spirit, one key methodological guideline would be: if you want to understand contemporary media technological culture, look at its science and military contexts, instead of the content of what is consumed as entertainment media. For example, in terms of war, the history of media conflates with that of modern combat:

> Phase 1, beginning with the American Civil War, developed storage technologies for acoustics, optics, and script: film, gramophone, and the man-machine system, typewriter. Phase 2, beginning with the First World War, developed for each storage content appropriate electric transmission technologies: radio, television, and their more secret counterparts. Phase 3, since the Second World War, has transferred the schematic of a typewriter of predictability per se; Turing's mathematical definition of computability in 1936 gave future computers their name. (Kittler 1999: 243)

Such a claim is, for sure, controversial, and not entirely historically accurate. Think of the multiplicity of modern technologies from telegraphy to telephony, from visual media to broadcasting, and consider if you can always find only one causal chain that connects them to military contexts. Reducing computer history to the singular point of Turing's invention is as dubious. Yet such generalizations serve a theoretical point, and illuminate the specific way of extending the media-historical agenda into a mapping of the wider modern history of scientific–military institutions and experiments (see Winthrop-Young 2002 and 2011: 129–43 for a thorough explanation and critique of Kittler's relation to war, and media as 'drill and distraction').

In addition to a military perspective, Kittler's viewpoint stems partly from a consideration of such engineering pioneers as Shannon read as a media theorist who prioritizes signal processing over semantics. What's more, this theoretical realization is embedded in the historical development of modern technical media themselves, and should hence guide the way we write about modern media (cf. Gane 2005: 26–8). One can find repercussions of such developments in a variety of German media-theoretical writings, and this is where Kittler's ontological posthumanism stems from: engineering, mathematics and the primacy of system design over any hermeneutic perspective that looks for interpretation and meaning in the fashion understood by nineteenth-century literature interpreters – or the modern hermeneutics of Gadamer, for that matter. (On recent German media-theoretical writing on Shannon, including on his playlike automata, see Roch 2010.)

Mathematical media ontology

So what if we should not, paradoxically, start studying media from media but from science and the military, and if we should not start studying media use from human beings, but from something else? Kittler's media-materialistic archaeology can give keys to understanding the modern conflation of communication with technology (Gane 2005: 34), and its implications for information materialism that takes as its starting point a more posthuman position. Bernhard Siegert gives one response to the post-human dilemma of conflation of communications and technology in terms of 'standards', which already *seems* like a slightly 'softer' and more social version of media systems than that of Kittler's. But the link to Kittler is clear too. Siegert manoeuvres around the question of the human and focuses on *systems* of communication, and especially on the postal system as such a discourse network. In the midst of this network, the practice of standardization acted as a surpassing of the Individual as the starting point of posting – and was replaced by the System. More closely, the system worked through technical standards which, in fact, define the self-sustaining circulation of the postal network (Siegert 1999: 108). This (post-)structuralist move assumes not that meaning stems from intentions, or individual acts of interpretation – that there are people using the systems according to their own volition – but that the system is subjecting the user to its structure, or in this case: standards. In other words, language is not the only system of subjectification: we can look at technology, or such institutional networks as the postal system, through a similar methodological prism. To paraphrase Siegert (1999: 109), technology, or standards, precede meaning, and enable it – similarly to how they enable the being of the subject. We exist as postal subjects because of a system, a media system, called 'the post'. In concrete terms, this is what the postal system achieved and what we could then see as an archaeological phase in terms of a surprising genealogy of the posthuman: penny postage in 1840 standardized the (pre)payment, mailboxes standardized the procedure of input to the system, and subsequently the whole routine of communication travelling through a predefined system as standardized packages ensured a tighter control of the time required for sending and receiving, as well as its spatial coverage within a nation and soon internationally. The posthuman does not always have to be thought through the digital-media discourse of cyborgs and cyberspace, and we can go much further back in time than to computers in our analyses of digital culture. As Siegert notes (1999: 121), the only thing missing from a perfect posthuman machine was some kind of a reading machine at the end and 'all of England's written communication would have been completely standardized and mechanized, from production right through distribution to reception'.

So in other words, only that what can be posted, exists (Siegert 1999: 119). What Siegert proposes is an understanding of the posthuman even before technical media per se, but through a more general feature that defines network cultures too: objectification through such *standards* (see Fuller 2005: 93–5) and what Alex Galloway (2004), in a more Internet-specific way, has called the protocological nature of contemporary control mechanisms of technicality. It is, of course, unconventional to consider the postal system as indispensable to the way we understand media culture but this is emblematic of what these kinds of media-materialist accounts of communication practices afford: thinking media outside the box, in a variety of guises, and focusing more on the process of mediation and such defining characteristics as standardization at the core of this materiality. This is what media archaeology at its best establishes: a problematization and a rethinking of such fundamental questions as what even counts as media.[2]

But with technical media, the posthuman gains further momentum. To be sure, these media theorists do not refer to this as 'posthuman', which is more an invention of American academic language. But the theoretical link is clear. If Kittler, and others such as Siegert, have established that the Foucauldian and poststructuralist message of the primacy of systems, or institutions, is what posits subjects, a further twist comes with digital media that is at its core mathematical. In Kittler's writings on software culture, he already makes the move concerning archaeologies of the present not only towards a historical reading of how we have ended up in a digital culture, but also in terms of how the machines themselves structure our everyday experiences. Kittler's influential texts, for example 'There is No Software' (1995), outline such ontologies of post-discourse network 1900 technical media now turned digital: a general codification system that is able to turn all media into digital code, and a general numerization and programmability of what the psychophysical media were able to quantify already. To paraphrase Kittler (1999: 1–2), computers are not only a remediation (cf. Bolter and Grusin 1999) of existing media such as typewriters and film, despite their interfaces (keyboards) and content (audiovisuality), but also introduce new standards in data transfer, programming and storage.

More specifically, this new state for media analysis is outlined in the first lines of Kittler's (1995) software article: texts do not exist any more in time and space that we human beings can perceive, but only in computer memory and, because of that, we no longer have direct access to writing. Due to complexity and high-tech demands, even the building of such machines is no longer understandable with old notions of skill or handcraft, but takes place through Computer-Aided Design, which, furthermore, points to the complexity of the hardware and software environments in which we live. It takes one to build one. Even so, Kittler states in the text that software does not exist, which as a provocative claim suggests the other side of his argument, which stems from the complexity of the structures inside computers. Writing technologies are to be understood no longer through natural languages, but through software languages and programs such as our word-processing ones – during Kittler's writing WordPerfect, but nowadays, more or less, simply Word. Yet, such software programming language turned into applications and programs requires a further layer of operating systems, which themselves, continues Kittler, are to be understood only in relation to the fundamental input and output operations governed through BIOS – the first piece of software that exists and allows the operating system to be bootstrapped into full swing in specific hardware settings. Hence, 'In principle, this kind of descent from software to hardware, from higher to lower levels of observation, could be continued over more and more decades. All code operations, despite their metaphoric faculties such as "call" or "return", come down to absolutely local string manipulations and that is, I am afraid, to signifiers of voltage differences.'

One could do a similar analysis of 'descent' of other mediatic elements as well. For example, as analysed in chapter 2 regarding visual culture, algorithmic constellations of images demand new perspectives. In this context, we can map the existence of a pixel as such an element in post-World War II visual cultures for basic raster screens which form intensities of red, green and blue, and are organized through bitmaps that further assemble them into coordinated systems for the human perception system (Harwood 2008). This is why on the media studies agenda a whole new set of difficult objects demand analysis – such as video codecs (MPEG-1, MPEG-2, M-PEG4, H.264,

DivX, WMW, several of which are based on the H.261 coding standard) that temporally channel and structure how we perceive visuals and sound (Mackenzie 2008; see Cubitt 2010).

Hence, to understand 'descent', which is a key term in Foucault's genealogical method, one does not only track historical descent, but also descent in terms of computer infrastructures, and how the supposedly immaterial notion of software is hooked up to the very material reality of hardware. Media archaeology goes back not only in time, but inside the machine. While there is room for a critical debate about whether this is a 'techno-determinist' view we are talking about,[3] we can flip it to illustrate the important political economic implications of where our computer-age discourse networks are embedded, and how the fact that power is now circulated through software to hardware is inseparable from the proprietary industries that produce the platforms on which our media for seeing and hearing are governed. For Kittler (1997), this leads to an analysis of the 'protected mode' at the core of Intel processors since 80286 was introduced in 1982, which, in contrast to the Real Mode, protected the processor from users. This particular analysis can be seen highlighting a more political side of Kittler's take that taps into the constitutive archaeological features of media technology: that our world is governed not only by language or even the hallucination of control through software languages, but by hardware, and, even more so, the proprietary logic that shuts off the machine from the end user through the protected mode, but also through graphical user interfaces, or application culture as Jonathan Zittrain (2008) has recently argued in relation to Internet and mobile-device culture. In application culture, we do not program anymore, but are programmed, as merely users/consumers of media (see Franklin 2009 on rethinking the division between users and programmers).

More widely, this is, of course, a question of media ontology as mathematical. Through an implicitly rather Derridean supposition, Kittler (2009) maps how Western metaphysics since Ancient Greece has neglected writing, but also mathematics, and hence technology, from its considerations. Yet, in the age of mathematical machines, i.e. computers, we need to rethink such fundamental metaphysical notions as form and matter that we inherited from Aristotle (384–322 BC), and focus more on ontologies of media provided by computer pioneers such as John von Neumann (1903–57). Indeed, the materiality of the informatic machines is suddenly not form and matter, but about *commands*, *addresses* and *data*, the basic structure we have inherited from the von Neumann architecture of computers: registers, busses and random access memory (Kittler 2009: 30).

These are the new architectures of power. Power becomes hardwired to technology.

Wolfgang Ernst (2003, 2011) explicitly places his theoretical work under the banner of media archaeology but, continuing a certain mathematico-materialist emphasis, insists on its difference from narrative writings of the cultural history of media. Mathematics being an underlying ontology of technical media is continued into a media-archaeological method through the interest in numbers and counting, which Ernst sees revived in the age of digital aesthetics. Like so many German media theorists, he does not offer an explicit theory of power in his media archaeology, but focuses on the techno-aesthetics of media. By referring back not only to old etymologies in which 'telling' (as in narratives) and counting coalesce, but also to one of the founding texts of modern writings on art, *Laokoon* (1766) by Gotthold Ephraim Lessing (1729–81), Ernst seems to suggest we need to pay special attention to time-specificity. By understanding the importance of counting, calculation and such processes that point back to the inherent link between mathematics and media, Ernst picks up on the division between spatial arts (painting and sculpture) and time-based arts (narrative). In the age of algorithmics, despite the temptation offered by an increasing visualization and graphical user interface metaphorics, we are again in the age of not only time-based, but *time-critical* processes, argues Ernst (2003: 42–4; cf. Ernst 2006). Hence, he moves further from the realization that mathematics and calculation are at the core of technical and digital media, to an elaborated argument that these are time-critical processes, especially when understood through the processual nature of the calculating machine or computer. Time-criticality refers to the internal, creative function of processuality of, for instance, digital machines. Ernst does not reduce computers to calculating machines and neglect the way in which they have become media machines, but argues that the media they offer in terms of visual, textual and sonic phenomena are, at the core, based in quantification, and hence numbers.

Ernst's way of articulating a specifically media-archaeological version of 'media materialism' is then not a direct assault on narrative theories, but a strong insistence on rethinking what we mean by narrative. He detaches it from a solely textual and meaning-based understanding to point towards how narratives and 'telling' are themselves processual *operations*: techniques as part of technological systems. Hence, as Ernst (2005) argues, media archaeology is not cultural history. Such methodologies might develop in parallel lines, but differ from theorists such as Stephen Bann in that the object is no longer people, discourses and narrativization as a method of bringing the past alive, but the archive. Ernst also differentiates himself from such media archaeologists of the digital as Lev Manovich who, he argues, is still doing linear histories of new media (see Lovink and Ernst 2003) – even if, we could add, Manovich (2001: 218–21) has given keys for a post-narrative way of thinking in emphasizing the database as the foundational form for new media objects and culture.

Indeed, Ernst is perhaps the first – following Walter Benjamin, of course – who explicitly insists on the centrality of the archive for media studies. The archive is a condition of any statement, and archives are monumental in the sense we have seen Foucault already arguing: they record that which has existed. Such recordings become the monument of time in terms of how it conveys documents not as narratives but as concrete, factual objects. This gets further complicated with technical media which accurately record, as Kittler argued regarding the phonograph, all kinds of other things besides meaningful statements. Every kind of storage, recording, carries with it in a very scientific sense as well 'time' and the original event of recording, and hence is non-linear itself. For Ernst, it is in all this that falls outside meaning that media archaeology picks up its epistemology and its methodology: 'Media archaeology concentrates on the non-discursive elements in dealing with the past: not on speakers, but rather on the agency of the machine' (Ernst 2005: 591; see also Ernst 2011). The techno-episteme starts from the machinic archive, even if, problematically, this conceptualization does not extend to discussing the aspects of politics in such an epistemology. We will elaborate on these questions concerning the archive in technical media culture in chapter 6.

Hence, it suffices here to point towards how the mathematics and temporal processuality of mathematics on our laptops, and desktop computers, smart phones, networks wired and wireless, are forcing us to think anew media epistemology. As flagged above, the new understanding of 'descent' is not only genealogical, but archaeological in the sense that a recent wave of media archaeologists have started to look at time-critical processes *inside* the machines and in the circuits of contemporary technology. Media archaeology goes *under the hood*, so to speak, and extends the idea of an archive into actual machines and circuits. Perhaps still hardware enthusiasts, and definitely materialist, but continuing their archaeological methodologies by hardware hacking and circuit bending, this new kind of media archaeologist moves from historical time to machine time such as network routing and channelling, Ethernet traffic rhythms, and processor patterns. This leads both to theoretical perspectives on 'time-criticality' (Volmar 2009) and to media-artistic/hacktivist methodologies such as with the Institute for Algorithmics – also addressed in chapter 7 in the context of media-archaeological methods for creative practice – or the Microresearch Lab and Martin Howse's methodologies for 'digital archaeology', such as 'carving' into data – for instance hard-drives. The final subsection of this chapter focuses instead on tying up some of the themes of German media archaeology with currents in contemporary Anglo-American media studies.

New media studies: medium-specificity

As briefly flagged at the beginning of this chapter, the recent years of cultural–theoretical debate have seen a renewed interest in matter, objects, material processes and the posthuman and non-human. The various brands of new materialism are not reducible to the material-ism of Marxist theories of the political economy of production forces in their historical development, and they are interested in the inten-sive materiality of bodies in motion and defined by *movement moving* (evident in the work of Erin Manning and Brian Massumi); the *abstract materialism* that draws from science-and-art collaboration (for example Luciana Parisi's writings on architecture and embodi-ment); *political physiology* that looks for connections between the 'social and the somatic' (John Protevi); radical empiricism of the wireless experience (Adrian Mackenzie); the writings on science by Manuel Delanda, Donna Haraway and Karen Barad; material feminists such as Rosi Braidotti, Elizabeth Grosz and others; and of course, for example, Bruno Latour's work that has had a significant influence – in addition to other theorist-philosophers such as Gilles Deleuze – on a rethinking of materiality (see Bennett 2010). Partly, this turn to materiality can be seen to correct the perceived immate-riality brought by digital culture, and by what postmodern theories flagged as the abstraction and immaterialization of cultural reality through a new kind of primacy of the sign, from money to simula-tory techniques. Such ideas were most visible in the work of Jean Baudrillard. Indeed, modern processes of abstraction and demate-rialization can be understood to be having effects as a crisis of the phenomenological, experiencing human body, and also to demand a different vocabulary that would take into account the *new* forms of materialities of the technical media age (Brown 2010).

What we have already seen emerging after the 1990s hype con-cerning virtuality of the digital culture is a new emphasis on software, platforms and the various relays and multiple media within the notion of 'digital media'. Hence, this new *medium-specificity* means keeping a more careful eye on the multiple materialities as well, as is evident in this account by Matthew G. Kirschenbaum concerning electronic media: 'A bibliographic/textual approach calls upon us to emphasize precisely those aspects of electronic textuality that have thus far been neglected in the critical writing about the medium: platform, interface, data standards, file formats, operating systems, versions and distributions of code, patches, ports, and so forth. *For that's the stuff electronic texts are made of* (quoted in Brown 2010: 56, emphasis in the original).

Hence, it is fruitful to see Kittler and the other 'media materialists' of the German school in this context that has insisted on new humanities vocabularies for digital culture. It would be unfair and silly to reduce the plurality of contemporary approaches to Kittler's influence but still one could elaborate a certain 'Kittler-effect'. Winthrop-Young (2011: 143–6) critiques the idea of a 'Kittler-school' of faithful followers of his work. Instead, he argues, it would more interesting to talk about the Kittler-effect in both German and international (he mentions especially American communication studies) academic discussions concerning media, in which Kittler's theories have acted as important benchmarks for providing a more solid technological basis for poststructuralist theories (Lacan, Foucault and, we might add, Deleuze), as well as radically historical perspectives on how we understand communication. One key benchmark, I would add, is how we understand the materiality of media from a historical, even archaeological, perspective – and the materiality of technical media, in particular. Despite the at times emphasized desire for distance from Anglo-American (although especially British) cultural and media studies, this Kittler-effect is visible in how some new forms of media studies are also taking bearings from Kittler in terms of the materiality of media. Hence, what we track here as 'media archaeology' – and the expansion of the concept – is of relevance for what could now be called, for want of a better term, '*new* media studies' which takes as its driving force the realization of the importance of concrete software and hardware processes and platforms in media studies. It is thus no accident that the more recent wave of new media scholars in the US as well are saying that their work is not 'about information society, but about the real machines that live within that society' (Galloway 2004: 17). In cultural studies there has been an emerging discourse concerning the move from the Birmingham tradition of cultural studies to new cultural studies which means that the primary theoretical corpus and reference point consists of more recent theorists – Badiou, Deleuze, Žižek and indeed Kittler – and themes such as posthumanism and transnational and post-Marxism (see Hall and Birchall 2006), and in media studies we can decipher the existence of a new generation of themes as well. Kittler is included, for sure, but one can also say that a very medium-specific set of ideas is being articulated, from media archaeology to media ecology, and from software studies to platform studies.

With the impact of Kittler, and more recently Ernst, the emphasis on the materiality of the information society through its machines has given tools for expanding the media-archaeological interest of knowledge as well. Media archaeology becomes more than an interest in lost ideas, quirky technology of the past, or the imaginary media of poets and visionaries. In the wake of the Kittler-effect, media archaeology becomes a way to investigate not only histories of technological processes but also the current 'archaeology' of what happens inside the machine. Hence, despite the voiced difference, or uniqueness, of the particular German brand, a range of approaches in the US-based new media studies are picking up on similar points, and extending the original impetus into directions where disciplinary boundaries get further blurred.

Such ideas are evident in directions such as platform studies, software studies, the humanities computing forensics of scholars such as Kirschenbaum, and even in the developments by scholars such as Wendy Hui Kyong Chun. Chun has reflected on the relations of media archaeology to the more Anglo-American visual culture studies and positioned her work somewhere in-between, as a mediation of different streams and academic debates. In her short reflection, visual culture studies represents the more user-orientated approach that also 'treats the interface, or representations of the interface, as the medium' (Chun 2006a: 17). Media archaeology – and Chun identifies this especially with the Berlin school, along the axis of Kittler–Ernst – is, in contrast, interested in how the machine itself posits the screen, the interface, and, on a technical layer, gives us the phenomenological experience of visuals and sounds – a point Ernst (2006) emphasizes in the chapter he wrote for Chun and Keenan (2006). Despite being a simplification, such divisions are good heuristic tools for making sense of the complex interchanges between intellectual traditions and debates.

Indeed, it is fruitful to see the media-archaeological under-the-hood methodology as a link to how visual culture studies paradigms are changing. The rethinking of the visual medium through software, protocols and other technologies of control is at the core of such works as Raiford Guins's (2009) *Edited Clean Version*, which extends to affinities with work by Ernst. Yet, Guins is drawing his impetus from the theories of governmentality of Foucault and the rethinking of power as control by Deleuze, but implementing such ideas through software and protocol analysis. In other words, if for Foucault the archive was the place where statements and visibilities are controlled, then a logical step, also proposed by such post-Kittler theorists as Ernst, is for us to rethink the machine as the archive: the software, the hardware, the protocols and platforms which form the visibility, the audibility, the statements of what is. What Guins does – and such emerging forms of media studies as platform studies (Montfort and Bogost 2009) and software studies (for example, Wardrip-Fruin 2009) as well, in differing ways – is to bring a new medium-specificity to the analysis of digital media. Guins is able to connect that effectively to the wider political economy of consumer products in the digital age, echoing Kittler's software-writings, and hence to address some of the shortcomings of the German media theorists. Thus, media-materialist writings enable technically specific understandings of aesthetics in terms of television scan lines and graphics systems, of graphics rendering and memory restrictions – as with the Montfort and Bogost (2009) analysis of the 1970s and early 1980s gaming platform Atari VCS – and of the new forms of temporality circulated by the cycles, processes and object and data worlds of computers (Wardrip-Fruin 2009).

Furthermore, such questions are ones not only of *ontology* (What constitute digital media? What are their defining features?), or of *politics* (What are the new forms of control and governmentality in the software age?) but of *methodology*: how do we study such phenomena? As Wardrip-Fruin (2011) continues from a software studies perspective, archaeologies of digital media should not be limited to readings of representations of old digital media, but be able to tap into their defining features, i.e. operationality and processuality. In a manner that resonates strongly with some of the positions taken by Ernst, Wardrip-Fruin (2011: 302–3) writes about digital media archaeology as a way of also understanding futures of digital media studies: we need to develop tools that understand digital media as processual: 'Digital media are not simply representations but machines for generating representations.'

Media archaeology has to be medium-specific, argues Wardrip-Fruin. This is exactly what so many materialist theories of recent years have started to call for: more specific and nuanced analyses of the modalities of materiality in which we are embedded in cultures of abstraction. Kirschenbaum's work is again exemplary of these new waves in media studies that stem from some of Kittler's and related analysis of technical culture but develop it into directions where it rediscovers relevancy for thinking about storage, cultural objects and processes in the age of information technology. Insisting on mapping their materiality through a close reading method, Kirschenbaum's methodology is here close to what we will address in more detail in chapter 5 concerning the conjunction of rethinking of archives and media-archaeological methods.

Kirschenbaum suggests a methodology and vocabulary for these processes of the informational culture which, again, take as their starting point informational materialities which resist mere apparatus-focus but still are able to tap into the specificity of the time-critical processes in which contemporary cultural products – texts, images, sounds – operate and are stored. Hence, this means a media studies vocabulary that acknowledges that the inscription technologies of our age demand a (digital) humanities understanding of random access, signal processing, differentiality and chronographics, volumetrics, rationalization, atomization, motion-dependency and the non-volatile nature of contemporary regimes of memory (Kirschenbaum 2008: 89). Perhaps contemporary media archaeology of digital culture starts not from the traditional archive, but from the hard drive – a characteristic which Kirschenbaum here describes? Perhaps the future archaeologist does not start her excavations by going to an archive filled with books and documents, but opens up a PC from the 1980s, inspects its circuit board, and starts forensics work on the hard drive.

Such software and hardware activities seems to be an increasing trend in media-archaeological research, and an emerging amount of work is focusing on archaeologies of software and digitality – not as cultures of the immaterial, but very much through the machines, processes – and standards, commands, addresses and data. Indeed, what we have outlined here as some of the contributions of Kittler and the 'Kittler-effect' on media archaeology applies to other ideas emerging in media studies as well and shows how media archaeology has relevance for a wide range of other theories and methodologies of analysis for contemporary media too. Chapter 6 continues these discussions.

Summary

Friedrich A. Kittler is a key thinker of the material discourse networks of 1800 and 1900 – notions that he developed to understand the specificity of technical media. Even if he did not recognize himself as a media archaeologist, Kittler's work has given key concepts for later developments. More recent theorists such as Bernhard Siegert, Wolfgang Ernst and Claus Pias are continuing similar themes and media-materialist approaches, but similarly a range of 'new materialist' media studies theories are emerging: software studies, platform studies and others. A variety of media studies methodologies are now insisting that we should not only engage in textual analyses of media culture, but be prepared to tackle what goes on inside the machine as well. The method of 'descent' as Foucault introduced it is becoming adapted not only to historical research, but also to such techniques of analysis of technical media that take the media archaeologist 'under the hood' of software, as well as hardware. From this perspective, media archaeology is a methodology that insists on medium-specificity.

Further readings

Bennett, Jane (2010) *Vibrant Matter. A Political Ecology of Things* (Durham: Duke University Press).

Kittler, Friedrich A. (1999) *Gramophone, Film, Typewriter*, trans. Geoffrey Winthrop-Young and Michael Wutz (Stanford, CA: Stanford University Press)

Kittler, Friedrich A. (2010) *Optical Media*, trans. Anthony Enns (Cambridge: Polity).

Lovink, Geert (2008) 'Whereabouts of German Media Theory' in *Zero Comments* (New York: Routledge), 83–98.

Parikka, Jussi (2011) 'Operative Media Archaeology: Wolfgang Ernst's Materialist Media Diagrammatics' *Theory, Culture & Society* 28(5), 52–74.

Winthrop-Young, Geoffrey (2011) *Kittler and the Media* (Cambridge: Polity).

5

Mapping Noise and Accidents

Media archaeology is interested in the anomalous, the non-main-stream in media cultures. An important precursor for such *media analysis of and from the ruins* includes Walter Benjamin's cultural historical method which itself takes waste, rubble and ruins as its starting points for a multi-layered excavation of the slow emergence of modernity. For example, his unfinished *Arcades* project, which itself remains a collection of fragments, is emblematic of this multi-layered approach to the natural history of commodity objects (cf. Gabrys 2011). Methodologically, it picks up on the theme of the fragment when writing about the ruins of modernity, mass culture, emergence of media cultures, and capitalism that surround us, and constitute our living world. Benjamin illuminated this idea of analysis from the ruins already in his earlier work, and in his doctoral thesis in 1928 on the German baroque *Trauerspiel* ('Mourning play') theatrical genre. He uses the term 'allegory' in a complex and far from simply comparative way, and in one passage on 'ruins' refers to how 'allegories are in the sphere of thought what ruins are among things' (Benjamin 1977: 354).

Whereas Benjamin goes on to explicate this in the context of the eighteenth-century theatrical genre, for us this has media-archaeological implications in how it ties together the ruins of material culture as part of the ecologies of thought. In a way, it illuminates some of the ways in which media-archaeological research and cultural histories of material culture have tried to engage with these themes. We live among layered historical times of which spatial architectures are one example, but we can extend that to architectures and ruins of media culture too, which demonstrate what the historian Fernand Braudel (1980) called the various durations of history. The long duration, the intermediary, and the time of the event intermingle and mix, and the seemingly contemporary is of the past as well in a way that does not fit in with either linear or cyclical notions of time. The same applies to ways of thinking, which reside in ruins and where the notion of 'archaeology' is more apt than 'history' for carving out the layered constellation in which the cognitive and the affective experience take place.[1] In this sense, the allegorical, as understood by Benjamin, is a parallel, partly competing, partly complementing concept to those master concepts of media archaeology proposed by Huhtamo (cyclical topoi) and Zielinski (variantology, the minor genealogies of media culture), and even Bruce Sterling's dead media approach that looks at the ruins, the fossils of media cultures that have been deemed unsupportable from a business point of view (Ludovico 1998).

This is a chapter on noise and disturbances, on anomalies of media culture. In this chapter I try to show one way of conducting media-archaeological analysis, namely a certain kind of archaeology of noise. As such, it is meant as a methodological exercise as well to demonstrate how media archaeology can be used to find the neglected: in the midst of celebrations of communication and the frictionless digital culture by such entrepreneurs as Bill Gates in the mid-1990s, such disturbances as viruses, spam, fraudsters, tricksters and scammers have become as essential a part of our technical communication landscape as the dreams of unending and unlimited connectivity. Noise and lack of connection are with us from the sonic to the informatics, and the cultural practices listed above – from viruses to spam – are often rhetorically connected to the idea of 'noise' in the communication channel.

The analysis of the dark sides of technical media culture is not without predecessors. We find good indications in the writings of Wolfgang Schivelbusch and Paul Virilio already. For Schivelbusch (1986), the invention of the train – which also can be considered a media technology that transforms the way we understand and experience time and distance – was instantly shadowed by the possibility of a train accident, which constitutes a key phenomenon in the way the whole system of trains and train movement was introduced in the nineteenth century. Paul Virilio has become famous for his more philosophical writings concerning the primacy of the accident, and the form of the accident becoming a defining feature of technological modernity – even to such an extent that he calls for an institution of museums for accidents (Virilio 2004). Such perspectives relate to the manner in which it is possible to analyse the specific forms of accidents – such as computer viruses (Parikka 2007) – of digital culture – and its predecessors.[2]

The sound of noise

Before turning to the main emphasis of this chapter, which relates to network communication, interference and the existence of unintended *and* intended noise as part of the modern communication systems, let's take a quick look at where noise seems to be an intuitive part of technological culture: noise as it rings, disturbs and hurts in our ears and bodies. An increase in meticulous analysis of sound in media cultures has been able to map more closely the relations between sound and noise – and sound *as* noise as well. This more acoustic approach to noise has spurred interesting and important writings on how we can use sonic perspectives to develop a thorough understanding of the ephemeral materialities of modern technical media, and how sound can act as a way to further insights to the link between modernity, noise and embodiment. As such, sonic noise has become more than an acoustic phenomenon for human ears, and itself an indicator of technological spaces, urbanity and modernization (Thompson 2004) – as well as having a crucial role in the birth of electronic culture.

Indeed, the nineteenth-century technologies of sound recording were instrumental in creating a new sphere of sounds far more comprehensive than one of music, or voice only, and this created the possibilities of time-axis manipulation of recorded material (back, forth, cut, paste, that are no longer techniques restricted to sound but characterize digital culture aesthetics more widely). Here, phonographic methods inscribed not only music, voice and comprehensible sounds, but also noise – whether that of the body or of the medium itself – and hence opened a whole new non-hermeneutic regime of soundscapes and analysis (Kahn 1999: 9–10; on the origins of sound reproduction, see Sterne 2003).

Paul DeMarinis has elaborated how this double emergence of analogue sound recording and sound-multiplicity happens on so many machinic levels: in addition to what people *intended* to have on the recording surface, another level was the unintended environmental noises that crept onto the grooves – then,

> a third set consisted of the various squeaks and rumblings of the machinery itself, the whirring of gears and the bumps of unwinding steel springs; and fourth would be the sound of overdubbing that soon emerged in public presentations where a single cylinder was recorded over and over again during successive demos, the new sound not totally erasing the memory of previous markings. (2011: 221–2)

Whereas DeMarinis suggests that we can unravel a whole media archaeology of control of noise-sounds in '[m]icrophones, high-signal-to-noise-ratio media, padded recording booths, and sound-stage protocols', he also points to the tactics of cultivating scratches and noises, an integral part of modern sound arts.

In other words, as Kittler has analysed extensively, the gramophone picks up not only the meaning inherent in human speech but, just as effectively, the whispers, the noises of the body, the 'extras' of communication, so to speak, that come with every opening of the mouth. Long before John Cage (1912–92) forced spectators to listen to the uneasy noisiness of their bodies and the environment as they 'listened' to *4′33″*, the technical recording of the trace of the body purged itself of meaning and intentionality. Indeed, as Geoffrey Winthrop-Young and Michael Wutz (1999: xxviii), the translators of *Gramophone, Film, Typewriter*, explain, this is part of the materialist ontology of the Kittlerian cosmology that we also addressed in the last chapter.³

Connected to the valorization of noise, the regime of noises was identified by such avant-gardists as Futurists as the sound of

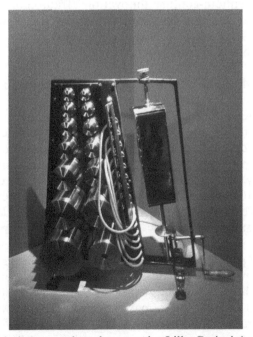

Image 5.1 Helmholtz's sound analyser at the Lille Curiosités Acoustiques exhibition, 2010.

modernity – the soundtrack of cultures of factories, urban movement and progress – in a manner that celebrated its futuristic promise, most visibly present in *Art of Noise* (1913) by Luigi Russolo (1883–1947). What Russolo pointed towards was that we need an appreciation, and careful classification and understanding, of the variety of noises – a whole science of noises, which are part and parcel of modern life. In Doug Kahn's (1999: 20) words, 'the trouble is that noises are never just sounds and the sounds they mask are never just sounds: they are also ideas of noise. Ideas of noise can be tetchy, abusive, transgressive, resistive, hyperbolic, scientistic, generative, and cosmological.' Fundamental to the new deciphering of noise in its multiplicity and as an object of knowledge was the creation of technologies of inscription and recording, also outside the actual phonographs. For example, the visual ways of inscription of sound were in this sense closely linked to the selective task of classification of sounds vs noise – what is useful, what is not, what is included, what is filtered out (Kahn 1999: 68–9; Levin 2003). In a way, one could see how the methods of inscription were also giving ways to find the medium-specificity that sound demanded – an idea cultivated by the emergence of new technologies specific to sound, such as the early twentieth-century innovations Trautonium, Sphaerophon, Atherophone and the Theremin, as well as artistic discourses such as that of László Moholo-Nagy (1895–1946) in the 1920s: what are the specific possibilities of sound as a technological formation (Levin 2003: 45)?

As such, the issue of noise expanded from being just an unwanted element to a more defining feature in how sound is being understood, as well as the knowledge of sound cultivated, even in such grim practices as sound torture. Sound and sonic technologies are essential to so many cultural formations: from knowledge production, which now seems new with the emerging sonification of data patterns but was actually part of the nineteenth-century science culture already (Volmar 2010), to sound as an integral part of the emergence of computer cultures. Historians such as Gerard Alberts (2010), have convincingly demonstrated how understanding of computer processes through the rhythms and sounds they made was an emblematic part of the early post-World War II mainframe computing culture in following the processing of instructions, as well as detecting anomalies and problems. Computers process sounds: what seemed noise to uncultivated ears was full of patterns and signals to someone like an IBM mainframe repairman in the 1950s. Next we are going to turn to a more informatics-centred perspective in considering what noise is – formally.

Primacy of noise

One is tempted to say that there is something German – in the sense of material media theory – in how several theorists like Kittler insist that the 'founding event' of modern media culture is the mid-twentieth-century model of communication and noise developed by Claude Shannon (1916–2001) and Warren Weaver (1894–1978). The technical formulation of diagrammatics of noise and noise reduction acts as a recurring reference point for explaining the novelty of signal transmission and media in the age of technical telecommunications.

In the 1940s Shannon presented a formal model of technical communication that also involved the formalization of the components of a communication system: sender, receiver and channel, as well as noise. Communication systems are noisy systems by definition, as demonstrated in a technical context by Shannon in his paper 'The Mathematical Theory of Communication' (1948) that was only the last phase of a much longer interest in communication theory in the age of vacuum tubes. For Shannon, the new theory of communication had to be designed to take into account 'in particular the effect of noise in the channel' (Shannon and Weaver 1949: 3).

Shannon's well-known diagram of a general communication system is in this sense illustrative. Even though noise is seen as coming from the outside and invading the mediating powers of a communicative act, it still is diagrammed as an integral part of the system. Hence it is accorded a position *within* the diagrammatic framework instead of residing as pure noise outside the communication act. In this sense, conceptually, noise is a modality of modern communication systems that by definition deal with *signals*, not with signifying, meaningful signs. This focus on signals came out of earlier pioneering work with vacuum-tube-enhanced voice communication (Mindell 2002: 111–12). In other words, this way of understanding communication was scientific and engineered – not human-oriented. Technical media machines and channels transport, first of all, signals, which then for us humans are signs that can be interpreted, talked about, and debated.

Through careful archival work with Shannon's papers, Axel Roch (2010) has offered a meticulous insight into the birth of the mathematical theory of communication – and how such scientists as Shannon were developing their ideas in the midst of the World War II mass mobilization of not only troops on the battlefield, but scientists into labs, which produced both atomic weapons (with the help of new calculating machines, computers) and improved, more secure forms of communication: from the new visual technologies such as the radar

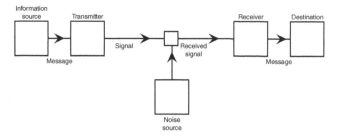

Schematic diagram of a general communication system

Image 5.2 The Shannon model of communication as a diagram that includes noise as an essential part of any communication situation. Redrawn by Ian Bennett

to cryptographic solutions so much needed in the electronic battle-field. For writers like Kittler, the link between modern media and war was already assumed as more than intimate – our media always stem from war, whether in terms of the work on effective communication and signal processing/encryption/decryption, or the mobilization of the body and the senses: 'Modern media drill, reshape, and mobilize the human body, its sensory apparatus, and its nervous system to make it more compatible with the requirements of modern electronic warfare. In short, we are dealing with drill and distraction, but the distractions are always already part of the drill', as Winthrop-Young (2002: 838) writes about Kittler's media theory in relation to war.

But the work on signals and communication predates World War II. Shannon's *alma mater* Bell Labs, which grew from the original telephone research lab into one of the most significant hubs of innovation for twentieth-century transmission media, had since the 1910s and 1920s been a key site for telecommunications research. One could say that the work there shifted the emphasis from psychological and semantic issues in transmission communication to mathematics and physical engineering. Transmission of intelligence and cultural products had been a topic in physics since the experiments with electrical telegraphy that one can, of course, track to way back before the nineteenth century as part of the wider history of experimenting with electrical matter and conduction (Fahie 1884). Yet, partly due to physical requirements for a better quality of transmission, partly for state and business security reasons, from the early experiments with telegraphs to those with vacuum tubes in the early twentieth century, combating weak signals and noise was at the top of the agenda of communications engineering. Research focused on various noise types in vacuum tubes.[4] In addition to noise inside and from technical components, looking for noise even from atmospheric conditions such as the sun or the weather became a top priority in electrical engineering. As the people at Bell Labs soon noticed, noise was everywhere (Cohen 2005).

For Shannon, this was an important realization too – that you can draw a connection between the mathematics of communication and noise, and the earlier physical theories of entropy developed by Ludwig Bolzmann (1844–1906) from 1872. Mathematics of communication is after all embedded in physical engineering, and hence physics: thermal noise, as part of the movements of electrons in circuits and vacuum tubes, is of great significance for any communication event (Roch 2010: 114–17). As part of its physical nature, during the early part of the twentieth century, communication was gradually perceived as a system event and feedback control. In the 1920s, Nyquist (1924) and Hartley (1928) of the AT&T Research and Development and Bell Labs teams presented in their respective papers the basis for a general theory of communication. They had been instrumental in the early work on strengthening signals – that no longer had to be only voice, but could be any signal of sound, text or image – over longer and longer distances, and through carrier multiplexing that allowed the packing of more separate conversations on one line in different frequencies (Mindell 2002: 112–114). Additionally, Shannon formulated the principle of systems of communication in which the received signal-message is formed as a function of transmission *and* noise: $E = f(Sn,N)$ (Shannon and Weaver 1949: 34). In its practical context, which aimed for system predictability, it fitted in with realizations in mathematics and physics. Such engineers worked with very concrete problems concerning network signals and communication becoming for the first time signal-based, paving the way for our digital culture. And yet, such problems seemed to be identified across a range of so many scientific and cultural fields. In 1900 David Hilbert (1862–1943) had argued for a system of mathematics that was complete, consistent and decidable, but the rationality of this calculative system was soon challenged. In mathematics, Kurt Gödel (1906–78) proved in 1931 that every system was by definition incomplete in that it could not be coherent and consistent by its own making. This realization had repercussions far beyond mathematics in the fields of computation and communication systems. (Gere 2002: 17–18). Hence, some years later, Shannon and Weaver's ideas were part of a larger field of modern thought in which noise and incompleteness were beginning to be considered as integral to any functioning system.

After World War II, cybernetic models of feedback were designed to isolate disturbing anomalies from systems' processes. But at the same time, continuing the earlier engineering work, this task produced a veritable science of noise. Just as someone creating electronic music knows the difference between white noise and pink noise, early pioneers in computing machinery distinguished several different modes of noise, and for each, an 'optimum filter' mode of managing that noise (Tuller 1952: 111).

The information scientists tried to battle the various kinds of disturbances in the communication channel with redundancy. As Warren Weaver proposed in his paper 'Recent Contributions to the Mathematical Theory of Communication', which followed and commented on Shannon's formulas, *redundancy* functions as a guarantee that messages will be received relatively intact at the other end. Uncertainty was seen as a basic characteristic of communication that could be countered by strategic repetition:

> Since [the] English [language] is about 50 per cent redundant, it would be possible to save about one-half the time of ordinary telegraphy by a proper encoding process, *provided* one were going to transmit over a noiseless channel. When there is noise on a channel, however, there is some real advantage in not using a coding process that eliminates all of the redundancy. For the remaining redundancy helps combat the noise. This is very easy to see, for just because of the fact that the redundancy of English is high, one has, for example, little or no hesitation about correcting errors in spelling that have arisen during transmission. (Weaver 1949: 112)

Problems of technical media, then, proved to be different from the ones in oral media. Engineering and programming are not situations of conversation. In retrospect, it is interesting how the forms of redundancy that aimed to combat problems of signal transmission actually turned out to be part of the noise of later technical media in the form of programmatic redundancy, such as mass spamming or viral programs. Redundancy has in itself spurred a problem of distinguishing the proper information from the presumably unwanted flow of messages with dubious origins, and various kinds of filters and scanners are trying to cope with it. Such software techniques as flooding and trashing (earlier terms for spamming) have been used to overflow BBS's, blogs, MUD, and chat rooms, as well as e-mail inboxes, in addition to constituting a core element of some forms of Denial of Service attacks, part of the current practices of online guerrilla actions. They are not merely noise but actually reveal a logic in which *excessive multiple posting* is a potential function of the software environment.

These kinds of problems with automated executions of code are evidently a crucial part of the digital network culture and force businesses to invest heavily in security and training of staff, and national governments to put increased emphasis on cyber security and new defence measures against online attacks.

Interestingly, with filtering programs and semantic Web applications that distinguish 'dirt' from proper messages, the communicative act is happening increasingly only between programs: the mass-mailing systems that distribute spam messages and the filtering applications that receive and analyse them and potentially forward some of the messages to the user. Media archaeology, by insisting on connecting the social aspects of communication with an understanding of the technical a priori – the technical conditions of existence – is then able to carve out important medium-specific details concerning contemporary media ecology.

The physics of noise

Noise, redundancy and predictability of messaging become key contexts for modern communication. One can track such ideas through scientific contexts: the realizations in modern physics crucially paved the way for seeing unpredictability as an ontological problem but one that could be partly addressed (even if not thoroughly solved) through practical solutions. The work done in the early twentieth-century telecommunications engineering laboratories was a good example (Mindell 2002). Such contexts produced the possibility of actually creating and managing communications as a signal – and hence removed from the human body and its energy – but, more widely, the emergence of modern media is intimately tied up with modern sciences. Hence, in addition to the histories of the media corporations and industry, we should recall names such as Maxwell, Faraday, Helmholtz, Fourier and Bolzmann – all key scientists of the nineteenth century who contributed to innovations and ideas that formed the backbone for later technical media devices.

Shannon's ideas can be seen as a continuation of attempts to find the most efficient way of transmitting statistical, quantitative and physical messages from transmitter to receiver, a problem that had been the overall encoding problem ever since the optical telegraph (Mattelart 2001: 56–7). At the same time, the issue of efficient encoding was also on the security agenda, where fast message transmission codes were supposed to be safe from cracking. Here the mathematical problem of efficiency and reliability of signals went together with security concerns.

Shannon himself drew directly from thermodynamics and the notions of entropy. The second law of thermodynamics, which argues for universal entropy and a gradual increase in disorder, had already been discovered in the the mid nineteenth century by Rudolf Clausius (1822–88). In a development that was important for Shannon's ideas, the physicist Bolzmann conceptualized the problems of closed systems in terms of entropy, meaning the tendency for any system to dissipate with time, to lose its structure. Interestingly, Bolzmann's early conceptualization of information took into account the dynamics of such systems: because of the huge number of interactions, a clearly deducible account of a system's functioning cannot be known a priori (Terranova 2004: 21). Bolzmann's agenda revolved around heat engines, but Shannon was able to use many of the ideas directly in his quest for reliability in information systems. As John Johnston (2008: 27, 136–9) explains, there is a direct link between the two, and statistical mechanics provided the needed measures of information, choice and uncertainty. Roch (2010: 114) argues that Shannon transported realizations from physics into electronic cryptography, learning from the patterns of diffusion, dissipation and thermal noise when designing his communication solutions.

The etymological relationship of *noise* to *nausea* brings in the idea of irregularity of movement, which emerged as a key theme of physics in the early twentieth century. Stochastic processes and Brownian random motion at the molecular level suggested that the universe consisted primarily of processes that were unstable, noisy. But when the physical realizations were turned into engineering issues, irregularity became a problem. To produce stable systems of communication and automation, one needed to control noise. Hence, for instance, Norbert Wiener (1894–1964), who spent his wartime years investigating how to control and shoot down the Brownian movement of enemy airplanes, turned noise into a nearly metaphysical evil. Communication engineering became a branch of statistical mechanics. The question became how to control the amount of entropy in a system, or, in other words, how to ensure that the degree of disorganization of a system did not rise too high (Wiener 1948: 17–18). Even though the practical aims might have been similar, this approach differed from Shannon's mathematical formulations (which, as pointed out, borrowed from physics as well), in which information always had, by definition, a relation to noise, and that noise was potentially a source of new information for the receiver – hence providing a sense of its own beyond the sender's intentions. Communication always takes place in environments, and is more atmospheric than just a clear message getting through – even if that is the pragmatic aim. Such ideas were later developed in the contexts of second-order cybernetics. Scientists such as Heinz von Foerster (1911–2002) saw that new forms of order could actually be born from noise (see Johnston 2008: 138, 189).

In any case, cybernetic feedback, which permeated not only technical systems from the 1940s and 1950s onward but also a whole field from social sciences to economics to psychology, became a model of noise control. In an ironic fashion, the science of steering (*kubernetes*) became one of the chief tenets in combating seasickness (*nausea*, the etymological origin of *noise* in Greek). Yet, despite this strategic effort – a very important one to be sure – communication and networks are never frictionless. Whether we are talking in the language of physics (leftover noise, or 'three-degree blackbody radiation', indicating how the universe is continuously expanding) or philosophy (e.g. the Serresian agenda of 'parasites'), or practical security measures of a company or some other institution against spam, intruders, crackers, etc., noise is there. In a way, the ontology of physics (and hence digital culture as well as rock music) of the twentieth century is crucially about noise.[5] Similarly, cybernetics, in its attempts to provide solutions for controlling noise, was inherently tied to the idea of noise as disorganization. Wiener's early interest in Brownian movement also suggests how cybernetics can be characterized as an 'archival task' of inclusion via exclusion. So much of cybernetics was based on the realization that the universe is probabilistic and only metastable. There is no ultimate possibility of getting rid of the intervening effects of noise, as it is a basic feature of the physical world (Hayles 1999: 88–9). But there are always ways to examine, map and constrain that noise.

Whereas Shannon's chief concern was reproduction of the signal, Wiener's was cybernetic homeostasis. Despite the fact that they are now seen as formative, cybernetic and signal processing stances, the conservative basis of both approaches had already been questioned in the early Macy conferences (1940s and 1950s), which were in a key position to debate and distribute cybernetic models across the social field. As N. Katherine Hayles (1999: 63–4) argues, John Stroud of the US Naval Electronic Laboratory pointed to the problem that dualist models of signal vs noise promoted. In Shannon's model, homeostasis was privileged over change. The exact replication of a message over space and time was theoretically defined as the task of communication. Yet alternative models more prone to think of change as positive emerged: for example, idea of information as the change that the message achieves proposed by Donald MacKay (1922–87).

On a philosophical level, this impossibility of self-identical signal transmission connects with the idea of transmission, *trans-mettre*, the in-between that happens in the media event. *Transmitting intelligence* was a term often used from the end of the eighteenth century onward, but there was a constant danger of transmitting false intelligence as well. How could one be sure that the message received was the message sent, and that no one and nothing had 'tapped the lines' between the communication's departure and arrival points? The concern was expressed, for example, in 1881 in the British *Blackwood's Magazine* (in an article entitled 'Freaks of the Telegraph'): 'The telegraph is not always, or to everybody, the unmitigated boon and blessing enthusiastic admirers have represented it to be. ... There is always more or less uncertainty attaching to a telegram, both in regard to the length of time it may be on its journey, and in regard to the way in which the wording may be reproduced' (quoted in Otis 2001: 138).

Guaranteeing the identity of transmitted information was a crucial requirement of communication in optical and electric telegraphs. At the same time, however, such a guarantee implied the danger of 'non-identical' communication, of something disturbing the presence between interacting partners. In various cases this was due to either meteorological conditions or insufficient sunlight, as with the optical telegraph. With the electric telegraph, the technical channels provided their own physical noise, but other, non-technical issues were just as relevant. In other words, the technical understanding of noise on the twentieth-century agenda set forth by information science and physics needed to take into account as well that noise as interference had been an aesthetic-political problem since (at least) the optical telegraph. Conscious interference and production of noise expressed a key fear[6] – but also a tactic of modern technical media.

Noise as interception

The nineteenth century experienced a boom in cryptography in the midst of such inventions as telegraphy and photography, and the 'accompanying sense of the general dematerialization of signs' (Gere 2002: 34). Various systems of encoding were used to enhance the efficiency of transmission in the form of standardized short codes, but also to provide encryption possibilities. A ping was, after all, in a narrow channel, easier to send through than a semantic message; hence, in a way, the formation of short codes and encryption is an intimate part of how signal-based modern communications was born (see Pias 2011 on 'ping' in modern communications).

Of course, interceptions and noise were already part of the transmission system of letters and the rise of the postal system: the Pierre Choderlos de Laclos (1741–1803) novel *Les liaisons dangereuses* from 1782 depicts very well an early interest in capturing telecommunication messages – even though dealing with the letters of lovers. Similarly, such notorious historical characters as Cardinal Richelieu was infamous for his 'system of espionage' (Fahie 1884: 12) – espionage being a practice no history of communication should neglect. Some years later, optical telegraph communication encountered related anxieties of interception. A famous case from 1836 told the tale of two dishonest bankers who bribed operators to send falsified information on interest rates, and profited from such hacking of information. This opportunity to hack communication channels was made possible by the standard routine of decoding and recoding messages at every signpost – a routine designed to decrease transmission errors (Flichy 1997: 37–8). The incident represented perhaps the first case in which deliberate errors (as false information) were introduced into communication patterns to achieve financial gain. Some proponents of the semaphore system, however, were convinced that the electric telegraph was more prone to noise in the form of vandalism, as one Dr Barbay stated in 1846:

No, the electric telegraph is not a sound invention. It will always be at the mercy of the slightest disruption, wild youths, drunkards, bums, etc. . . . The electric telegraph meets those destructive elements with only a few meters of wire over which supervision is impossible. A single man could, without being seen, cut the telegraph wires leading to Paris, and in twenty-four hours cut in ten different places the wires of the same line, without being arrested. (Quoted in Sterling 1994: 12)

Or even if the wires were dug inside the earth, there was still the danger of 'rogues':

Could any number of rogues, then, open trenches six feet deep, in two or more public high roads or streets and get through two or more strong cast-iron troughs, in a less space of time than forty minutes? . . . If they could, render their difficulties greater by cutting the trench deeper: and should they still succeed in breaking the communication by these means, hang them if you can catch them, damn them if you cannot, and mend it immediately in both cases. (Fahie 1884: 140)

Such 'hackers' raised passionate feelings already in the nineteenth century!

In a business context, securing information was an imperative. As Karl Marx notes in his *Grundrisse*, written in the 1850s, capital was keen on creating modes of exceeding spatial boundaries and finding new physical modes of exchange (communication and transport) that were increasingly based on new technologies such as the telegraph (Crary 1999: 140–2). At least from the mid nineteenth century, the stock exchange and commercial communication represented the majority of telegraph traffic in both Europe and the United States. As an 1882 French report on the famous US Gold and Stock Telegraph Company noted, guaranteeing the *identity* of information to all telegraph information subscribers was seen as a key feature in the early business telecommunications sphere ('La Telegraph de Bourse', *La Nature*, 23 September 1882; quoted in Flichy 1997: 69).

The issue of hostile noise as interception of messages was intimately tied not only to business but to war. Ever since the optical telegraph of Claude Chappe (1763–1805) had become functional in the early 1790s, the telegraph was perceived to be a key element of military operations and national security. To underline the importance attributed to this communication system, it was not authorized for civilian use. The codebooks were strictly guarded, and only the senders and receivers were supposed to have knowledge of the code keys (Mattelart 2001: 23). The telegraph allowed a new kind of a communicative overview of the battlefield in which the commanding general moved to a command centre behind the soldiers, coordinating movements and wiring battle units together via telegraph. Such a novel communication sphere needed protective measures, and especially the cipher, as a cheap and effective solution provided the much-needed secrecy of communication instead of the rigid nomenclator system (Kahn 1967: 191).[7] But even though military communications became more effective with the telegraph as the binding force, the probability of interception was higher. A commander could merely sit down and 'tune his radio to the enemy's wavelength' (1967: 298).

Nineteenth-century telegraphy occupied a special place in the quest for noiseless transmission and uninterrupted mediation. The electric telegraph especially was envisioned early on as a security medium for preventing train accidents (Winston 1998: 23; Fahie 1899: 112). Security was also raised as a question relating to the contents of transmission. As David Kahn explains in his extensive history of cryptography, one year after the first messages of Samuel Morse (1791–1872) in 1844, his promotional agent published advice on secrecy in correspondence.

Similarly, a few years later, the English *Quarterly Review* emphasized the importance of security in telegraphic communications:

> Means should also be taken to obviate one great objection, at present felt with respect to sending private communications by telegraph – the violation of all secrecy – for in any case half-a-dozen people must be cognizant of every word addressed by one person to another. The clerks of the English Telegraphy Company are sworn to secrecy, but we often write things that it would be intolerable to see strangers read before our eyes. This is a grievous fault in the telegraph, and it must be remedied by some means or other. ... At all events, some simple yet secure cipher, easily acquired and easily read, should be introduced, by which means messages might to all intents and purposes be 'sealed' to any person except the recipient. (Quoted in Kahn 1967: 189; see also Story 1904: 95–6)[8]

The universal medium – as the optical telegraph was envisioned to be in full Enlightenment mode – was not supposed to support accidents or accidental signals. From the optical telegraph to the electric, and on to the first ideas about the wireless introduced by Marconi (1874–1937), the telegraph was seen as point-to-point communication that was to be protected against outsiders. In the early twentieth century, the wireless made the situation even more ambiguous, for it seemed to create novel possibilities for tapping into the transmissions. Point-to-point transmission was hard to secure as radio waves spread throughout the ether; indeed, anyone with sufficient equipment could receive such messages. The realization of the possibility of tapping into Maxwellian electromagnetic waves and fields presented a whole new situation of removing obstacles to communication – walls were suddenly pierced by modern communications – and revealed also the difficulty of aiming: how do I know the message goes only to the intended party (Fahie 1899: 197–9)?

Whereas governments and the navy in various countries were keen on securing the wireless sphere for themselves, the emergence of radio amateurism raised the urgent problem of how to keep uninvited visitors off the airwaves. Even if the wireless prepared the way for broadcasting, early pioneers such as Marconi saw the potential intrusion of strangers as a key problem for this medium (Huhtamo 1992: 8–10; Fahie 1899: 198). The dangers in such 'wiretapping' were demonstrated by the *Titanic* incident (1912). The ocean liner's SOS message was transmitted on the wireless, but it was also intercepted by radio amateurs, who were later accused of interfering with the rescue efforts. Soon after the incident, the government started to address the

'anarchy of the waves' by requiring examinations for wireless operators. The licensing was designed to stop the wasting of airwaves. As
the *New York Times* reported on 15 December 1912, 'The effect of all
this restriction will be to clear the air of the incessant wireless chatter
of the innumerable amateur stations.'

The tactic of intended noise, then, was not restricted to military
powers; it was also in the reach of (self-)educated operators. Here
the figure of 'tinkerer boy-heroes' can be seen as a good example of
concerns in the early moral panic over 'tapping the wire'. According
to Susan J. Douglas (1989: 187–216), however, these early 'hackers'
were not regarded as one-sidedly malicious: they could also be seen
as positive models of appropriating media technologies to private
use. Whereas communication systems were much characterized by
secrecy and the need to guarantee an interference-free channelling
of information, the amateur operators were able to tap the secluded
lines and the secret world of business and military communications.
Such grassroots action used the official lines for the amateurs' own
purposes, as a 1907 article in the *New York Times* reported in describ-
ing the actions of a young amateur tinkerer, Walter J. Willenborg:
'Messages from everywhere to everywhere and back buzzed into
our receiving instrument. Only those in cipher escaped.' The article
further described how Willenborg was able to destroy other messages,
as demonstrated by his intercepting and interrupting a message from
the Atlantic Highlands:

> Willenborg has achieved such high frequency of wave force, or oscil-
> lation, that he can, when picking up a message, send shooting into the
> receiving machine taking it such a clamor that the message is imme-
> diately destroyed. . . . The aerial above the shack on the roof began to
> shoot forth airwaves that crowded each other with great violence. He
> kept this up for about thirty seconds, and we returned to the receiv-
> ers. ('New Wonders with "Wireless"', New York Times, 3 November
> 1907)

Such concerns had already been part and parcel of late nineteenth-
century communication discourse. Worries about the transmission of
false intelligence and the threat of capture of intelligence included
people as elements of distraction. The danger of *parasitizing*, of using
telegraph networks for unauthorized goals, was a threat that also was
repeatedly raised, as Laura Otis notes in her take on the relations
between physics, media technologies and fiction of the nineteenth
century. Stories of individuals parasitizing public networks were published repeatedly, and this human link was deemed the source of error

in networks that aimed at technological, social and national unity. People were essential but flaky. As *Blackwood's Magazine* wrote in 1881, 'The human element plays so considerable a part in matters telegraphic, that the human propensity to err finds proportionately wide scope.... It evidently to a great extent depends on the turn of mind of the operator which way [the messages] come out' (Otis 2001: 142–3).

When considering the gender aspects in the cultural formations of early network media, women especially occupied this position: the conceptual and material place of *in-between* in transmission (see also Zoe Beloff's art projects on the gender of the medium/media of the nineteenth century). As telegraph operators, typists, secretaries, and in other administrative positions central to new forms of communication, women entered the world of technical media. At the same time they were very ambiguously portrayed. As Carolyn Marvin (1988: 30) notes, poems that served as light fillers in electrical journals often identified women as technological *objects* under male *control*. Yet the huge number of women working as interconnectors in telegraph offices, as secretaries with typing machines, and later as telephone switchboard operators were uncertain elements, probably because of their imagined cultural status as unreliable and emotional (1988: 26, 31).

Uncanny communication objects

What the telegraph age introduced was a novel assemblage of technical communication media constantly susceptible to noise.[9] Of course, this was due not merely to technical reasons but also to political and economic ones. There was a keen interest in the nineteenth century on promoting and securing the emerging technical media networks for capitalist and national interests. Yet at the same time the circuits seemed (at least on symbolical and imaginary levels) to support a variety of unauthorized communication events. Even though the 'Victorian Internet' did not include such 'parasites' as worms and viruses, the discursive position of the anomalous was filled with other kinds of near-mythical instances of the media-uncanny. As Jeffrey Sconce (2000: 57) has shown in *Haunted Media*, the communication channels of the nineteenth century had already encountered the anomalous.

The electric telegraph system and later also the telephone network advanced stories and concerns of what went in and on the wires. Often these were part of the folk culture of the new media rather than official concerns, in the same way that our digital culture has had its fair share of network myths. Several stories in the collection *Lightning Flashes and Electric Dashes: A Volume of Choice Telegraphic Literature, Humor, Fun, Wit and Wisdom* (1877) deal with issues sometimes neglected in the more formal and official accounts of the networks of telegraphs. Intended for people affiliated with telegraph companies and also as promotional material, the goal of such a volume was to evoke positive emotions concerning the new technology, and accounts of accidents are few. Yet the short story 'The Volcanograph' introduces how weird objects of network culture had already spread in the nineteenth century. The short story depicts 'hobgoblins' who keep disturbing proper communicative events. The unwanted intruders that keep 'breaking in' on the channels are given a lesson with the aid of a telegraphic bomb, a countermeasure of a kind: 'Science now comes to our relief in the shape of the volcanograph, a 2,000 cell dynamite battery, worked by a lever and crank in the main office' (*Lightning Flashes* 1877: 7). The pranksters are given a lesson with an explosive electrical bomb, delivered by wire. The story articulates several interesting themes, from annoying spam

BUT THE VOLCANOGRAPH CUT HIM SHORT.

Image 5.3 The volcanograph electric bomb from *Lightning Flashes and Electric Dashes* 1877.

prankstering to electrical pre-cybernetic warfare, taking place on and through the wires.

We have analysed some of these anomalies already in chapter 3 on imaginary media. The supernatural was part of the high-tech of telegraphy and other innovations, and later extra-terrestrial entities also seemed to bug the wires. In the 1890s, there was debate over the effects of the Sun's electrical storms on telephone communication, but also speculation concerning other kinds of 'strange mysterious sounds' that remained inexplicable. The new electrical networks promoted such speculation concerning aliens, as for example with Mr Preece at his talk at the Society of Arts in 1894:

> If any of the planets be populated with beings like ourselves, having the gift of language and the knowledge to adapt the great forces of nature to their wants, then, if they could oscillate immense stores of electrical energy to and fro in telegraphic order, it would be possible for us to hold commune by telephone with the people of Mars. (Fahie 1899: 159)

As technologies took over and automated cultural activities and daily routines, they were increasingly imagined as living entities. The technological medium, the literal in-between, was acquiring qualities that portrayed it as uncanny and alive. Perhaps this was a reflection of how the new technologies had been seen since the mid nineteenth century; the communication systems were constructed as if autonomous, self-sustaining organisms, networks, and the technical principles governing the fast movement of messages were hidden from the human eye.

Noise and archive

So why study noise, and what does a media archaeology of such seeming non-communication provide for media and communication studies?

There are several potential approaches to a cartography of noise: it spreads out as an aesthetic, technical, political and acoustic phenomenon. Noise was seen as nearly metaphysical but formally controllable, and even evil by some cyberneticians such as Wiener. Yet it was promoted as an aesthetic revelation by avant-garde artists from Russolo to Cage to composers of glitch music and, according to writers such as Sven Spieker, as an integral part of how artists reimagined the order of the archive through the marginal and the contingent. The emergence of trash and contingency is a theme of modernism that Spieker analyses through artists such as Duchamp and the Surrealists. Thus, modernism is actually a mode of knowledge about the archive: it 'promotes the idea of an archive that does not so much collect facts as reveal the conditions for their discovery, an archive whose peripheral objects become visible or audible to the extent that they conform to the archive's own protocol' (Spieker 2008: 173) In such perspectives, as with the sound noise archaeologies briefly mentioned above, noise becomes a way of understanding how normal communication works. This realization is connected to the increasing attention paid, since the 1980s, to the so-called 'anomalies' of network culture: not only spam and bad software, which are often, somewhat metaphorically, described as the 'noise' of desired communication, but also cyberwar and the war on cyberterrorism. Networks are increasingly framed as vulnerable, metastable constructions, and the future of the Internet is portrayed as dependent on the 'noise question' and various methods and techniques for filtering, managing, and redirecting 'noise'.

On a diagrammatical level of communication having to do with transmission, noise became formalized in the mid twentieth century (although physics had been interested in stochastic patterns since the early part of the century). This formalization by Shannon and Weaver can be seen as a key point when the issue of noise entered the archive of technical media culture. Yet, as we have seen, noise has been an important, although not clearly defined and articulated, tactic of modern communication media at least since the late eighteenth-century optical telegraph. A longer genealogy reveals the importance of a politics of noise in communication systems and the organization of modern media. Since the optical telegraph noise has been a military issue, and it soon became also an economic one, playing a role in a vast panorama of issues in the United States and Europe.

To apply the Foucauldian idea, developed further recently by Ernst, the archive is the condition for our knowledge, perceptions, memory and other cultural processes. Due to its centrality in technical media, noise is an essential part of that 'archive', in the sense that it constitutes a key theme of modern technical media culture. Through noise, through anomalies, we are able to decipher a range of crucial issues concerning politics, aesthetics and cultural processes of media.

The *I Love You* project at the Frankfurt Museum of Applied Art serves as a key example of the diagrammatic and archiving logic of noise in the twentieth century. In 2002 the museum embarked on a novel archival project when it announced that it had started to collect viral code. Whereas the museum was already renowned for its classical collection of ceramics, books, and Islamic and East Asian art, its new mission was an expression of a seemingly novel interest in practices of digital outlaws.

The collecting task was part of the *I Love You* exhibition, which has since then also toured other museums. The exhibition was designed to introduce and analyse the aesthetics and cultural practices of viral programming, a task connected to the cultural status of source code in digital society; it also addressed the meaning of programming as a key cultural technique of the information age. As the curator Franziska Nori noted, the archival function of a museum is not merely to document but also actively to articulate a society's modes of communication and memory (www.digitalcraft.org/iloveyou/, accessed 26 Nov. 2011).

Gustav Metzger, in his 1960 'Manifesto for Auto-Destructive Art', had already appropriated self-contradictory forms and patterns as part of a logic of creation. Although Metzger's ideas were not directly about virality, he addressed the idea that disorganization was an integral part of any system. Time-based media were constantly vulnerable to the potential disorganization that in the nineteenth century was expressed in terms of the physical notion of 'entropy', and in the informatics of the twentieth century as 'noise' that threatened the clean calculations and communications of cybernetic systems. In recent years we have seen a range of viral art, from the American artist Joseph Nechvatal's algorithmic, viral images, to 'biennale.py', the computer virus exhibited at the 2001 Venice Biennale by 0100101110101101.org, to other pieces of net art, for example by the artist duo Jodi, who use the dysfunctions and the potential breakdowns of network software for their artistic potential. All these examples are continuing the experimental work of earlier avant-garde artists who amplified and discussed new perspectives on arts and media culture.

So, in terms of such concepts as 'discourse networks' (Kittler) and 'the archive' (for Ernst), the seeming non-communication is as important as communication. Signals are always surrounded by noise, even to the extent that we cannot always decipher which is which. Already film in its relation to archiving of time can be seen to introduce a world of archiving singularities and contingencies, instead of just the 'value and meaning' that we needed to rethink the relation between noise, materiality and media (Doane 2002). Technical media are embedded in noisiness, in terms either of how Kittler and Kahn write about sound recording technologies, or of how we can consider other kinds of algorithmic, programmable noise to be part and parcel of software cultures and the archive of network culture.

As such, sonic noise as the sound of technological modernity finds itself echoed in digital network cultures: noise for ears can also be noise for machines, exemplified in some of the media-archaeological takes on glitch art in software cultures (for instance Rosa Menkman's work), as well as the rhythmic cartographies of digital signal processing – sonification as the work of mapping algorithmic culture, as the Institute of Algorithmics in Berlin is occupied with (Miyazaki 2011). We will return to such examples in the chapter on media-archaeological art (chapter 7), and now turn to the question of the archive in media archaeology.

Summary

This chapter offered a case study of an important theme of modern media culture: noise. It shows how one can media-archaeologically approach some neglected and less benevolent practices of media. Despite the mainstream focus on frictionless communication and connecting in social media cultures, noise, interruption and cyber warfare are equally important themes through which to understand modern communications since the telegraph. This chapter offers methodological insights into the primacy of noise, and how to use an eclectic source base to tackle this phenomenon that touches on history of science, technology and the arts. The chapter extends from the earlier discussion of Kittler and Ernst, but also flags briefly some insights from, for example, media archaeologies of sound fostered by Douglas Kahn, among other prominent writers.

Further readings

Fuller, Matthew and Goffey, Andrew (2009) 'Evil Media Studies' in *The Spam Book: On Porn, Viruses and Other Anomalous Objects from the Dark Side of Digital Culture*, ed. Jussi Parikka and Tony Sampson (Cresskill: Hampton Press), 141–59.
Kahn, Douglas (1999) *Noise Water Meat. A History of Sound in the Arts* (Cambridge, MA: The MIT Press).
Parikka, Jussi (2007) *Digital Contagions: A Media Archaeology of Computer Viruses* (New York: Peter Lang).

6

Archive Dynamics: Software Culture and Digital Heritage

Media archaeology starts with the archive – the implicit starting point for so much historical research that it itself, as a place and a media form, has been neglected, become almost invisible. This is the fate of media that become too effective in what they do. They vanish from view, do their job of mediating, and leave the illusion that all there is is content passing through the channels. Immediacy is the shadow side of mediation (cf. Bolter and Grusin 1999). In media-archaeological writings, the archive has not been much debated – although, now, more recently, Wolfgang Ernst[1] has been flagging the need to rigorously rethink the concept and practices of the archive in the age of audiovisual and software media, Cornelia Vismann (2008) touched on the media archaeology of the archive in her take on law and media, and media archaeologists such as Erkki Huhtamo have been demanding that scholars meticulously do their homework – but not only at home: first-hand use of original sources, materials and collections is demanded by Huhtamo as a crucial guideline for his emphasis on media archaeology as a historically empirical enterprise (see also Røssaak 2010a).

The centrality of the archive for any cultural and media archaeology is to a large extent a follow-up to Foucault's expansion of the concept from the concrete physical places of storage of cultural data to the discourses that govern modes of thinking, acting and expression. Traditionally the archive was a place for storage, preservation, classification and access (Røssaak 2010b: 11). More concretely, we can see how the archive has been a key node in relaying and storing data of modern culture, and hence acted as a key medium in itself – very much connected to the bureaucratic mode of control alongside registering and manipulating data, primarily in offices and through office technologies: typewriters, calculators, spreadsheets, carbon copies and, later, databases, software-based applications, etc. (Vismann 2008). In various accounts of media history, computers themselves are regarded as part of the lineage from papyrus to paper, to printing and the need for advanced information management systems to organize the massive amount of printed materials; from the Dewey Decimal System of 1876 to the computer as an internalization of a long media history of paper, printing and libraries, and a storage unit for companies and organizations (see, for example, Sly 1976: 27–9). In a way, Lev Manovich's (2001: 218–20; see also Ernst 2011: 252) theoretically more elaborate claim that the database is the primary form of organizing and expressing reality fits the same bill: instead of the narrative, the structural collections of data we call databases form new kinds of information realities enabled by computers.

The history of the archive relates to record-keeping, which, during the ancient Roman administration, was focused in the Aerarium near the Capitoline Hill – a reminder of the concreteness of the birth of archives as a state treasury of a *varia* of things, from metals to reserve funds, insignia, senate resolutions and other administrative papers (Vismann 2008: 57). As such, the archival institution was a way of turning important things such as notebooks into *monumenta publica*, and, as Vismann (2008: 58) argues, *mementos*, reminders of the past of the empire in a similar way to how the Prussian archival system in the nineteenth century turned itself into a subject of history through writing 'itself into history' (Vismann 2008: 120). This classical form of the archive was territorial, spatialized and walled – where the wall of the institution was also the border of its symbolic functions, as Vismann analyses in her media archaeology of files and record-keeping: 'The wall designated to surround the symbolic order of the law once the codification is complete turns everything outside into rubbish and file trash' (2008: 64). The modern archival theory, practices of preservation and frameworks for selection and preference were articulated throughout the twentieth century.

However, with the emergence of such new social media 'archives' as YouTube, Flickr, etc., the notion of the bureaucratic archive has changed (Gane and Beer 2008: 71–86). Modes of accessing and storing data have changed from centrally governed and walled spaces to distributed and software-based. The trash that was trash because of being kept outside the walls gives way to new forms of less official archives in social media cultures. One (wo)man's trash is another's retweet, or a shared link on Facebook – less official, but no less formal, however, as the formats have changed to more technical ones. In addition to the bureaucratic techniques of offices, the new archives have to take into account formats, medium-specificity, as well as various software-related themes such as encoding. Similarly, despite the distributed nature, one can argue that power still resides in the archive, which is now embedded in architectures of software, and the political economy of social media platforms whose revenue streams are based on the fact of individual everyday contributions through activity: Facebook, YouTube, Google, etc., gathering data on user patterns, preferences and consumer desires, for further evaluation, reuse and reselling purposes.

This chapter investigates new notions of the archive as modes of inscription of information and culture, connected to the new modes of economy and capitalism that frame the relations to more personal and easily accessible databases. Archival theory is a specific discipline for archivists, theorists of cultural heritage and cultural memory, but I will not touch on that significant context.[2] Instead I take a media studies approach to archives. What are the implications for our notions of cultural heritage from such a shift in the practices and discourses of the archive, and how does media archaeology lend itself to discourses concerning the archival and the museum in software cultures? As we will see in this chapter, the theoretical problems of recent media archaeologies of technical media and software along with a rethinking of the archive, go hand in hand with the practical challenges faced by cultural heritage institutions and professionals: how do you archive *processes* and culture which is based on both technical processes (software and networks) and social ones (participation and collaboration, as in massive online role-playing platforms as cultural forms). Both media archaeology and digital humanities seem to be interested in this territory and such questions.

Dynamic media archives

The darkened room echoes with a computerized voice that seems to be reading lists – a form of ordering of information itself. There is something about this monotonous voice that reminds of a Samuel Beckett play, as does the litany of things being talked about. Slightly cold, distanced speech, that in ways connotes bureaucracy, lists everyday things, fragments, texts that have lost their context, circulating. A huge wall of over 200 vacuum tube screens is itself filled with text – same thing again: fragments, words, typos, scrolling, still flashing at points. This is *The Listening Post* (2003), Mark Hansen and Ben

Rubin's media artistic installation permanently situated at the Science Museum, London. The voices and screens are only the end result of a direct feed from various Internet platforms such as chat rooms, bulletin boards, forums and anything that is based on text. *The Listening Post* is not only for our listening, but represents itself a machinic form of listening to text. It has no ears, except the data streams then only synthesized for our ears, so it seems more than listening in the anthropomorphic sense. It listens as much to 'us', or the data stream we initiate on the Internet, as we listen to it. Similarly, its narration is an algorithmically mediated form of calculation and listing.

Housing a piece of sonic installation art in a science museum – which more often has been traditionally organized around still objects, from instruments to technological tools – is in itself an interesting enterprise, as it smuggles in processuality and duration as part of the collections. The liveness of the piece is a feature in itself, and flags the theme of streamed online information as one crucial 'set' of data of contemporary culture, as well as, on a phenomenological level of experience, the time-based nature of acoustics. Furthermore, it acts as a time-critical piece of software art due to this synchronization task. Per se, it is not about storage, as Michelle Kasprzak (2005) pointed out when reviewing the piece after it won the Ars Electronica Golden Nica award of 2004: 'The poetry of Listening Post derives from the fact that the communication of the chatters lives outside of the chat room, but only for a moment, and it is not archived. . . . The Listening Post has no memory, it is a monument only to the present.'

Despite the lack of memory – and seemingly being more about transmitting and calculation, which are the two other components through which we can decipher the characteristics of 'communication media', according to Kittler (1996) – *Listening Post* does actually act as a good entry point to discussions concerning memory. As a monument to the present, however, it addresses the bifurcation of that temporal category into a multitude of microtemporal operations at the core of our contemporary media, which, according to Wolfgang Ernst, constitutes the new regime of cultural memory. The present is not a stable 'now-time', but a process that in our technical media culture is characterized by processes of software, streaming, encoding and decoding of data (codecs for audiovisual material, for example), and other ways of handling the stream of data as a temporal process. Data are not stable, and this is why the regime of processing becomes intimately entangled with questions concerning memory. As Ernst (2006: 118) writes, 'the multi-media archive deals with truly time-based media (which are images and sound), with every image, every sound only existing for a discrete moment in time. Freezing an electronic image means freezing its refresh-circle.'

At the heart of this transmission of information from various Internet platforms as part of *The Listening Post*, the installation represents one take on the process of streaming as a particular challenge to the archival institutions and cultural memory: in other words, how do you represent, archive and curate time-critical processes? What is the relation between memory and storage (Chun 2011b: 133–73)? This question was already asked by Doron Swade, the Science Museum curator behind the reconstruction of the Difference Engine in the early 1990s, differentiating between objects and the new processuality of software culture thoroughly conditioned by the quick obsolescence of hardware on which to run the programmes: 'The intractable fact of the matter is that in terms of archaeological time scales the operational continuity of contemporary hardware cannot be assured even when suitable specimens are available to begin with. What meaning, then, does an archive of bit-perfect program software have if the material cannot be run?' (Swade 1998: 201–2). Swade flags that there is more to archiving software cultures than focusing on the bits themselves – this form of culture is also about execution, and hence temporality.[3]

The presence of time inside the museum has been evident in at least two ways. On the one hand, the archive and such institutions of modern memory as the museum are of course monuments of time in the sense of restoring, recording and maintaining various objects, documents and other materials. As part of modern institutions such as the nation state, and as forms of biopolitics, archives and museums have been instrumental mechanisms of order. On the other hand, time also exhibits itself through deterioration. Old papyrus scrolls, paper material, nineteenth-century technical media inventions from photography and film deteriorate. Their chemical materials react to air humidity, and pollution, and represent an interface between the world of chemistry and physics and cultural memory.[4]

Every material thing decays, and this decay is in itself a sign of radical temporality that cannot be regained, despite restoration projects. This is accepted by curatorial practices concerning objects (Swade 2002: 229), and even more so in archaeological collections that are based on the premise of fragments, fragility and decay. Yet, for those 'objects' whose primary context has been machine-operated process, or even storage, decay is a significant problem for archiving, especially in the era of computing-based storage, as Swade (2002: 229) writes: 'Magnetic media, the most common means of information storage for machine-readable software and data, are notoriously impermanent. In the US in the early 1980s banks, required to retain computer records for audit purposes, were advised that no archived magnetic medium over three years old should be regarded as reliable.' This was identified as a problem already when the consumer-driven software discourse was starting to talk about immateriality of bits and the regime of the digital as independent of the physical world. Yet anyone dealing with storage and worrying for the sake of future archaeologists of digital media knew better. Referring to Jeff Rothenberg's *Scientific American* article from January 1995 ('Ensuring the Longevity of Digital Documents'), Swade (2002) continues, about magnetic audio-tapes, video-tapes, magnetic disks and optical disks:

> Two figures are cited for each medium: 'time until obsolete' and 'physical lifetime'. In the case of optical disk, 'time until obsolete' is estimated at ten years and 'physical lifetime' at thirty years. So even the most durable of our current 'permanent' media offer storage durations that qualify as ephemeral when measured against the archaeological time scales of our custodial ambitions and there is a fundamental incompatibility between the life-expectancy of magnetic media and the long-term custodial needs of museums.

The situation is not completely new, even if we have moved from object-based preservation to an increasingly process- and time-based process preservation (or perhaps, as with software, to object-oriented-software-based preservation). The modern museum – since the French Revolution of the 1790s, and sharing a parallel history of emergence with the telegraph (Daniels 2002: 16–19), developing in the nineteenth century as part of Victorian culture – is itself part of the regime of modern technical media of reproduction and preservation, as Michelle Henning (2006: 74) argues, writing about recording and archiving as technological drives which are part of 'Victorian historicism and overaccumulation'. Cultural heritage focuses on preservation of inscriptions, and investigating the specific nature of such inscriptions is a mediatic question. Media material decay can be taken as a media-archaeological topic of research, as well as the remediation that is done under the rubric of 'digitalization'. Indeed, digitalization represents a curious wave of practical interest in maintaining important materials for posterity, even if at the same time it leads into crucial foundational questions: how does the encoding of film material in M-PEG introduce a new kind of image conception (see Cubitt 2010), and what about the fact that the digital is, despite hype in the 1980s and 1990s about immaterial virtuality, itself a very material notion that includes hardware, software and other material contexts, and is prone to deterioration? We still have to measure the lifespan of such storage media as CDs and DVDs in years (statistical estimates range from 5 to 20 years), which gives an index of the need for continuous maintenance in any process of archiving.

This is a point that software theorist Wendy Hui Kyong Chun (2011a) makes as well. She argues how the idea that digital media are based on a new permanence of memory (inherently connected to programmability) was to differentiate them as new media compared to the old media of, for example, television. Hence, digital media were to provide the solution to the problem of this temporality at the core of earlier analogue memory and archives, and solve all the decay, scratches and degradation in our celluloid, vinyl and a variety of other material in which our cultural memory was inscribed – only to present a further problem with the realization that digital memory storage was also limited. Indeed, this strategic mistake of assumed correspondence between memory and storage is more than acciden-tal, as Chun (2011a: 184) writes:

> Also key to the newness of the digital is a conflation of memory and storage that both underlies and undermines digital media's archi-val promise. Memory, with its constant degeneration, does not equal storage; although artificial memory has historically combined the tran-sitory with the permanent, the passing with the stable, digital media complicate this relationship by making the permanent into an enduring ephemeral, creating unforeseen degenerative links between humans and machines.

The digital is not eternal, nor is it simply ephemeral. The enduring ephemeral is for Chun the figure through which to understand the specific nature of digital media in relation to the archival logic of con-temporary culture. She is not denying that digital media are formed through a specific relation to memory that has been meticulously discussed and designed, from pioneers such as John von Neumann and Vannevar Bush (1890–1974) to materials from vacuum tubes to CD-ROMs and hard drives. Yet, despite the ongoing enthusiasm for preservation and archiving at the core of digital culture, 'from online museums to the YouTube phenomenon Geriatic1927, from Corbis to the Google data banks that store every search ever entered (and link each to an IP address, arguably making Google the Stasi resource of the twenty-first century)' (Chun 2011a: 188), we need to argue that, instead of assumed permanence, the key characteristic of digital memory is the coupling of degeneration with renegeration. Chun wants to argue that only because, even on a technical layer, digital memory never just *is* but also degenerates and hence needs to be maintained, regenerated and rejuvenated, the whole ontology of memory and archives is closer to a dynamics of renewal than just of mere storage. Another way to sum up the difference between analogue media archives and digital ones is to use the words of Paul DeMarinis (2011: 223): 'analogue media, to be preserved, must not be played: each replay is a partial erasure and a new recording – an overlay. Digital preservation relies instead on the frequent rereading, erasure and rewriting of the content.'

Unlike the earlier formations of the archive which can be said to focus on freezing time – to store and preserve – these new forms of archives in technical media culture can be described as *archives in motion*. The notion suggested by Eivind Røssaak (2010b: 12) captures well this new archival situation: such archives are not only archives of motion (in the sense that the nineteenth century was already interested in capturing, storing and processing human and other forms of movement as part of its scientific culture) but archives that themselves are dynamic, changing forms.

Projects archiving digital material – such as the Library of Congress archiving Twitter-material from all those numerous 140-character–maximum signals of everyday life – also face the sheer dynamically growing immensity of the task.[5] This challenge has not stopped such pioneers as Brewster Kahle's Internet Archive project, and, for example the Wayback Machine that offers snapshots of web pages at regular intervals and stores them for later retrieval. His important ideas and projects relate to digitalization of material, and proceed via the various media types produced for storage – books, films, music, software and so forth. What Kahle (see his 2007 TED talk online at www.ted.com, accessed 26 Nov. 2011) is furthermore able to underline is how such archival projects relate to new forms of publishing, as with material made available for ebooks, and later remediation of books into digitized versions and then into print-on-demand products, as with Bookmobiles and such new technologies as the Espresso Book Machine (www.ondemandbooks.com, accessed 26 Nov. 2011). This link to books becomes even more 'natural' when we realize that the Internet Archive is modelled more like a library than an archive – based on the idea of being indexed and searchable, and hence emphasizing not only storage but use (and transmission) (Ernst 2010: esp. 66.)

What can be seen as the biggest threats to traditional ways of thinking and doing archiving – collaborative modes of production, distributed network forms of the new cultural artefacts that are more processual than thing-like, and the sheer number of potential items to save – can be turned into a possibility as well. As William Uricchio 2009b) argues, the network form itself can be one way of rethinking the archive and how culture is reproduced through the archive. Referring to the idea of Thomas Jefferson (1743–1826) – from a letter in 1791 – Uricchio argues for the possibility of the distributed archive where the peer-to-peer (P2P) logic of production is turned into one of storage as well: instead of centralized vaults for objects, the massive number of computers and storage media connected through the network protocols can itself be turned into a form of P2P-archiving. In a way, such ideas were already present in the 1966 film *Fahrenheit 451* by François Truffaut (1932–84), in which the book as a media form survived by being orally distributed to as many people as possible, as well as in the art group etoy's *Mission Eternity* project (launched in 2005, http://missioneternity.org/, accessed 26 Nov. 2011) that deals with how preservation becomes sharing and co-production (Bosma 2011: 174–6).

In social network culture, documents, files, and increasingly things too (the Internet of Things tagged with RFIDs) are ever more track-able and searchable. This has emphasized the interest in digitaliza-tion which is just another form for new methods of retrieval, as well as metadata for search purposes. Yet, as discussed by Chun, there is more to the theme of memory and storage than the work of digitali-zation and cataloguing material with the help of metadata method-ologies (for an archival critique of metadata, see Boast 2011). The fact that digital data online can in some platforms, like Wikipedia, be tracked down through their edit history gives the illusion of pos-sibilities of digital archaeology made easy as with Wikipedia turning ten years old in 2011 (see 'Internet Archaeology: Dig into Wikipedia's deep past', 14 Jan. 2011, www.newscientist.com, date accessed 26 Nov. 2011). Yet this 'history' functionality of wikis is surrounded by the more important theme of dynamics: that digital media are in them-selves available to change, manipulation and variation, as with socially distributed processes like Wikipedia itself, constantly changing; and that digital memory itself, on its socio-technical level, is vulnerable to limited duration and decay, and in need of constant maintenance. In social media culture, new forms of production, sharing and organ-izing content through, for example, the folksonomy of tagging prac-tices presents again something far more dynamic than the traditional content and knowledge management procedures that literary cul-tures were used to (cf. Uricchio 2009b). This issue, which relates to fundamental changes in cultural memory in software culture, can be approached through some of the questions concerning new media art as well. It relates both to the social dynamics of interaction in technological culture, and equally to the media ontology of digitality and process-based technical media.

Software, net art and archives

The discourse concerning net- and software-based art documentation, curating and archiving raises core questions concerning cultural memory in the digital age.[6] Hence, we are able to use that discourse as a stepping-stone to discussing the relation between media archaeology and the archive in contemporary culture. So far, much of the debate in digital cultural heritage has revolved around user experience, and the digital object's relation to affects (understood in this context as emotions), as well as the new possibilities afforded by participatory, collaborative involvement in the cultural heritage (see Cameron and Kenderdine 2007). Such questions are clearly part of the influence of the wider Web 2.0 culture which also forces established institutions both to open up to the possibilities of not only Internet technologies but also practices, and to acknowledge that a huge amount of cultural heritage work now takes place in amateur and other non-traditional platforms on the Internet. In fact, for experts of digital art curation such as Sarah Cook (see CRUMB – the Curatorial Resource for Upstart Media Bliss, www. crumbweb.org/), the whole division between analogue and digital media – as defining, for example, Internet or software art – is problematic, and needs constant refining in terms of paying careful attention to which particular role technology plays in such art works – as a tool, or the medium of the work, or the wider practice-context (Cook 2007: 116)? Instead, she suggests paying more attention to the 'alternative non-medium specific *practices* employed by artists' (2007: 116) which takes the whole issue to another level of discourse, avoiding some of the problems in trying to grasp the specificity of medium-specificity.

Indeed, we cannot assume to automatically have the answer to what medium-specificity means: is it the technology, some components of the technology (software that can be emulated, the platform which affords its aesthetics), the unfolding in use of – for instance – game systems, the social context, practice, or what that defines the medium? Any answer to such questions would have important implications for the archival strategies taken (cf. Bearman 2007: 29).

In addition to intensive discussions in the new media art histories and curating field, Wolfgang Ernst (2009b) has given a media-archaeological perspective to this issue. With a different emphasis from Cook, Ernst adopts a medium-specific approach, which picks up on the fact that archives are now remixable and regroupable. On the one hand, this points towards the previously mentioned 'participative form of archival reading' (2009b: 81), and, on the other, to what Ernst calls the *micro-temporal* level enabled by the digital media technology. Ernst is less interested in the experiential level of participation and social media than in the mathematics of archives in network culture, which he connects to a wider media-archaeological agenda of cultures of counting and calculating (2003) that extend back in history, as well as to the micro-temporal layer of where the archive of contemporary media experience is formed. According to Ernst's argument, which he explicates in relation to the *Netpioneers 1.0* project on archiving, contextualizing and re-presenting net-based art (www.netpioneers.info, accessed 26 Nov. 2011), the archive is becoming less a stable storage place and increasingly a function of 'logistical interlinking' (2009b: 85). Archives are suddenly not only about storing and preserving, but about transmitting (Ernst 2010).

Instead of being a place of storage, Ernst argues – in a manner resembling Chun's position – that the dynamics, permanent updating and conflation of storage with search define the archive in current digital network culture. The algorithmic searchability of archives transforms them to an instance of real-time computing, which underlines that, instead of being collections of objects in the traditional sense, 'net archives are a function of their software and transmission protocols rather than of content' (2009b: 85). Referring to Alex Galloway's work on protocols as the defining logic of Internet culture, Ernst argues that every archive object on the Internet has to work through a given set of protocols of storage and transmission. Furthermore, he draws a distinction between documentation and archiving – whereas the videoart of Nam June Paik (1932–2006) can perhaps be archived in its media-material form, the installation of which the video-tape is a recording can only be documented, along with contextual information and so forth (Ernst 2009b: 87). Such points could be said to repeat basic realizations in museological and archive practices that various protocols order the logic of the archive and exhibition, and that contextual information is needed alongside the actual artefacts, but Ernst argues that in technical media cultures the question becomes ever more complex. The protocols are now concretely technical, not just part of the practice, and the materiality of the artefact itself becomes rethought because of time-critical art pieces, and software-based projects that are also time-critical: based on execution, dynamics and operationality of code.

When it comes to net art and new media art archives, the emphasis on dynamics and liveness can be found in other accounts as well. Christiane Paul (2009: 105) refers to the need to understand the archive 'as a "living" environment that can itself adapt to the changing requirements of the mutable "records" it contains'. Such a stance points to similar themes as Ernst: contemporary *archives in motion* (Røssaak 2010) incorporate dynamics into the archival form that traditionally was based on stability. The documentation of the variation inherent in digital-based arts and the practices of net art is isomorphic to the ontology of the digital, itself based on variation, modulation and the constant possibility of updating. Capturing the 'event' of so much of net-based art is a practical problem stemming from the ontological nature of both the technical media contexts, and the art practice:

> This type of archive would need to document the different versions of a work that develops through user contributions – for example, by keeping copies of the project in its different states; and it could potentially document aspects of the 'environment' in which the work existed at different points in time, such as discussions of the piece on blogs, mailing lists, etc. The contextualization and archiving of Net art require new models and criteria for documenting and preserving the process and instability of works that are often created by multiple authors and constantly develop in time. (Paul 2009: 105)

For Ernst, 'time' is at the core of his media-archaeological approach to new media arts, and archives in network culture. As mentioned, he is keen to track the emergence of the micro-temporal layer of media archives, which is a supplementary and deeper layer in relation to the traditional historical, conserving macro-time of the archive as traditionally understood (Ernst 2009b: 89). What this means is a turn from object-centred archiving to objects in the software sense, their searchability and transformation into forms that make them viewable and experiential through encoding, streaming and other software techniques. This transformation of how objects and things become, for example, streamable is where Ernst sees the key media-archaeological points of the digital archive. What are the measures, the technical contexts that enable such a transformation and deliverability of data from the archive? In fact, this points to the earlier argument at the beginning of the chapter that the computer itself has become an archive in the way its memory system allows us to store and find objects:

> Computers themselves represent 'storage and retrieval' systems – for people as users and as an essential part of memory programmability. Apart from sequential access (the old magnetic computer tapes) there is immediate random access (matrix memory). Every computer is already a digital archive. The archiving occurs in the RAM of the familiar computer, not in the emphatic sense, but rather as the precondition for any calculating process taking place at all. (Ernst 2009b: 90)

As Ernst underlines, he is not interested in the content of the specific art pieces, but in their technical conditions, which are also conditions of their archivability. Hence he differs from the more experience-based and phenomenological accounts in cultural heritage discourse and media archaeology. To make things slightly more complex, his approach is to think of the machine as an archive as well. Media-archaeological writing starts with the agency of the machine: technical media are themselves technological constellations that are able to store and process data in ways that are beyond our cultural analytical tools – an old phonograph captures much more than we can decipher semantically, and analysis through Fourier transformations and other mathematical tools reveals completely new layers of hitherto unperceived non-semantic data. Instead of the phenomenological approach to material – what we can see with our own eyes, and understand with our own ears – we rely on mathematical tools to decipher, analyse and calculate archives. The things we see on-screen, the so-called 'multimedia', are only an effect of the more fundamental pre-history of media, in which, according to Ernst, 'this "pre-" is less about temporal antecedence than about the techno-epistemological configurations underlying the discursive surface (literally, the monitors and interfaces) of mass media' (Ernst 2011: 239; see also 2006).

Net and software art relates to the discussion about 'born digital content'. In more practical terms, considerations concerning the agency of the machine and ontology of software are elaborated in questions of 'born digital content' which further differ from products that are digitalized from original or electronic forms.[7] Ernst's media-archaeological methods and theories relate to the wider situation in which cultures of memory find themselves – how do we make sense of this technical media layer, for both interpretation and preserving? Writers such as Ernst are not content with non-technical solutions to this archival problem, and look at theoretical frameworks that go beyond user experience, hermeneutical interpretation and narrative.

Hence, it is interesting to read his media-archaeological theories in relation to such new digital humanities debates and methodologies as the Lev Manovich-led Cultural Analytics initiative, and Alan Liu's various projects in literature studies and computer forensics that are making an entry in both cultural analytical methodologies and archival institutions: for example the British Library is engaging in computer forensics methods in their archival work, being increasingly aware of born-digital content by authors.[8]

Forensics and the materiality of digital inscriptions

Matthew G. Kirschenbaum's (2008) approach to storage and archives tracks the forms of inscription we find in our digital culture. As such, it partly draws from Friedrich Kittler's methodology of analysing technical forms of inscription, but takes that into new contexts, which still retain a high relevance for our consideration. Kirschenbaum is, like Ernst, a critic of 'screen essentialism' (Nick Montfort's term) in new media studies, and insists we need a more detailed account of the processes in which storing data – and hence cultural content, whether electronic art or electronic literature as in his own field – takes place. Going 'behind the screen' means for Kirschenbaum a methodology of close reading of technological forms of inscription that we find in our magnetic-based storage technologies, familiar from the history of computing from von Neumann to later floppy-disk cultures and current hard drives too. Similarly to Ernst (2003), who talks about digital forms of computing as non-semantic narrating of calculation, Kirschenbaum's interest is geared towards forms of writing that are technological; data inscribed on a magnetic tape are not directly readable for human eyes, but it is clearly still an inscription (2008: 29–39). This is literacy in the age of digital humanities and software. Data always have their *areal density*, which in current hard drives is around 100 billion bits per inch (Kirschenbaum, Ovenden and Redwine 2010), a major leap from the 1960s figures of some few hundreds of bits per inch, as well having its intensity of magnetization (measured as its coercivity, in Oersted-units), much as storage media have ideal speeds (floppy disks, for example, around 300 to 350 Revolutions Per Minute, and current hard drives, for example, around 7,200 RPM). (On the practicalities of 'digital archaeology', see Ross and Gow 1999.) In digital culture, storage never just *is* – it moves, is intensively reworked continuously and enjoys a temporal duration technically known as *hysteresis*[9] while being packed in a very material substrate.

Instead of just the screen content for retrieved documents, we have software and hardware cultures through which inscription, hence storage, hence archiving is conditioned. A digital image that you might approach and analyse through its screen content – whether on your computer screen, or on your mobile, or rectangular television box – is for the technically tuned cultural analyst or media archaeologist a constellation of material information. To paraphrase Kirschenbaum (2008: 12–13), an image consists of a pixelated bitmap, metadata of how it was created, a digital watermark perhaps, and other forms of details that one can view with different software functions (whether through the Show Header function, or through a 128-bit encryption key). Throw in considerations of the protocols, display settings and multiple platforms on which images unfold and you are approaching key questions of what the image is in software culture.

Hence, the methodology of combining humanities and computer science expertise, and therefore of relevance to the wider debates concerning digital humanities starts in this case from questioning even what the object of our archival desire is. Referring to Kenneth Thibodeau's (2002) way of defining digital objects from the perspective of preservation, Kirschenbaum (2008: 3–4) highlights that theories and methods have so far focused primarily on the idea of digital objects as conceptual – in a way, the social, interpretational ways in which we see for example a digital photograph on-screen. Instead, we can also take into account digital objects as physical (the concrete inscriptions on magnetic tapes) and logical (referring to the ways in which, for example, software works, and bitmaps offer information that is of analytical relevance for humanities too).

Besides offering close readings of electronic literature, Kirschenbaum is able to provide a needed complement to Ernst's media-archaeological account to illuminate points about the archive in software cultures. As has been said, Kirschenbaum focuses on inscription, but in doing so is able to question the dilemmas concerning the so often preferred screen-essentialism, and also to address the multiple, relational ontology of informational objects. Indeed, the idea of forensics suits both practically and epistemologically, the media-archaeological idea of going deeper and deeper into the materiality of the informational systems. In the case of file systems, this would mean not being contained by searches through standard directory structures, menus and so on, which do find file-based data but neglect so much of the data actually on the disk:

> Instead, an investigator will want to create a so-called bitstream image of the original file system. A bitstream is exactly that: every bit recorded

on some original, physical instance of storage media is transferred in linear sequence to the copied image, whether it is part of a file currently allocated in the FAT [file allocation table] or not. This means that all of the other ambient data on the original media is retained as part of the forensic object, including even (if the process is done right) data in 'bad' or corrupted sectors no longer otherwise accessible. (Kirschenbaum 2008: 53)

In other words, even bad data has value in algorithmic culture (see the previous chapter on 'noise').

For methodologies of media archaeology of software and, for example, net art and software art, these are inspiring ideas. The dynamics of archives is complemented with a view towards the meticulous ways in which we can track down effects of inscription on material platforms. In the words of Patrick Lichty (2008: 182), 'Even a work that is intrinsically ephemeral leaves physical records, and those are potential 'objects of desire' for the museum, the collector, and the archive because they ground the technological artwork.' In this case, desire circulates materially. The idea applies more widely to computer and software culture as well, and asks the very tricky question: where do we start? How do you research something that at its core seems to be so fluid, so ephemeral, so dynamic that it fails to stick to those methodological nets that are aimed at capturing solids instead of processes? This is naturally a problem for software studies more generally, but also for archaeological research interested in histories and conditions of media culture. One option is to engage in all the institutions, people, blueprints, plans, design processes, ideas, patents, Requests for Comments, marketing material, reviews and other discourses in which software is contextualized – as well as understand the various platforms, protocols, program languages, operating systems, applications – and of course, hopefully to focus increasingly on the non-Anglo-American world of media histories.

Yet we can argue that this does not capture all of the defining characteristics of software cultures. At least in a media-archaeological vein, we need to be medium-specific, and our understanding of archives needs to do that as well. So many of the characteristics of computer and software cultures demand that we look beyond the surface and tap into the processuality of technical media culture, which has been an increasingly central feature from the early 1960s. As Noah Wardrip-Fruin argues, in a similar vein, even if we have managed to extend archaeologies of hypertext from Tim Berners-Lee's key role in developing the World Wide Web to the earlier ideas of Theodor H. Nelson, Andries van Dam and Douglas C. Engelbart, we are missing out on the more processual side to these media – source code compiled and processed, for instance (2011: 320; see also Chun 2004 for an archaeology of programming and software).

In the next section, we will dig deeper into this question of operationality.

The operational archive

One of the dilemmas raised about preservation of digital objects has to do with their ephemeral nature. As we can see from above, this does not, however, mean immateriality. Quite the contrary – we can decipher the physicality of digital technologies as a crucial component of their nature (Thibodeau 2002) which expresses itself through the deterioration of the substrates of storage (from magnetic to optical storage technologies), as well as through the processuality of the digital. Thibodeau (2002; cf. Chun 2004: 46) notes how the digital object can never just be retrieved as a still object – any retrieval is always, in a computer and software environment, a *processing* of that object and introduces dynamics and change. This applies to physical objects as well. Despite the fact that archives and museum collections have been more or less branded by object-centredness, where the stillness and stability in preservation and curation of the object is of primary value, time – and hence change – affect how heritage institutions have to deal with alteration (Thibodeau 2002). As Robin Boast (2011) reminds us, a continuous maintenance work in the heritage institution is supporting, reproducing, taking care of such objects and producing its own dynamics of circulation and maintenance around even supposedly still objects.

Yet, with post-World War II cultures of computing, we are facing a situation in which the dynamic nature of the world seems to constitute an integral part of how things work, not just break down. Computers, and software, are good examples of such things. This is the big future task for such museums of science and technology as The Science Museum, building a new gallery of Modern Communications (planned for 2014 opening), which will also feature computing and networks (especially the World Wide Web). As we have seen above, the ontological problems surrounding how to understand and theorize net art, for example, are closely related to the practical problems, and the cultural heritage sector is faced with this challenge more widely (the previously mentioned born-digital content). In a way, archivists and curators have to face the dilemma outlined by Chun

(2004) concerning software and coding: the (source) code does not equate with execution, and software itself is involved in so many genealogies of computer culture that one cannot reduce it to the logical set of instructions commanding hardware. Indeed, software, and its development from concrete wiring of mainframes every time you wanted a new kind of process to the huge industry of the past decades, involves so many shifts in the usage of the term that we just cannot easily pinpoint what it is.

Visibility of software is called into doubt by Chun, who argues that despite software being a crucial affordance for our visual culture, it remains invisible itself. The history of programming is a bundle of things which demands a complex methodology to unravel the various scales on which it moves, culturally and technically, from the concrete work of female programmers to automatic programming involving not only code but also interpreters, assemblers, compilers and generators, writes Chun (2004: 30), referring to the early UNIVAC programmer Mildred Koss. The fact that, with automatic programming, code becomes iterable across machines and contexts and hence occupies a seemingly autonomous and even viral quality contributed to the idea of its immateriality for sure, but at the same time probably only added to the problem of archiving and curating such cultural forms.

How do you conserve something that is not visible, but allows things to be seen and heard? That is a fundamental question for any archaeology of knowledge, and, for us, *technical media* archaeology. Expanded into a wider question concerning time-critical processes, this last section returns to Ernst's media archaeology and its 'operational arm' in the Operational Media Archive of 'epistemological toys' (http://mw.turing.culture.hu-berlin.de/foswiki/bin/view, accessed 26 Nov. 2011) at the cellar of Media Studies, Berlin.

In contrast to museums of still objects of technology and media, and to private collections (several media archaeologists have extensive collections as well), this archive, or 'Fundus' as it is also called, is somewhere between an engineering media lab for old technology and a repository for media archivists. The collection houses a variety of technologies, which are in operation or engineered to work. The variety of things and devices ranges from gramophones, calculators, stereoscopes and computers to cathode ray tubes, oscilloscopes and a Korg synthesizer. Visual media traditionally familiar to media archaeologists, for instance a magic lantern and a praxinoscope, are complemented in the collection by a range of objects and devices from the electronic media age: tubes, valves, diodes, cables, connectors and antennas.

Image 6.1 The Media-Archaeological 'Fundus' as part of the Berlin Humboldt University Institute for Media Studies – a repository and a tinkering space for old media technology, and a step in the direction of media archaeology moving from a textual method into engineering and analysis by making operational. © Lina Franke

Branded as an archive of media-epistemological toys, the name captures the two-fold mission of the place, materiality and play/ learning: first, through a concrete hands-on approach to investigating the non-linguistic modes of media objects, that they do not speak in human languages, but their seeming silence as artefacts can hide a very active, other kind of processuality; and second, that this epistemological gaze is seen as a playful attitude of engagement and a didactic media-archaeological method of learning how hardware is coupled with discourse: in other words, how modern (technical) media are a coupling of symbolic mathematical operations with the hardware in which they become an engineered signal.

The archive is an operational pair to Ernst's theories, and exhibits well what he understands by such key concepts as the monument, the diagram, time-criticality and the primacy of the signal to any cultural semiotics geared towards meaning. The objects are monuments in the way in which the archival institution was based on monumentality – as mementos of a past. At the core of Foucault's idea of archaeology of knowledge, and now in Ernst's theory of media archaeology, the media-technological artefact as a monument is a reminder from a past media culture, and as such carries with itself pastness. This is another way of saying that the archive occupies itself with inscriptions and these inscriptions are what media archaeologists also focus on. This pastness is not only of indexical, textual value, but an operative machine that has transported its technological, as well as the underlying scientific, principles with it. To put it simply, the machine is not a textual description of a past technology, but itself a concrete form of the principles, diagrams, examples of past media in action.

One concept that Ernst uses for this brand of media archaeology is the diagram. We can think about this in very concrete terms: the diagrams of circuits and machine functions, which are abstract descriptions of the operational principles of modern technology. Ernst emphasizes that this is not a structure – instead, perhaps slightly in the fashion that Foucault and Deleuze would have argued, the diagram is a guiding principle for the potential actions a machine might take. It hence refers less to a static state of a machine (even if, as we know, most engineering diagrams look very static) than to the potential connections that a machine might make. In other words, and echoing many recent themes in software studies (Chun 2004, 2011b), a machine is not just its source code, blueprint or diagram, but how that diagram functions in process, when it is being executed: whether this is a software program compiling the piece of code, or an old Russian submarine radio still able to receive low-frequency transmissions. Such a link between old technology and contemporary (still, as long as there are analogue transmissions available) networks makes the machine an active, diagrammatic articulation of past and current time.

The diagrams are Ernst's way of guiding our attention to the technical contexts, the archive, for our modern media. This includes time-criticality – that our modern media are always defined by how they unfold in a process, whether we are talking about a radio receiver and its mode of signal processing, or, for example, a computer and its execution of processes (see Volmar 2009). As we have argued above in relation to the dynamics of software culture, the way we understand technical media culture objects is through how they engage in processes and hence cannot be pinned down as stable artefacts only. Things that we recognize from music and sound – intervals, rhythm, speed and slowness – characterize our technical media as well, from computer storage (from the earlier mercury *delay* line technologies to RPMs of hard drives) to refresh rates (that define how we see, for instance on cathode-ray-tube displays), from processor speeds to streaming content online (Ernst 2009a). Time is then not only the external framework of history through which we can understand media development, but a technical characteristic governing the machines.

The downside of such epistemological and archaeological toy research is, of course, that it can easily 'forget' itself in the world of hardware and information sciences. As an approach to media, it seems radically different from that of Raymond Williams and a whole tradition of Anglo-American cultural and media studies – and hence media archaeology as well. The problem is that such a focus on machines, despite making a very refined point about the technical conditions of perception, does not effectively connect this to themes of political economy, or for instance subjectivity and subjectification. These are technologies that contribute to the archaeology of cognitive capitalism, but such links have not really been elaborated yet. Indeed, this 'Berlin-Humboldt-approach' focuses on the technology in media. It might prove extremely fruitful – to rethink power/knowledge through the circuits and technologies in which it is embedded, instead of only the normal source-base of critical theory and humanities – or a huge problem, if it altogether neglects such social issues.

With these methodologies for media archaeology, we are introduced both to a fresh idea of what the archive is and to how we can analyse modern media. The operational archive, supported by Ernst's theoretical work, enables us to think more widely about the processual nature of technical media. That this is a big question for contemporary cultural heritage is one thing – another benefit is that it expands far outside digital computing into contemporary culture. Digital culture is opened by its deeper archaeological layers of technical media – including also *analogue* computing. In any case, the archive is being rethought in its role as a public institution connected to other institutions of transmission of cultural heritage like the museum, but also renegotiated through everyday practices of network culture. As flagged earlier, participatory cultures force us both to rethink the practices of production of cultural content as dynamic, shared and defying the traditional author function, and also offer new ways of organizing data – also dynamic, changing and grassroots-emergent, as with folksonomies. The way we think about archives – and go about archiving – is a function of their technological context, which is a point emphasized from Jacques Derrida to Wolfgang Ernst, but we should pay as much attention to the political economy of this archival situation.

The archive is indeed becoming banal – as it refers more generally to everyday storage needs, and the various devices, from portable flash memory drives and external hard drives to cloud computing, in which storage is a new business, for files and documents, family photos, and personal collections of other digital material, for example music files. Archiving everyday life is a theme of technological media culture that one could track from the multiplication of mundane memories in photographic cultures to home videos and more. What is more, the political economy of the archive is connected to production in one more sense: remixing as one key feature of digital aesthetics is reliant on there being something to remix, and the appreciation of repositories as potentials for novel repurposing, remixing and remediation. Such an idea can be found already in Huhtamo's media archaeology, when he writes how reactivation of cultural themes is constantly 'aided by easier and easier access to cultural archives' (2011: 38). Yet the increasingly easier access to digital content – whether from YouTube or some other repository of audiovisual, textual and sonic material – is at the same time shadowed by strict copyright legislation and procedures. The media ontology of the archive is not only about technicalities, but about the legal as well as political economic aspects of reuse and transformation. This is also where media archaeology, as a transdisciplinary methodology for analysis of media culture, has to develop most.

Summary

The archive can be approached through its technological context: memory, too, is conditioned by technological platforms and forms of inscription. In contemporary culture, this points towards the urgent need to think of digital-born content as a specific case for new ways of archiving processes instead of just artefacts, and the implications this has for media ontology. Software is one special case of process-based, time-critical technical media, which cannot be reduced to just one aspect of its technicality, for instance source code. One could, however, say that technical media are more widely time-critical, as exemplified by the collections of the Media-archaeological Fundus at Humboldt University. Media-archaeological objects are revived and understood through their processual, time-critical nature. How best to benefit from the media-archaeological methodologies in order to understand the materiality of the process-based archival situation that we are faced with? How could media archaeology contribute to some of the debates in digital humanities?

Further readings

Chun, Wendy Hui Kyong (2011b) *Programmed Visions. Software and Memory* (Cambridge, MA: The MIT Press).

Ernst, Wolfgang (2011) 'Media Archaeography: Method and Machine versus History and Narrative of Media' in *Media Archaeology*, ed. Erkki Huhtamo and Jussi Parikka (Berkeley, CA: University of California Press), 239–55.

Kirschenbaum, Matthew G. (2008) *Mechanisms. New Media and the Forensic Imagination* (Cambridge, MA: The MIT Press).

7

Practising Media Archaeology: Creative Methodologies for Remediation

A lot of media-archaeological work is executed in artistic ways. Already the earlier interest in historically as well as theoretically rich investigations into resurfacing patterns of use, hidden and neglected inventions, as well as the multitemporal histories of devices and media technological contexts, were accompanied by original artistic practices that were creating archaeologies of media in the present. A lot of media-archaeological theory has been open to accepting a range of media artistic avant-garde as part of the archaeological inquiries, in which the methodology becomes a way of critically questioning new technologies; Siegfried Zielinski (1999: 22) writes of 'those among the avant-garde of electronics in whose heads and hands the new techniques do not become independent ends in themselves, but are constantly irritated and reflected upon: artists like Valie Export, David Larcher, Nam June Paik, Steina and Woody Vasulka, or Peter Weibel'. Addressing media-archaeological creative practices, this chapter presents some of the work in this stream of interest, from Paul DeMarinis to the more recent young wave of media-archaeologically attuned practitioners, and taps into the question of how media archaeology can work as a method for artistic engagement in present-day media culture.

Several influential media archaeologists, such as Siegfried Zielinski (Cologne, Berlin) and Erkki Huhtamo (UCLA), have primarily worked in art institutions, which has left its mark on both the students adopting media-archaeological methods and the scholars' own work. Such fields as media art histories (www.mediaarthistory.org/, accessed 27 Nov. 2011) have brought together a range of scholars with practitioners, and a number of contemporary creative practice methods can be seen to be related to media archaeology. Festivals such as Ars Electronica, Transmediale and ISEA have also played their fair share in a similar kind of support for artistic work and theoretical debates concerning media archaeology.

In addition, the discourses and practices are not restricted to the term of media archaeology. For example, the concept of 'remediation' as developed by Jay David Bolter and Richard Grusin already sounds intuitively a good way to investigate intermedial relations and media historical borrowings across time and media in a fashion that is not only about *writing* about media. In short, you can critique media through making media – and even doing media *history* differently. Instead of media-historical ways of imposing unity, avoiding contradiction, assuming non-constructed naturality and preferring holistic linearity and integrated narratives (I am here paraphrasing from William Uricchio 2004: 34), media-archaeological art wants to suggest a more non-linear way of understanding past-presents. As flagged in chapter 3, this takes place in relation to imaginary media research and art, but we shall continue that theme here too through an elaboration of media-archaeological art, art practices and practitioners' views of how they perceive their working methods.

Assembling the present past

Practitioners such as Paul DeMarinis, Bernie Lubell, Zoe Beloff, Catherine Richards, Perry Hoberman, David Link and a range of others have for a long time – since the 1990s – been identified as media-archaeological artists (Huhtamo 1995). Similarly, recent years of mediatic arts have seen a younger generation of practitioners bring in a new set of ideas and agendas, partly also because of the influence the earlier wave of theories and art filtered through institutions and texts. Rosa Menkman, Garnet Hertz, Morten Riis, and the Berlin scene that includes practitioners such as Shintaro Miyazaki, Martin Howse and Brendan Howell are just some of the emerging generation who are adapting ideas from media-archaeological theories of Siegfried Zielinski, Erkki Huhtamo, Wolfgang Ernst and others in their studies, and have shown 'the applicability' of media archaeology as an art method. Similarly, practitioners such as London-based Sarah Angliss and Aleksander Kolkowski[1] can be seen engaging with media-archaeological themes in their work on cultures of recording, sound and technology, even if not explicitly contextualizing it as such.

Yet exactly what media-archaeological art means is less often articulated. We know it deals with engaging with the past and learning

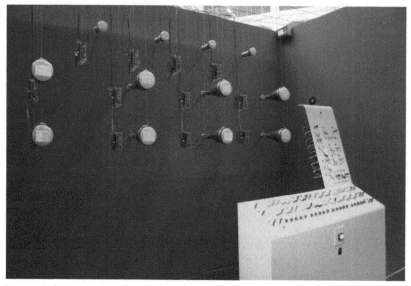

Image 7.1 An image from the German theorist and artist David Link's installation *LoveLetters_1.0* (2009) of the early generative-text program on the Manchester University computer (1948). © David Link

from the past media cultures in order to understand present mediated, globalized network culture through artworks executed in various media. But what, more specifically, have been the works we could see as media-archaeological? As a form of brainstorming (and with help of such early texts as Huhtamo 1995), I tried to come up with at least six different ways in which one can see old media technology and themes resurrected in the contemporary context – whether in galleries, festivals or online. Of course, several of the projects in these categories overlap with each other, and the list is not intended to be anything more than a heuristic tool to illuminate what is being talked about in this chapter.

(1)　Artistic works that visually engage with historical themes; for example in more cinematic pieces, such as Lynn Hershman Leeson's *Conceiving Ada* (1997), which reimagines folds of time between digital culture and the past heroine of early computers and software, Lady Ada Lovelace (1815–52). Also, in the wider popular culture, media-archaeological themes can be found in such products as the popular online clip 'Pixels' by Patrick Jean and Onemoreproduction (www.onemoreproduction.com/) in which 8-bit characters invade New York. Retro-themes can be seen linked to the media-cultural nostalgia drive (Suominen 2008).

(2) Invoking alternative histories, which are able to offer critical insights into the assumed-natural state of digitality – whether technological or social – through the art piece that goes against the grain in terms of the materials it uses, or the narratives of use. Good examples include Zoe Beloff's cinematic constructions of gendered histories of technology, of mediums and devices of control; Paul DeMarinis's *The Messenger* installation (1998/2005) investigates telecommunications from an alternative perspective; various steampunk-themed ideas, performances and devices kicked off by Gibson and Sterling's *The Difference Engine* novel as a phantasy of the information age of the nineteenth century.[2]

(3) Art of/from obsolescence: pieces and practice that use obsolescent materials and solutions to engage with emerging media cultures – or just investigate the potentials in reusing and hacking electronic media. Examples could include: Vuk Cosic's ASCII[3] art that refers directly to media-archaeological investigations into remediation of textuality, marginalized technologies and 'useless' media solutions; the Refunct Media installation (by Klomp, Gaulon and Gieskes) that rewires obsolete media into a new media ecology (http://vimeo.com/27417437, date accessed 5 Nov. 2011); festivals like the Art of the Overhead Projector-series in Sweden, organized by Linda Hilfling and Kristoffer Gansing, on obsolete image media; 8-bit sound cultures as inspiration for thinking about 'new' digital culture and its artistic practices, as well as more recent but still out-dated examples, such as Alexei Shulgin's live rock performances with a 386dx processor computer and Windows 3.1 Operating System in 1998. Perhaps we could even consider Bernie Lubell's various wood installation works across the years as a case in point – using an 'obsolete' material to construct 'high-tech' machines.

(4) Imaginary media that are constructed and not just imagined: devices that are dead, or were never built, being reconstructed and re-employed, for their curiosity value but also to investigate the nature of progress, change and the novelty-obsessed technological culture that is still, however, embedded in (planned) obsolescence; we already tapped into this theme in chapter 3

with, for instance, Gebhard Sengmüller's *A Parallel Image* installation. DeMarinis's works, such as *The Edison Effect* and *Gray Matter*, modulate already existing ideas in sound recording and electrical communications into inventive directions and concrete assemblages. Julien Maire is as clearly a media-archaeological artist with a fascination in re-investigating past apparatuses, but modified in creative ways. Bruce Sterling's influential *Dead Media* project and such artistic parts of it as the online interactive 'Embrace the Decay' work, can be seen dealing with themes of technological disappearance and remediation (www.moca.org/museum/digital_gallery.php, accessed 27 Nov. 2011).

(5) Media-archaeological art that draws from concrete archives – in other words, artistic practice informed by archival work and historical materials, a direct way of working like a historian but for artistic ends. Such work is well documented in Sven Spieker's (2008) art-historical take in his *The Big Archive* (see also Merewether 2006), and visible in works of such contemporary artists as Gustav Deutsch (*Film ist*), Bill Morrison's work with 'orphan film material' (for instance in the film *Light is Calling*, 2003) and that of Sarah Angliss, who is able to draw on her background at the Science Museum, London, and through her sound and robotic performances develops themes from media history. In addition, for example, there is the work of David Link, addressing the Manchester 'Baby' (Small-Scale Experimental Machine, more officially) computer, which was the first stored-program computer, and the Love Letter Generator-program by Christopher Strachey (1916–75). As an artist, Link works almost like a historian, but one who does not express himself (only) in writings, but in constructions – history becoming media art.

(6) Media-archaeological art methods that dig not only into the past, but also inside the machine and address the present – but technically 'archaeological' – buried conditions of our media culture. Such projects that focus on opening up the machines, as well as speaking to a range of important contemporary processes, protocols, software and hardware environments with art/activist practices that at times come close to circuit bending and hardware hacking include, for example, The Institute for Algorhythmics and Microresearch Lab in Berlin; Rosa Menkman's projects such as the *The Collapse of PAL* performed as part of the Transmediale 2011 festival; Matthias Fitz's investigations into electromagnetic fields in his installation

work (*Re-Creation of an Unstable Universe*, exhibited at the Art Claims Impulse-gallery in Berlin in Spring 2011); and, for instance, even Cory Arcangel's interventions into game cultures, such as hacking the Super Mario console game in *Super Mario Clouds* (2002).

There is a need for a stronger articulation of media archaeology not only as a textual method, but also as an artistic methodology (Parikka and Hertz 2010). As utilized by DeMarinis (2010, 2011) and others already for a longer period, such methods are at times even more effective than writings in bringing forth a multitemporal and layered mode of executing past media as alive in contemporary culture. This is what all these approaches share in different ways, from narrative content to material assemblages. The notion of practical execution of the ideas was articulated as one characteristic of a way of doing media history that is not only historical. Indeed, as shown by Inke Arns (2008) in her text on some recent Eastern European artistic projects of media-archaeological spirit, these projects are not about offering the stability of history only as a story leading inevitably to the current, but one about seeking potentials – things, ideas, relations that were never actualized.[4]

Indeed, the idea of potentiality is clearly present in how Paul DeMarinis and, for instance, Zoe Beloff and Julien Maire approach past media – new media in parallel lines. DeMarinis's work is emblematic of most of the 'categories' listed above in its way of tying in historical source work with narratives that are, however, executed through concrete installation works and assemblages. No wonder then that Erkki Huhtamo has called DeMarinis's style and artistic methodology 'thinkering' that is an experimental, but completely rigorous and well-researched, approach to rethinking media technologies past and present – outside the mainstream. In Huhtamo's words, emphasizing DeMarinis's fascination with obsolescence that invites a reimagining of media histories:

Using anything at hand, from secondhand electronic components, old record players, radios and electric guitars to datagloves, he constructs artwork-machines that sing and speak and resonate – emotionally, intellectually and culturally. An example is a piece called Four Foxhole Radios, an ambiguous commentary on human inventiveness in dire circumstances (like a concentration camp), and the need to overcome isolation. The work consists of functioning radio receivers created by applying burnt out light bulbs, mesquite barbeque charcoal, rusty batteries, eighteenth century nails, packs of chewing gum, discarded CD's, votive candles, whisky bottles and shot glasses. (Huhtamo 2010: 33)

What stands out is the use of mixed materials in assembling new forms of media apparatuses that are outside the mainstream understanding, and yet tap into the very scientific basis on which modern storage and communications media are built. In his *Rome to Tripoli* installation (2006), DeMarinis has built a radio transmitter based on early twentieth-century models by Q. Majorana and G. Vanni, successfully creating a technically curious and aesthetically interesting mechanism in which 'a stream of sulphuric acid mechanically vibrated by sound, reproduces the interruptions of the vocal frequencies as a series of droplets' (DeMarinis 2010: 183). In terms of its political significance, it taps into the political histories of the long-distance (nearly 1,000-kilometre) communications that were instrumental to the Western colonialist enterprise that transmitted European culture, such as opera, to North African listeners. The airwaves, the mechanics, the bits of acid instrumental to the transmission, and the whole technical wireless communication were part and parcel of this assemblage as a non-human actor, but completely political (cf. Bennett 2010).

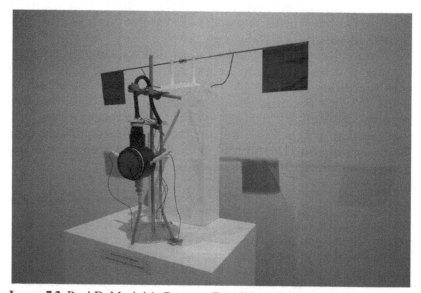

Image 7.2 Paul DeMarinis's *Rome to Tripoli* installation assemblage. Image courresy of Raitis Smits, RIXC The Centre for New Media Culture.

It would be easy to pick plenty of examples of mobilization of similar historical, but strangely current, instances of media-technological interventions from DeMarinis's work. Even his very early work, *The Pygmy Gamelan* (1973, electronic circuit composition), showed signs of his interest in both circuits as the crucial element for understanding modern communications and power, as entangled together. It showed the desire to think of media outside their normal framework. In that piece, a custom-made electronic circuit picks up electrical fields, whether from bodies organic – such as people nearby – or cosmic – such as stars and galaxies – and, based on its reception, plays variations of a five-note melody. We can say that the piece 'begs a series of archaeological questions' (Turner 2010: 23) about the cultural conditions in which the work emerged, its relation to repurposing already existing consumer technologies, and the relation of the circuit-piece to folkloric themes.

Fred Turner continues to elaborate *The Pygmy Gamelan* in relation to 1960s and 1970s counter-culture in the California area, and also in relation to the ideas about 'comprehensive design' of Buckminster Fuller (1895–1983). At the core of those ideas was the political need for artistic–scientific repurposing of objects and 'products of industry', which resonates with DeMarinis's work in terms of design: appropriation of 'the same wiring and the same circuits that supplied mainstream Americans with their consumer technologies and for that matter, their weapons' (Turner 2010: 25). Works like this tapped into that novel regime in which persuasion, power and politics are active through mass media but also through experimental appropriations:

> Like a radio, the Gamelan tunes in frequencies of electronic activity that are otherwise invisible. Yet unlike a radio, it orients the listener to patterns of energy far beyond the control of corporate America. Its five-note melodies sound the invisible forces of the universe, the same forces that affect humans as species. At the same time, they do so using a small device, an individual, even personal module. (Turner 2010: 25)

We could talk about such pieces in relation to a longer lineage of mobile media, in which earlier artistic and experimental works were testing out ideas that later on were consolidated into the more standardized mass consumerist version of mobile entertainment as it currently stands. The same applies to DeMarinis's *The Music Room* (1982) sonic instrument, which does not require any actual musical knowledge, paving the path for later Guitar Hero-type game systems. And yet, perhaps at least as interesting as 'predecessors' to what later became part of the wider consumer market, are the ways in which various media-archaeological art works by DeMarinis are able to illuminate a variety of these devices and their technological relations as part of regimes of biopolitics and affect: they can be seen as archaeologies in this sense as well, investigating how technology and technological media aesthetics stand as a crucial force in terms of management of what we feel, perceive and dream. While tapping into the irrational and imaginaries of media, they are also perceptive of the wider scientific-political ways of governing in current society

Doug Kahn (2010: 51) has aptly summed up DeMarinis's contribution to the field of media arts and archaeologies. Kahn emphasizes that, alongside normal literary, written media archaeologies, DeMarinis is, as well as deconstructing, also reconstructing (alternative) histories and promoting a way of thinking through the practice of building things, new assemblages. Furthermore, an important part of this is the point about politics which is a germinal part of these investigations, in contrast to some other work regarding which I agree with Kahn (2010: 51): 'media archaeology rarely gets its hands dirty with anything besides pithy surrogates'.

Media-archaeological art as time-machines

Media archaeology is always in danger of veering towards excavations of curious instruments and odd gadgets just for their own sake and hence losing the wider political contexts in which technology takes part in governing bodies, affording perceptions and building platforms for social relations, work, entertainment and identity. All of these are questions which cultural studies has identified as crucially political in the sense of the politics of everyday life. Politics of media-archaeological art *has* tapped into gender (Zoe Beloff), the aesthetico-scientific basis of technopolitics (DeMarinis) and ideologies of technological progress (a wide range of different artists), as well as environmental issues (Hertz). Furthermore, I am interested in the ways media-archaeological reconstructions and 'thinkering' (Huhtamo 2010) can mobilize new forms of temporality, which act as subtle ways of rethinking myths of progress, linearity of time and teleological assumptions concerning evolution of media culture that underpin the more mainstream ways of seeing how media technology is part of our lives.

Also outside media-archaeological discussions, remix and remediation have gained a strong foothold as key aesthetic processes and artistic practices of digital culture (Campanelli 2010; Bolter and Grusin 1999). These can be seen as emblematic of aesthetic practices that focus on the use of archives and existing material for creative purposes, and, as such, also rethink the notion of creativity outside myths of romanticized originality. Novel assemblages consisting of already-existing material – whether material that is found, or that is intentionally preserved in archival institutions – can be seen as fresh, interesting and even political. Such remix-practices in media arts have produced a number of interesting works. For instance, Paul D. Miller, DJ Spooky, is a prime example of thinking through both DJ culture and theory, as well as the historical layers of media culture evident in such works as the Errata Erratum remix-machine that draws on the ideas on creativity of Marcel Duchamp (1887–1968), and extends to thinking of musical storage media such as phonographs as 'memory game devices' (www.moca.org/museum/digital_gallery.php, accessed 27 Nov. 2011). Of course, in everyday culture, remixes are part of the wide possibilities offered by digital tools and online platforms – YouTube is filled with creative amateur remixes, that are rethinking originality, remastering, mash-ups, and hence new and old, in curious hybrids. This is why we need to be aware of the wider infiltration of what were traditionally seen as art methods as part of everyday creativity in post-Fordist cultures where a lot of avant-garde art discourses and views have been adopted in how we work and perceive labour (see Lazzarato 2008).

In terms of media-archaeological art, lots of the ideas seem to mix historical time scales intentionally. Laurent Mignonneau and Christa Sommerer's *The Life Writer* (2006) mixes up mechanical typewriter technology with production of genetic algorithms; Julien Maire's *The Inverted Cone* (2010) is a complex assemblage that investigates the nature of time, and clashes pasts and presents in its Henri Bergson-influenced visual worlds. In addition, Tom Jennings's *The Story Teller* is here a useful way to illustrate the idea of media-archaeological art as *an assemblage*, a curious time-machine (Huhtamo 1995) that does not always transport us back (or forth) in time, but involves multiple temporalities in itself.[5] *The Story Teller* reuses ideas and obsolete material from media history, including a teletype machine, a paper-tape reader, and a speech-phoneme processing system. While the performance piece, which includes reciting eight hours of narrative about Alan Turing, can be seen to touch on the history of computing, and Turing's idea concerning the infinite paper-based calculation machine, it also involves a more complex mix of media. Referring back not only to computing, but to telegrams, punched paper, old storage forms, as well as the mechanical basis of computing, the piece is itself a multiple layer of different technologies and hence time scales. It fits in with a notion of history proposed by Fernand Braudel (1980): history as

a multi-layered, multi-rhythmic, concerted plurality of various times
– a polyphonic history.

This polyphonic temporality in *The Story Teller* is described by
Garnet Hertz as *speculative conglomeration*:

> These technologies reconstruct a blend of dead media from the past
> that are not replicas of an exact time and location, but a speculative
> conglomeration of lost forms of communication from the history of
> computing. Jennings goes to considerable lengths to present artifacts
> that appear that they came from the past, including the functionality
> of paper tape and teletype, the careful use of historical materials like
> Bakelite, Micarta and brass, and building of handcrafted enclosures
> from oak. Together, the *Story Teller* system is a hybrid blend of obso-
> lescence where unfamiliar time periods are layered into a functional
> system that is almost impossible to differentiate from an actual histori-
> cal artifact from the 1950s. (Hertz 2009: 127)

The Story Teller illustrates how technology is often not just old, or
new, but always assembled together from various pieces – and this
applies not only to specifically experimental pieces in gallery settings, but to everyday media as well. It presents a different kind of an
idea of temporality, that I see both as characteristic of a lot of media-
archaeological art and as well illustrated by the French philosopher
Michel Serres: we need to be equipped to understand a complex, per-
colated vision of time that does not just flow in one direction. Serres
talks of 'foldable diversity' as another characteristic of this non-linear
way of understanding temporality – and as what is distinctive of even
technology such as cars that are only contemporary as an aggrega-
tion of various temporally disparate scientific and technological ideas.
From the Neolithic invention of the wheel to recent electronics, the
car is itself an assemblage.[6] We imagine our technological cultures as
modern, contemporary or even progressive, but such approaches are
simplifications. Instead, Serres gives important philosophical support
for projects that want to complexify our notions of temporality:

> we are always simultaneously making gestures that are archaic,
> modern, and futuristic. Earlier I took the example of a car, which can
> be dated from several eras; every historical era is likewise a multitem-
> poral, simultaneously drawing from the obsolete, the contemporary,
> and the futuristic. An object, a circumstance, is thus polychromic, mul-
> titemporal, and reveals a time that is gathered together, with multiple
> pleats. (Serres and Latour 1995: 60)

What media-archaeological practices are good at doing is forcing us
to think about time as *pleated*. Outside the linear 'earlier–later' time

axis, this shows that time spreads in all directions. Hence, many of the important discussions in society concerning machines and technology have to do with convincing people what is new and what is obsolescent, and finding subtle ways to impose such categories – through marketing, legislating and political measures. One of the most urgent debates since the 1990s has been the temporality of the network culture, and the various attempts to capture 'Internet time' as a specific form of speed – of both progress and work processes.[7] The unfounded belief in the permanence of the digital as a material grounding for long-term storage is constantly questioned by things breaking down, and was addressed already in the previous chapter. Hence, ephemerality seems a more apt description of the workings of memory and time in digital culture – but not without a material grounding again (see Chun 2011a). Projects that engage with slowing down time, address digital to analogue translations like the *Embroidered Text Message* (2009) by Ginger Anyhow (gingeranyhow.com/textmessages.html, accessed 28 Nov. 2011), or then investigate durations that are beyond our human time-span are as much emblematic of this problem of time and storage in digital culture as the ideas presented in previous chapters. As we will see below, these are also crucial questions concerning information technology waste and the political side of research into the 'deep time relations of media' (Zielinski 2006a; cf. Gabrys 2011).

Dead media or zombie media?

Siegfried Zielinski's concept of 'deep time' is adopted from geological research and a focus on a horizon of durations of not only thousands, or millions, but billions of years of history. For Zielinski, this idea points towards the need to look at media too in terms of their long-term relations that radically steps out of the short-term use value that is promoted by capitalist media industries. As a political and ecological twist to this, one project that takes its impulse directly from media-archaeological and dead-media debates is the Dead Media lab by Garnet Hertz – the already-mentioned California-based artist and writer. Hertz's creative practice is informed by deep involvement in various 'tinkering' methodologies, from circuit bending to DIY robotics, and he has been able to connect that with media-archaeological interests – something we have, in collaboration, also called 'zombie media' of the living deads of media culture (Hertz and Parikka 2012).

Hertz's project picks up Bruce Sterling's call for a sustained interest in knowledge of media that are dead, and discarded outside normal use in everyday life – but still can have much artistic and other value. Hertz twists this further into an ecological project, or even ecosophic in the sense that Félix Guattari (2000) talks of ecosophy as reinvention of the various transversal relations between the social, the psyche, the economic and the environment. Dead Media Lab becomes hence much more than a lab for repurposing information technology – Hertz quotes the statistics on the hundreds of millions of still-operational devices that are discarded in the US alone. It is also a social laboratory for those practices that engage both in thinking about future green information technologies and in promoting community engagement in DIY methods that are inventive everyday reuses and appropriations of the art methods of the early twentieth-century avant-garde – repurposing existing media and 'readymades' becomes less about Duchamp and more about circuit bending and hacking workshops at community centres. It closely relates to the 'rematerializing' tendencies in electronic waste that force us to think about the *natural* history of electronics, well analysed by Jennifer Gabrys (2011).

The link to media archaeology becomes most clearly voiced in this part of his Dead Media Lab call – innovation through media history:

> The history of obsolete information technology is fruitful ground for unearthing innovative projects that floundered due to a mismatch between technology and socioeconomic contexts. Because social and economic variables continually shift through time, forgotten histories and archaeologies of media provide a wealth of useful ideas for contemporary development. In other words, the history of technological obsolescence is cheap R&D that offers fascinating seeds of development for those willing to dig through it. This lab encourages the study of obsolescence and reuse in media history as a foundation for understanding the dynamics of media change. (www.conceptlab.com/deadmedia/)

As cheap R&D, media-archaeological ideas about memory, time, duration and obsolescence are part of a wider artist–activist engagement. Less a textual method, circuit bending and hardware hacking are related to thinking about media history in fresh ways that also engage with the important question of how we are able to reuse devices that too easily and too quickly end up in waste sites.

Hence, work such as Hertz's ties in to both the lineage of media-archaeological artists such as DeMarinis, who has also been interested in the wider environmental ideas concerning media (nature as media) and equally to such initiatives as, for instance, the Mediashed in the UK. Mediashed key activity revolves around the call for 'free media' that are outside the proprietary platforms, and hence open both legally and technically. Mediashed's work has focused on both software and reusing waste and junk materials (such as electronic devices and parts) for community and artistic purposes. In addition, they have shown an interest in 'obsolescent' forms of communication in their EcoMedia theme days and projects that expand the idea of communication to various techniques, from shouting, spitting and smelling to pigeon communication, all found in natural bodies. (For a connection to media archaeology and imaginary media, see Parikka 2011a.)

In such projects, we are moving farther away from what has usually been the safe ground of media archaeology. Even if 'redundancy', 'obsolescence', 'time' and 'dead media' connected the approaches of both free media activists and media archaeologists, the latter have, as Kahn too flagged, been reluctant to be that political. Yet to me, this link that Hertz is able to make is of crucial value in expanding media-archaeological theory and art methods. Hence, in addition to Mediashed, another clear link would also be the UK-based Redundant Technology Initiative (http://rti.lowtech.org/intro/) that grounds all of its activity in 'technology that they could acquire for nothing'. As such, it has meant concrete spaces for Free Media tinkering (Access Space is characterized on their website as 'an open-access digital reuse centre' for learning and teaching), as well as projects that recircuit back to recent media history, even in the form of Mac Hypercards, ASCII-text, 28.8K faxes repurposed as part of an imaginary TV-feedback system, and manifestos promoting 'low tech' (http://rti.lowtech.org/).

As we argue with Hertz (Hertz and Parikka 2012), techniques of media-archaeological art like circuit bending are crucial for a wider environmental consciousness. The aesthetic tactics and various 'minor' methods such as circuit bending, hardware tinkering and so forth are important links to a wider activist stance towards technical media. The increasingly closed nature of consumer technology (see Guins 2009) is the other side of the coin in this call to reuse old technology. This closedness is what really defines proprietary platforms. A large amount of current consumer technology is not meant to be opened, tinkered with and reused, and this is guaranteed through various measures, ranging from Digital Rights Management that legally restricts users' possible actions to the various design strategies that make it very difficult to engage in, for instance, circuit bending. Such techniques can indeed be seen as 'minor' but they are important for illuminating how technological solutions relate to power relations. Even design solutions – using glue instead of screws – are part of this wider regime of controlling patterns of (re)use (cf. Kittler 1997).

Furthermore, this relates to the wider politics of 'planned obsolescence' (Hertz and Parikka 2012), which can be seen as the background for much of consumer society, including technology. In such perspectives, the wider history of reuse in avant-garde art from Duchamp to DJing and VJing not only is about innovations through remixing and mash-ups, but is set against the demand for originality and newness that drives production of technology. As a form of governing production and demanding constant replaceability, 'planned obsolescence' has, since the 1930s, been seen as a form of enforced obsolescence and as supporting new product design. Yet, during the last decades it has become even more evident that such a drive for creation is unsupportable in terms of the ecological load it creates and distributes very unevenly as part of the global economy.[8]

Signal-based media art

As the above section, as a brief glimpse into various activist contexts of addressing obsolescence, demonstrates, the importance of the 'material' is very central to media-archaeological artists. As addressed in earlier chapters, the materiality of technical media is, however, in itself problematic, and was addressed for a long time as 'immateriality'. The 1990s cyberculture was keen to address new information technologies as virtual, which I believe was merely a euphemism for 'imperceived' and led to a lot of neglect in terms of trying to understand the ways in which power was circuiting itself through the technologies. Kittler's as well as media archaeologists' influence was to give insights into how the seemingly fleeting and ephemeral was grounded in politics of hardware, code, signal transmission and protocols.

Artistic practice has always had to engage with a wide range of materials, and also to think through critically the various reuses and characteristics of the materials we are employing for our creative activities. From fine art to computer art, this has meant an experimental attitude towards the apparatus as well, and the twentieth century is itself a rich ground for excavations of the collaborations of science, technology and art. New institutions of the late twentieth century – not only the internationally recognized hubs of media design and innovation such as the MIT Media Lab, but also UK polytechnics (Mason 2008)– were in pioneer positions to experiment with computerized platforms.[9] A range of experimental work is now being done by smaller artist groups and young emerging practitioners, in addition to bigger institutions. As well as a lot of visual-based work in early media-archaeological creative practice, people such as DeMarinis and, for example, Bernie Lubell engaged in sound and physical structures of interaction for their excavations into longer histories of science and technology. But how to react artistically in a situation in which a lot of our media are losing their tangibility and becoming invisible – in the age of cloud computing, remote servers, ubiquitous computing that hides inside things, and, in general, such complexity in our media devices that most of the technical details are removed and become only an area of professional knowledge for engineers.

As a further move away from the visual, recent media-archaeological art has turned towards networks, algorithms and the signal. Hence, such works as the Institute for Algorhythmics' sonic archaeologies, the MicroResearch Lab (www.1010.co.uk), and, for instance, Rosa Menkman's work with archaeologies of technical signals, image protocols and glitch aesthetics show a new interest in technical media tightly interwoven with the earlier-mentioned two-fold understanding of media archaeology: as excavating longer time-spans in order to understand the conditions for the contemporary scientific media culture, and as excavating the technicalities of current technologies in order to understand how they frame our living world. Such methodologies pick up on some of the same principles as material media archaeology in digging into the machine. A good example is the idea of 'data carvery' (as coined by Martin Howse) as a way of investigating digital archaeology (see also chapter 6) that looks at the inscriptions on hard-drive technologies.[10]

The Berlin-situated Institute for Algorhythmics brands itself as 'listening and looking for an epistemology of everyday life' (www.algorhythmics.com/, accessed 27 Nov. 2011) which also reveals a further side to the media materialities of the information economy – not immaterial, but temporal:

> Algorhythms occur when real matter is controlled by symbolic structures like instructions written as code. Algorhythms show us that our digital culture is not immaterial, but divided in time. Time + music becomes important for understanding media. With enough scientific effort the invisible electronic or electromagnetic (wireless) signals can be made hearable. Listening to those digitally modulated signals, you can hear the rhythmic character of the signals of most digitally working devices and also of wireless consumer electronic networks like WLAN, GSM, UMTS, Bluetooth, digital TV and Radio et cetera. (Ibid.)

The Institute taps into two key themes in contemporary media arts and theory: sound and algorhythmic culture. As such, it is able to use aesthetic methods as epistemological investigations – formations of knowledge, or how we understand and know about our technical world around us that is often structured as 'imperceptible', except for the content of what is being transmitted to consumers.

These practical methods for epistemological investigations into contemporary culture also go by the name of 'Sonic Archaeology' (www.sonicarcheology.net/, accessed 25 Nov. 2011) as coined by Shintaro Miyazaki (2011). Sonic Archaeology investigates various software and hardware methodologies through which to map the quite often invisible and imperceptible electromagnetic waves, as well as investigations into computers, mobile phones, mp3-players and digital cameras. Hence, archaeology becomes a way of understanding how such devices structure the everyday worlds and temporal sequences in which we live in technological societies – but instead of speaking generally about technological society, they look at the concrete processes and gadgets in which such traditional cultural studies concepts as power now reside.[11] Archaeologies of the present do not focus only on historical time, but also on the way in which contemporary technologies are archives that store, process and distribute information. There is a parallel development that at least implicitly picks up on Kittler's tripartite 'commands, addresses, data' division (chapter 4) as the methodological guideline: media archaeologies of looking at media history through technical terms that apply to institutionalization or systematization of what we used to call 'power, subjects and experience', and, concretely, how such new forms of concepts for humanities' analysis of technology afford investigations into the insides of machines as well.

In a similar manner, Rosa Menkman's work such as *The Collapse of PAL* is intriguing as it taps into a quite often neglected feature of media culture – the encoding formats for colour televisual content. Such topics are usually tackled in terms of policy analysis and design, but this time are adopted as part of discussions concerning technological progress, nostalgia and standards. Menkman transforms our angle in a McLuhanesque way, from what is being seen (content) to how it is being encoded, modulated and transmitted (media as encoding standards and signals).

PAL stands for Phase Alternating Line and was designed in the 1960s as a specifically European system for colour TV. As such, it formed an intimate part of the formation of the analogue TV broadcasting culture in post-World War II Europe, and became a specific aesthetic regime in its own right. The technical standard defined the frequency rate (50 hertz, or 50 cycles per second) for scanning the picture lines, the colour characteristics (tint, hue, etc.) and error correction through a technique called phase reversal.[12] Now, with the emergence of digital television as both a technological and aesthetic project throughout Europe, the signal type is in danger of becoming 'dead media'.

Menkman's *The Collapse of PAL* is a video performance on two screens that investigates this process of becoming obsolescent. It adopts both a technical aspect in the work by offering modulations of the signal through various devices and techniques from a Nintendo Entertainment System (NES), 'a dysfunctional digital camera, digital compression artifacts, video bending artifacts (DV, interlacing, datamoshing and black bursts) and feedback.'[13] For sound, various more or less obsolete media were also used, such as a Cracklebox (small audio synthesizer gadget, originally from the 1970s), a European telephone signal and an old keyboard. As such, the performance was embedded in using old devices and systems, and through such a performance of old(er) media-technological solutions, the tension between old and new was analysed. What Menkman was able to bring forth were screens filled with electronic signal landscapes, waveforms and at times recognizable figures. The narrative of the otherwise technical, abstract video performance revolved around 'The Angel from the Future', a Benjaminian figure of critique of progress, who, as the narrative voice and spectral, distorted presence, painted a history of the PAL signal as loser to, for example, the Digital Video Broadcasting (DVB) signal in the MPEG coding format. The terms such as 'losers of history', 'history excavated in the midst of rubbles', 'storm of progress

Image 7.3 Rosa Menkman's *The Collapse of PAL* performance. © Rosa Menkman

which works to hide the multiplicity in history' all point directly to Benjamin's famous *On the Concept of History* text.

From a media-archaeological point of view what is most interesting is the ability to engage with archaeologies of signals and signal formats. Instead of a focus on devices, even if lost and outside the mainstream, we are seeing new perspectives that take as their focus components, processes and other such *minor, grey elements* of media history. Many of the elements that we have taken for granted or as specialist areas for scientists and engineers are being now focused on by artists and media theorists. Protocols (Galloway 2004), wireless technologies (Mackenzie 2010) or, for instance, computer forensics (Kirschenbaum 2008) have become part of studies in social sciences, humanities and media theory. The same goes now increasingly for the minor themes, or components, of media history in the hands of theorists and creative practitioners: signals, but also valves, tubes, antennas, telephone exchanges and semiconductors are revealed as much more than enabling technical parts. They can also reveal a lot about the social and power implications of technologies, and illuminate a very important transversal theme: the components are often the more fluid bits, that establish intermedial relations, and as such are temporally and media-archaeologically often more important than what we see as coherent media (televisions, computers, cinema).

Valves and tubes are *transmedia* components (cf. Ernst 2008) that were essential for the innovations from telegraphy to television and computing; antennas are the often neglected part of our wireless and transmission cultures; telephone exchanges are a similar 'switch' in terms of how communication works – a good example of mobilizing old exchange technologies into a politically hot topic is by the ex-Mongrel-group and UK-based artist trio Harwood, Wright, Yokokoji in their *Tantalum Memorial*, which ties old telephone switch technology together with Congolese alternative practices of 'radio trottoire' communication in the context of mining of Coltan, an essential mineral for our media technologies such as mobile phones, primarily found in the Congo.[14]

Or take semiconductors, the elements essential to modern technical media in terms of their material qualities that enable mediation between conducting and insulating the flow of electricity. One could see the emergence of modern mass media as one of experimenting, testing and producing such materials that are stable, and hence mass-producible, in terms of their capacities for conduction and insulation of flows of energy – and, as such, demonstrate the centrality of physics for media (and media arts). Hence, semiconductors can be incorporated into media-archaeological practices, as, for example, DeMarinis does in his elaboration of materiality of media, or, as he puts it in his own words in relation to the previously mentioned *Four Foxhole Radios* installation (2000):

> It turns out that semiconductors – the central discovery on which our communications culture turns, and among the most exotic products of materials science – are in fact everywhere to be found. I have made junction diodes from burnt out lightbulbs, mesquite barbeque charcoal, rusty batteries and eighteenth century nails; variable and fixed capacitators from packs of chewing gum, bibles and discarded AOL CDs; coils and variocouplers from votive candles, whisky bottles and shotglasses. These diverse materials serve to make the pieces both playful and instructive. They offer promise of communication and connection even in the direst of situations or in total isolation. They reveal that the manufactured material world is still part of the greater universe and that, unbeknownst to Bill Gates, semiconductor physics is unaccountably breeding in hidden places. Because they actually function as radios, they may help us to feel at home in the world. At any given time and place Frank Sinatra's voice can be heard in the radio waves. For the installations I add other sounds into the ether with small low powered transmitters so that you may as likely hear Joseph Stalin or Spike Jones. (DeMarinis 2010: 161–3)

In the quote, the dialectics between physics (that we are technically dependent on certain ways of mobilization of science for our media) and content (voices transmitted) is well illustrated. It also brings forth the willingness to dig into the grey areas of media culture, as mentioned above: not only to look at what connects and characterizes one specific medium, but to offer, through constructions, innovative interventions into non-linear media history – the relations between media, and across times, are much more multiple and pleated than often perceived, and this already calls the whole category of 'new' into question.

Scientist-artists, or just informed users?

Much of what has been introduced above – the projects, some of the methods, and themes that characterize media-archaeological art – begs the question: do we then have to become engineers to say and do anything interesting and accurate about current media culture? Luckily, the ways to engage effectively and critically with media culture are not that narrowly defined – but what these artists and projects flag is the need to dig deeper than textual analysis. In a way, much of the demand for a thorough, meticulous and disciplinarily open analysis and creation is expressed by Zielinski in his own way of feeding anarchaeological ideas towards practice. It is the step from consumption to production:

> The only effective form of intervention in this world is to learn its laws of operation and try to undermine or overrun them. One has to give up being a player at a fairground sideshow and become an operator within the technical world where one can work on developing alternatives. For artistic praxis with computers in particular, this means learning the codes they function with. (Zielinski 2006: 260)

This is an important call for media theory and practice, and resonates with some other voices of recent years: Alex Galloway and Eugene Thacker (2007: 100) claim that 'Today to write theory means to write code', whilst referring to Geert Lovink's earlier call against the 'vapour theory' of unspecified mysticism and rhetoric that fails to attach to the actual practices which constitute media culture. Similarly, one could say that designers are actually in a privileged position concerning media critique with the ability to create new media objects, processes and uses – in short, worlds. Several arguments seem to carry the same message: we need to understand the various modalities of our tools for thought – such tools are not only about text and writing. In the same way that university curricula and ways of assessing students are slowly taking into account that verbal and written works are not the only modality of expression, and that one can do media critique through production (audiovisual, software- and network-based, performance, installation and so forth), there is an urgent need to promote the understanding of such practices in/as research. And yet, having said that, I am a vigorous defender of the need for theory – traditions of philosophy, critical theory and innovative conceptualizations that are crucial ways to mobilize the technical and practical as part of resistance.

In terms of digital culture and society, the theme of 'media education' has been important for years. An understanding and basic knowledge of uses of, for instance, computers was on the agenda already in the 1980s with the emergence of the first computers. These were integrated into school curriculums too – from basic workshops I attended when at school in Finland (where the pupils often knew more than the teacher, who had not really used a computer herself before), to the wide implementation of cybernetics and training of programming in Eastern Europe,[15] and, for instance, in the UK the BBC Microcomputer and the educational programmes in schools and on television (*The Computer Programme*, BBC2, 1982).

Some recent projects have actually engaged in media education as well, but with a special focus on old media. A good example is the Science Museum (London) workshop on old 'groove' technologies of recording, from Edison wax discs to more recent types of inscription technologies. Together with scholar and writer Katy Price, Aleksander Kolkowski worked with a youth group as part of the Museum's Oramics special project (which in itself has tackled a media-archaeological theme, the female pioneer Daphne Oram's early British music synthesizing machine from the 1960s).

Here, the students were allowed a hands-on approach to obsolete recording technologies, which, as Kolkowski argues, is a way to start thinking about digital cultures of recording and sound as well. Kolkowski elaborates it as a kind of education about forms of listening and hearing – and perhaps also a problematization of the assumed universality of the digital.[16] Workshops like these, as well as the ones that Hertz has organized for a variety of different age and interest groups and communities, propose the idea of media archaeology as educating us about technology and media, not only as critical consumers who can hermeneutically interpret complex media content but also as producers who can actively engage in various media practices. A bit like the Kolkowski/Price workshop, Hertz's circuit-bending workshops investigate the possibilities of reuse of discarded old technologies, such as battery-powered toys modified into musical instruments, as well as acting as an easy crash-course in electronics and circuits – the fundamental features for media literacy in the age of technical communication. Even if the projects do not always reference directly the canon of media-archaeological theory such as Huhtamo, Zielinski, Grusin and others, they engage with similar themes and the persistence of media history in the present.

Summary

Media-archaeological art methods have been able to introduce a rich set of practices that not only write about past media in new ways, but execute it as well. Works by a range of practitioners from Paul DeMarinis, Bernie Lubell, David Link and Zoe Beloff to a more recent wave of artists have investigated new ways to think through obsolescence, myths of progress, the technical specificity of 'new' media and the wide range of alternative histories and potentials of the past that can be brought to life. As such, they are crucial both in terms of elaborating the conditions of existence of technical media (experimental tinkering, or 'thinkering' as Huhtamo has called DeMarinis's work) and as methodologies for remediation and reuse of, and reappropriating, the old. In addition, an increasing amount of media-archaeological art can be seen as political in the way it investigates the political economy of technical media, the blackboxing of technologies, their ecological consequences, as well as, for instance, neglected gender contexts. A key theme is understanding the complex temporalities of contemporary media culture – something this chapter approached through the notion of 'assemblage'. The chapter ends with the question of whether we could further develop media-archaeological art methods into ways of engaging with wider publics as well.

Further reading and links

DeMarinis, Paul (2010) *Buried in Noise*, ed. Ingrid Beirer, Sabine Himmelsbach and Carsten Seiffarth (Heidelberg and Berlin: Kehrer)

Grau, Oliver, ed. (2007) *MediaArtHistories* (Cambridge, MA: The MIT Press).

Huhtamo, Erkki (1995) 'Time-Travelling in the Gallery: An Archaeological Approach in Media Art' in *Immersed in Technology. Art and Virtual Environments*, ed. Mary Anne Moser with Douglas McLeod (Cambridge, MA: The MIT Press, 1996), 232–68.

Spieker, Sven (2008) *The Big Archive. Art from Bureaucracy* (Cambridge, MA: The MIT Press).

Art projects and artists websites

(Websites accessed 28 Nov. 2011)
Zoe Beloff, www.zoebeloff.com/
Paul DeMarinis, www.stanford.edu/~demarini/
Institute for Algorhythmics, www.algorhythmics.com/
David Link, www.alpha60.de/
Bernie Lubell, bernielubell.com/
Julien Maire, http://julienmaire.ideenshop.net/
Rosa Menkman, http://rosa-menkman.blogspot.com/
Micro Research Lab Berlin, www.1010.co.uk/org/
Gebhard Sengmüller, www.gebseng.com/

8

Conclusions: Media Archaeology in Digital Culture

Whilst writing this book, I was lucky enough to be affiliated with the Science Museum in London as a short-term fellow in early 2011. During that period, I was introduced to their storage house in London, and offered a glance at all that remains outside the actual museum exhibitions: rooms and halls filled with high shelves, ordered with miscellaneous objects of an experimental designer's dreamworld – but also abandoned, obsolete computers, grey plastic cover after grey plastic cover. Next to obsolescent computers: manuals, software and other *varia* that were not going anywhere at that moment. I was also introduced to the system: where objects come in, what happens in the first room, which room they go to next, and where then – how objects are tagged, and become actually part of a whole address space that involves locations, procedures, tracking and placing. Things in their place – and the place traceable through information management systems, of course – just like in any modern system from archives to offices.

I was left thinking of this in relation to digital culture more widely. The object management that we call archives still remains mostly hidden to the majority of museum users. Yet trends in digital culture are increasingly about generalization of such management ideas – so that with, for instance, the Radio Frequency Identification (RFID) devices the fantasy is of a world that is completely taggable, traceable and manageable. The world itself becomes a storage space – an archive, a database. Marcel Duchamp offered his own alternative, critical version of the museum-turned-into-a-mobile-suitcase in 'La boîte-en-valise' (1936), but now the mobility of the museum can be turned into the mobility of the informational patterns that attach to objects, and to subjects themselves.

Similarly, media archaeology does not itself take place only in media studies or film studies departments. Media-archaeological ideas – and scholars and other practitioners – can be found in a variety of places inside and outside institutions. From archives to art studios, museum spaces to junk yards, across disciplinary boundaries, geographically dispersed in academic institutions from US universities to Europe, from South America to Australia, Japan, Indonesia and more; from academic theory in the US to obsolescent Soviet-era technological cultures fossilized in Eastern European countries, to enormous e-waste piles being processed in China, to artists working with ideas concerning obsolescence and technical culture in Berlin; addressing a variety of practices, focusing on the periphery too; concrete institutions meshing with intellectual and critical agendas. In short, media archaeology *travels*.

As such, this is not only a book about media archaeology and mapping with historical methods the co-existence of new and old media cultures intertwined through practices, apparatuses and recurring ideas. It is also a book about history, time and the archive as a central concept for digital culture. Concepts too, travel (Bal 2002). Many of such archives are very mundane: the archives offered on clouds for the growing amount of holiday photos; the archives that social media platforms gather from us and our online behaviour as part of datamining, which is a key part of business models in network cultures; the microtemporal 'archives' as part of the processing events of our computers and mobile phones, for very short-term storage (RAM) (Ernst 2010).

Memory, experience and the subject – all basic concepts and ground for so much in the arts and humanities of recent years – are all being embedded in these new 'archives', and our cultural practices are nowadays really difficult to distinguish from the technologies and scientific discourses in which they are being embedded. The turn to science and technology can be a temporary financial requirement for so many university departments in the midst of the ongoing global funding crisis – which more broadly has to do with the running down of publicly funded institutions and the wider trends of neoliberalism – but the intellectual rewards for crossdisciplinary labs are great too. What I wanted to suggest in this work is that these concepts – and institutions – of archives, memory and cultural analysis are entwined with transdisciplinary regimes of knowledge – and for media archaeology to really carve its niche as a 21st-century humanities methodology, it needs to be clear and up-front about its special position at the crossroads of art, science and technology – and show the longer lineages in such border-crossings. Bernhard Siegert has described the early phases of media-archaeological research in 1980s Germany as branded by the Nietzschean notion of 'gay science', which wildly looked for new connections and ideas, dug up new sources, and left others to worry about what the underlying concept of media was (Siegert 2008: 28). We need to ask ourselves: how do we keep such a transdisciplinary spirit of curiosity and intellectual radicality alive and updated in a situation in which university degrees are being reduced to only being 'qualifications' for particular jobs?

On doing

My emphasis has been to look at what you can *do* with media archaeology – not only what media archaeology *means*. Sean Cubitt (2004: 11) writes in *Cinema Effect*: 'The task of theory today is no longer negative. The job of media theory is to enable: to extract from what is and how things are done ideas concerning what remains undone and new ways of doing it.' This leads to a rethinking and mapping of future potentials instead of merely histories. As such it is an emphatically political figure of knowledge, when future-orientedness (what can be done?) is itself understood as political.

Indeed, I am less interested in the traditional critical humanities and theory tools of *interpretation, understanding and critique* and more keen on those new forms of cultural and media analysis that want *to use, to pervert and to modulate* (Cf. Deleuze and Guattari 2004: 4). It is unusual to turn to Deleuze and Guattari when talking about historical modes of knowledge, which they are quite quick to label as a 'sedentary point of view' (2004: 25) which stabilizes, freezes and blocks becomings – those vectors through which we can think of something new. This has to do with alternative figures of knowledge. Do you produce knowledge (or any other creative act) to validate already existing mantras, or in order to enable change – track something that is fleeting, minor but, because of that, more significant, perhaps? This relates to what Deleuze and Guattari called 'nomadology': a mode of knowledge and production that emphasizes new connections that are not reproductions of what exists – but *produce new modes of existing, thinking and creating*. This cartographic mode of nomadic interest in knowledge does not trace, but experiments with, the world; for Deleuze and Guattari (2004: 13), and later developers such as Rosi Braidotti (2002) who has elaborated nomadic cultural analysis as a specific ethos for material and gendered humanities in the twenty-first century, maps and cartography are experimentations that foster 'connections between fields' and establish new dimensions for us, involving transformation and change at the core of knowledge creation. This ethos, to me, despite the seeming hostility towards history found in Deleuze's own writings, is something that can inform our future understanding of media archaeology as well.

This is why I call this an exercise in mapping, a cartography more than a history, and a mode of experimentation in a similar way to how so many media-archaeological works have looked at practices of experimentality between arts, technology and sciences – an ethos of 'the new' that refuses the narrow definition of new given to it in 'new media' discourses, and looks for a more fundamental, more insightful way to develop this idea. Furthermore, its not a simple case of articulating the persistence of the past in the present; instead, the temporal relations are much closer to Zielinski's (2006a: 3) call: 'do not seek the old in the new, but find something new in the old'.

In this book, this call for the new is applied to media archaeology. I have wanted to give insights into some of the defining theories, approaches and ideas that have helped us to establish new connections to old media apparatuses and cultural practices. In addition, I have wanted to find something new: where is media archaeology going, and how do we keep it vibrant and more than a subset of media history? Hence, there is much more than 'traditional' media archaeology in this book: in addition to referring to and talking about established theorists and artists such as Huhtamo, Zielinski, Elsaesser, Kittler and DeMarinis, I tried to talk of the more recent debates in theory and art – from Wolfgang Ernst's very technologically oriented emphases on archaeology and archives to Wendy Chun's software studies, from Matthew G. Kirschenbaum's computer forensics to artistic work by a younger wave of practitioners. Hence, we see media archaeology transported from investigations into old media towards cognate fields – such as software studies, platform studies and other debates in the new media theory of digital culture.

This book has also talked about the new politics in which such practices take place in relation to technology and machines – hence, in a way, responding to Timothy Druckrey's important point about the dangers of media archaeology becoming too self-congratulating, and a curiosity cabinet way of just being enthusiastic and embracive of quirky discoveries and 'oddball paleontologies, of idiosyncratic genealogies, uncertain lineages, the excavation of antique technologies or images' (Druckrey 2006: ix). Instead, we need rigorous methodologies.

On matter

I admit that this book tries to have its cake and eat it too. I try to include a lot of the best ideas from both some of the more social-constructionist versions of media archaeology and the technical and mediatic specificity and controversial innovations that come from German media theory. Such perspectives are often defining discussions about what communication itself is and what media are – for instance, Lisa Gitelman, who represents the first camp, defines them as follows: 'I define media as socially realized structures of communication, where structures include both technological forms and their associated protocols, and where communication is a cultural practice, a ritualized collocation of different people on the same mental map, sharing or engaged with popular ontologies of representation' (2006: 7).

Interested in materiality as well, her take produces, however, a different materiality from some of the versions coming from a German perspective. Kittler, Ernst and others constantly focus on different aspects where materiality lies – outside any metaphorics of the social or culture, they might add. One such starting point is the channel – as defined by Shannon and Weaver in an engineering-oriented way, and transported into a wider set of assumptions concerning how communication works. Such projects allow us to focus on a wide set of non-human materialities, making sure that the platforms of communication that are increasingly technical and restricted to 'expert-territory' are discussed from a critical media-scientific point of view too. Such ideas can be seen as political as well, but differing from, for instance, Gitelman's emphasis.

So where are we left if everyone insists on being interested in materiality? This begs the question – and already perhaps implies the answer – of whether there are various materialities at work:

- *Materialities of cultural practice*, of human activity as embedded in both cognitive and affective appreciations and investments, but also embodied, phenomenological accounts of what we do when we invent, use and adapt media technologies.

  Related to such accounts, various material emphases in recent discussions have extended such non-signification-based concepts as 'affect' to, for instance, labour as the domain of the gendered, sexualized, ethnic body, the material investment, so crucial to any immaterial creative economy.

- *Materialities of materials* – which sounds like a tautology, but points towards how we think of the constitutive non-humans that also, to riff off Bruno Latour, are part of what we call the social. Media history is a long story of experimenting with different materials from glass plates to chemicals, from selenium to coltan. What is more, such materials have their after-effects, nowadays most visible in the amount of e-waste we are leaving behind from our electronic culture.

- *Materialities of technologies* – media-theoretical accounts such as Kittler's have been instrumental in pushing us to be media-specific. This has meant digging into how technologies work, and finding structures of power through a technological analysis. Media archaeology is, for theorists such as Ernst (2011), reverse-engineering.

Instead of wanting to resolve such questions concerning competing materialisms, I hope to be able to use them as catalysers to think not only about materiality of things, or technologies, but also about the materiality of affect and the constitutive practices in which things, and media too, materialize. Hence, the question of our communication theories, through which we understand media culture and its design practices, has to do with where we start – which materialities we include, which histories and archaeologies of matter *matter*, and how can we stay sensitive to the various contexts – scientific, technological, artistic, social, economic, including labour, and natural/ecological – through which we *do* media, art and communication studies.

On temporality

In addition to the material, one of the things that interest me in this book and in media archaeology in general is how it mobilizes new senses of temporality. Amsterdam-based film theorist Wanda Strauven (2012) has flagged the same theme in terms of how media archaeology has worked as a critique of temporality through mapping '1) the old in the new; 2) the new in the old; 3) recurring *topoi*; or 4) ruptures and discontinuities', which reflects the various 'schools' of media archaeology from Huhtamo to Zielinski, to Elsaesser's New Film History-inspired field, to Kittler, Ernst and other material media theorists. These aspects have been introduced in this book too. In addition, drawing on a range of other writers – such as Fernand Braudel, but we could just as well nod towards Manuel DeLanda's (2000) accounts of thousands of years of non-linear history – the existence of times in radical multiplicity becomes emphasized. Jonathan Sterne (2009) has put this recently in similar terms: 'if the span of media history in human history amounts to approximately 40,000 years, we have yet to really seriously reconsider the first 39,400 years'. Such writers of digital culture and art as Josephine Bosma have also argued for novel temporalities. Bosma (2011: 169) refers to the Clock of the Long Now initiated by Stewart Brand, which functions on a layer of 'deep time' (reminiscent of Zielinski's rhetorics); similarly, Bosma refers to the American artist James Tobias's wonderful idea of 'queer clocks: devices that diagram, express and interpret unfamiliar temporal relations'. To me, this captures excellently the potential media-archaeological spirit of investigating non-human and fresh temporalities that are at the basis of how we see culture, cultural heritage and our lives in technical media environments.

Already, a lot of the archaeological methodology has demonstrated the ability to rethink the past in new ways and in new temporalities, as well as the possibility of considering the futures of media and media change – futures of the screen and other media in the reshuffling of the mash-up cultures of YouTube and other social media services (see, e.g., Uricchio 2009a). This meant, for example, taking old media practices and forms and reinventing them in software cultures: a good example would be Masaki Fujihata's 2003 piece, *Morel's Panorama*, which takes the nineteenth-century mass medium of panorama paintings – 360-degree virtual realities of sorts – and, with the help of a panoramic camera, transforms that spatial experience into a software-conditioned projection. It also means coming up with media devices of imaginary sorts that do not necessarily match with our expectations, but because of that make us think about the basic temporal and spatial characteristics of how media fine-tune our perception. Media-archaeological ideas can extend what media are from the confines of the familiar: see, for example, the extremely slow image-transmission rate of Gebhard Sengmüller's *Slow Scan Television* that has a frame rate of one per day, the *Exploding Camera* of Julien Maire which investigates the functionality of already dead media in the midst of cultures of war and death, the *Life Writer* (Laurent Mignonneau and Christa Sommerer) which spills out not only analogue letters from its mechanical system but also genetic algorithms: artificial-life creatures.

The next radical step is to expand towards non-human times. On the one hand, a focus on algorhythmic events, the temporality of machines and time-criticality that escapes our human frameworks is an attempt at that. On the other hand, addressing nature and nature-times is another way to tap into other materialities and temporalities than we have usually attached to digital culture.

In this context, I find Jennifer Gabrys's (2011) approach ingenious. Her *Digital Rubbish: A Natural History of Electronics* is a book about the various materialities of electronic culture. However, it executes this slightly differently, and focuses not only on how we use, interpret and debate about media – but also on how media relate to nature and waste. Hence, her subtitle, A *Natural History of Electronics*, besides being a paradoxical mix of naturalness and the artificial, is adapted from Walter Benjamin's 'a natural history of commodities'. Benjamin, in a true (proto)-media-archaeological spirit, dug through layers of the emerging consumer media culture in his theoretical work, and analysed, for instance, the objects – the fossils – that had fallen out of fashion and use. Now, with the extensive highly advanced technical work going into our media, such devices are fossils not only of curious interest but of toxic hazard. Waste is the residue of media culture, and points towards both the various practices through which obsolescent media are transported, recycled, ripped apart, abandoned, resold and reused, perhaps across the globe, and the various contexts of time and nature such obsolescent media embody. Instead of as glossy newness, we encounter media in places like the dump, the recycling centre, on a street corner abandoned, in attics and other places of disuse.

Gabrys points out that such a focus on electronic waste and obsolescent media forces us to rethink other temporalities than the usual set attached to new media. Instead of progress, processor speeds and the pace of efficiency, she focuses on such temporal materialities as dust and, for instance, soil. For Gabrys (2011: 105), dust is a more accurate marker of media technologies than the 'accelerating speed of information': covered in dust, obsolescent technologies remind of this other time – the remainder of technological use and 'progress'. She continues that dust might just 'be an underlying condition'. Can we start to unravel the 'conditions of existence' of media from dust? Or, more generally, from failure? Media, as Gabrys argues and as I have done similarly with Hertz (Hertz and Parikka 2012), referring to the underlying 'planned obsolescence' part of our modern media cultural condition, are programmed with destruction and being discarded.

Dust is not the only marker of such different temporalities. Packed with toxic materials and chemicals, discarded, obsolescent media are one of the growing problems of the current culture–nature condition. Just as the supposedly 'immaterial' digital technologies (for instance server farms) are actually embedded in massive networks of energy consumption (Cubitt, Hassan and Volkmer 2011), abandoned old media are a huge problem from another environmental point of view. Gabrys' perspective on a 'museum of failure' and archives of obsolescence addresses the politics of media archaeology – perhaps something not so explicitly present before (as flagged by Druckrey), but which should clearly be part of the new temporal agendas. The temporality of dust is then parallel with a focus on temporality of nature that surpasses that of human use value and becomes a time of the soil, which registers the 'material residues' (Gabrys 2011: 6) of our electronics.

Failure has been at the core of media archaeology, which has been keen to question the newness of new media by looking at alternative histories, forgotten paths and sidekicks of media history. This kind of research and artistic practice emerged in the early days of digital culture hype during the 1990s. Now, failure needs to be recognized as part of wider networks, which ideally can also be part of the media-archaeological agenda. Gabrys (2011: 164n41) herself does not explicitly affiliate with media archaeology, even if to me the connection is clear if we think it in the way I outline above. To quote Gabrys (2011: 106): 'Failure presents the fossils of forgotten dreams, the residue of collapsed utopias, and the program of obsolescence. Through the outmoded, it is possible to move beyond the more "totalizing" aspects of technology, such as progress teleological reasoning, or the heroism of invention.' Instead, we can start to focus on 'minor' practices such as reusing, remixing, rethinking our relations with old media (see Hertz and Parikka 2012).

As such, media archaeology has potential as an innovative 21st-century arts and humanities discipline that investigates non-human temporalities and does not succumb to individualizing stories of heroes, but wants to address those material and cultural contexts and forces that are beyond our control – but might suffer from our effects. The environment is clearly one example. As a nomadic enterprise, a travelling discipline that moves across disciplinary boundaries in order to understand complexities of matter and time, the media-archaeological agenda includes much more than the past and the present – it points to the archives of the future.

Notes

1 Introduction: Cartographies of the Old and the New

1 The Steam Punk Magazine: www.steampunkmagazine.com/.
2 See, in general, Mark Ward, 'Steampunks gather for Great Exhibition'. *BBC News* 30 March 2010, http://news.bbc.co.uk/1/hi/technology/8593 305.stm. For a very good introduction to steampunk in contemporary culture, see Bowser and Croxall (2010).
3 Philosophers Gilles Deleuze (1925–95) and Félix Guattari (1930–92) referred to such epistemological ideas as 'nomadic, minor science' that is experimental and transversal and set against 'royal science' (Deleuze and Guattari 2004).
4 'Are Record Clubs the New Book Clubs?' *BBC News* 18 January 2011, www.bbc.co.uk/news/magazine-12209143. For the Lost Formats Preservation Society founded in 2000, see www.experimentaljetset.nl/archive/lostformats.html.
5 Strauven (2012) has to an extent similarly mapped media archaeology through three disciplinary 'branches' of: (1) film history/media history; (2) media art; and (3) new media theory; these aspects are partly reflected in this book too and elaborated through the later chapters.
6 We can find a range of media archaeologically tuned writings investigating related themes: science and medicine practices as part of visual culture (Cartwright 1995), mobile media as part of a longer genealogy of urban mobility (Parikka and Suominen 2006), war as the driver for media culture (Kittler 1997a) and, for example, Rachel Maines's (1999) book on 'technologies of the orgasm'.
7 For a more comprehensive introduction to an archaeology of media archaeology, see Huhtamo and Parikka (2011). The introductory mapping in this book is partly based on the original work done for the earlier collaboration with Huhtamo.

8   In relation to media archaeology, interesting experiments that are some-where between archives and concept labs are emerging – for instance, the Humboldt University Media Archaeological Fundus (part of the Media Studies Institute) and Lori Emerson's Archaeological Media Lab in the US. Also in existence are various online projects that engage with media-archaeological themes, including, for instance, www.telenesia. com.

9   The work of the Institute for Algorhythmics in Berlin is emblematic of the art/hacktivist spirit of recent waves of media archaeology: www. algorhythmics.com/. See also http://sonictheory.com/?p=300.

10 See the California-based artist-writer Garnet Hertz's Conceptlab: www. conceptlab.com/.

2   Media Archaeology of the Senses: Audiovisual, Affective, Algorithmic

1   More generally, this can be connected to the concept of remediation as well (Bolter and Grusin 1999), which has a further link to what Alex Galloway (2009: 936) has summarized as an interface and a *layer model* concerning media. In such a perspective that draws on McLuhan, (media) history becomes layered, and consequently spatialized, into a system of relations of exchange, borrowing, reuse.

2   As an example, see Sutherland (1965) for early speculation about haptic and embodied display design in computer graphic environments, also mentioning displays based on smell and taste.

3   A good example is the artistic piece *Early Media Goes to Movies* by Paul DeMarinis (2008). The installation refashions Jean-Luc Godard's 1967 film *Week-End* in various ways: three long-duration shots are rethought and represented as panoramas, stretched time strips reminiscent of the works of Étienne-Jules Marey (1830–1904), and soundtracks are visu-alized as 'optical sound patterns' (DeMarinis 2010: 189). Furthermore, in the installation the remade shots are circulated through panoramic, peep-hole and 3D-stereographic apparatuses. Already the title of the piece hints at the overturning of the linear histories of development from cinema to (multi)media.

4   If the Brighton 1978 conference was a seminal event in terms of being a resource for the emerging New Film History, we can similarly empha-size the importance of a variety of collections of pre-cinematic devices and objects in archives of Werner Nekes, Bill Douglas, Peter Jewel and William and John Barnes; such collections expand not only histories of cinema, but also histories of objects and hardware that constitute key links between media technological arts and engineering (Christie 2007). In addition, several media archaeologists such as Erkki Huhtamo have been active collectors themselves.

5   For a very detailed archaeology of the panorama, see Huhtamo (2012).

6   Huhtamo (2005: 11) points towards the sexual implications of the Mutoscope, and the research by, e.g., Linda Williams into the Mutoscope as an imaginary masturbation machine.

7   For Grusin, the use of affect relates to his parallel readings of Benjamin and Kracauer as commentators of distraction as the key affective mode of early screen technological modernity, and anticipation as the mode in which experience and temporal sensation in network culture work. Whereas Benjamin was talking about crowds, and the sense of distraction in the urban experience and as part of how we relate to the cinematic spectacle, Grusin (2010: 128) argues that now the body is tuned to a different relation to media, with the affective state of *anticipation* characterizing social online media.

8   Interestingly, this of course bears some kind of a relation to the anthropological technics from which we could track some of the early forms of media theory as well, born in the nineteenth century. The pioneering work by Ernst Kapp (1808–96) at the height of the physiological interest in the material human body was articulated in his *Grundlinien einer Philosophie der Technik: Zur Entstehungsgeschichte der Cultur aus neuen Gesichtspunkten*. For Kapp (1877), the relation was the other way round: the internal human capacities provided the models for media technology, with the eye providing the architecture for inventions such as the camera obscura, mechanical steam machines imitating muscle power and distributed systems such as the telegraph network being modelled on the nervous system. This was also a predecessor to McLuhan's important theoretico-archaeological and poetic take on media history.

9   Often media-archaeological writers (see Huhtamo 2007: 72–4; Grau 2007b: 140) have a tendency to emphasize their work as mapping the cultural nature of perception and senses, in contrast to physiology, but I find that this opposition needs to be worked around in other ways – with theoretical frameworks and methods that do not separate the two (with a preference for one or the other) but see the physiological as already completely cultural, and the cultural as being embedded in the physiological. See, for instance, Schmidgen (2002), Crary (1999) and Kittler (1999).

10   We could see some of these implications in parallel to Elizabeth Wilson's (2004) research on the neurological body: not only reading the body as a surface of signification, but preparing cultural theories so that they can talk about the non-signifying biological body of muscular capacities, internal organs, biophysics and microphysiologies (2004: 8). Work like Wilson's also gives media theory the impetus for questions such as: what is the psychosomatic body for media theory and history, and how could media archaeology carry that into analyses of attraction, sensation and media relations as historically developing themes?

11   Good examples concerning the kinaesthetic relation between movement and early cinema are the 'phantom rides' – 'more than the movies', in the words of Lauren Rabinovitz (2004). They are part of the repertoire of various cinematic forms of moving the body, including, for

example, *The Haverstraw Tunnel* (1897), or then, as Väliaho (2010: 60) argues, Edison Manufacturing Company's *The Storm at Sea* (1900) which activates similar kinds of radical reshiftings of perception in the body in swirl.

12 For a good online resource on nineteenth-century life sciences, with a special focus on German-language research, see the Max Planck Institute research project-related platform, The Virtual Laboratory: http://vlp.mpiwg-berlin.mpg.de/index_html (accessed 23 Nov. 2011).

13 Sean Cubitt, 'The Raster Screen and the Database Economy', a paper presented at Anglia Ruskin University Trust's 'Identity, Security' seminar, 10 September 2009, online at http://barney.inspire.anglia.ac.uk/inspire_j/ds1.html (acessed 23 Nov. 2011). For an apt example from late nineteenth-century image transmission inventions, see the gridification and codification system for image-transmission purposes by L. H. Lowd (Bellet 1896).

14 Just as an exercise, consider the current Amazon Mechanical Turk (https://www.mturk.com) labour crowdsourcing platform in relation to such archaeologies of quantification and distributed labour.

3 Imaginary Media: Mapping Weird Objects

1 See Gebhard Sengmüller's *A Parallel Image Brochure*, available at www.gebseng.com/.

2 Ibid.

3 The nineteenth century can be said to be the period of the invention of the invention (as Kittler 2010: 127 coined it, referring to Thomas A. Edison) as a specific form of institutional practice, and a process of social life, as argued by Gabriel Tarde (1843–1904) in his curious micro-sociology. Tarde (1890) proposed an idea of invention based on imitation and contagion, and hence focused on the social interrelations, even on a micro-level, from which 'invention' as an ontogenetic fact emerges. The invention of invention was tied to a systematization of practices of turning scientific and technological ideas into commercial ends, as with Edison, whose systematization of teamwork and laboratory conditions in relation to innovations in sound, moving image and telecommunications technologies were exemplary of the directions in which the 'laboratorization' of media cultures was going; indeed, from media technology labs *à la Edison* to experimental psychology labs for measuring human perception, and on to clinical labs such as La Salpêtrière, modernity was also the birth of the lab as a special place of observation and creation. This logic of invention was followed by its hyperbolic, imaginary media counterparts, as with, for example, the protagonist Marial Canterel's Locus Solus garden labs for 'various fertile labours' (2008 [1914]: 3) in the novel of the same name by Raymond Roussel (1877–1933) – a place for the most bizarre inventions of imaginary media. In addition,

popular scientific education was on the agenda, demonstrated in such institutions as the New Urania in Berlin, founded at the end of the nineteenth century for distribution of knowledge during what was already then branded as the century of the natural sciences (Bendt 1896). Of course, the systematization of processes of technological imagination in the form of the laboratory and the experiment were paradoxically connected to a new media cultural phenomenon of the quirky scientist – Nikola Tesla (1856–1943) as a prime example enjoying a celebrity status already in the nineteenth century (see Thomas Commerford Martin, 'Nikola Tesla' *Century Magazin* (New York) 47 (February 1894), in Tesla 1961: 6–10).

4   See 'The 19th Century Iphone'. *BBC News* 17 May 2010, http://news. bbc.co.uk/2/hi/technology/8668311.stm.

5   An illustrative example is *Materialisations-Phänomene* (1914) by Baron von Schrenck-Notzing (1862–1929), which outlines – especially through a case study of a medium, Eva C – key themes of the medium of the medium, in its direct relation to media technologies, such as photography, as well as indirect relations to cinema through phenomena such as somnambulism and psycho-physiological disorders analysed by Väliaho (2010) and Crary (1999). 'Mediumship' becomes itself a practice of communication, and as such is presented by Schrenck-Notzing (1923: 12) as a speculative future practice closely related to science and apparatuses of recording and measurement. For a media-archaeological reworking of the Schrenck-Notzing case, and the medium Eva C, see Zoe Beloff's installation *The Ideoplastic Materializations of Eva C* (2004): www.zoebeloff.com/eva.

6   For more information on the project and the book series, as well as the network of institutions and scholars in the 'Variantology/Archaeology of Media' project (Berlin), please see http://variantology.com/.

7   In the play, Moon inhabitants have organized their scientific analysis of the Earth into the Society (a laboratory of sorts) for Earth Research, and work through advanced media technology: 'The technical equipment of the Society for Earth Research is limited to three units, which can be operated more easily than a coffee mill. First, we have a spectrophone, through which everything that happens on earth can be seen and heard; a parlamonium, which can translate tedious human speech into music for moon citizens spoiled by celestial harmony; and an oneiroscope, with which the dreams of the earthlings can be observed. This is important because of the interest in psychoanalysis prevalent on the moon' (Benjamin 1992: 38).

8   Zielinski (2006a: 261–2) points to this geographical distribution in his conclusion and emphasizes the importance of the postcolonial research agenda: 'Stated oversimplistically: both the philosophical and the practical foundations for the construction of modern media worlds stem originally from the Far East, particularly ancient Chinese culture, and from regions adjacent to the Mediterranean, such as Asia Minor, Greece, and Arab countries, including their outposts in southern and southwestern

Europe.' In this way, he is able to demonstrate yet one more key context for media archaeology as a travelling theory and set of methods: how the ideas, and knowledge that constitutes what we have more recently started calling 'media cultures' are ones that have travelled, and often from Arab and Asian countries to Europe and then the US as the birthplace of consumer-focused media industries. A further task in which Zielinski is successful is the heterogenization of the notion of Europe, and hence an implicit dismantling of the too hegemonic term 'eurocentrism'; European media history is itself a heterogeneity, and, for example, Eastern European media cultures offer inspiring insights on a rethinking of Europe. On postcolonial contexts for media archaeology, see Kusahara (2011), Nadarajan (2007); Marks (2010); Zielinski and Fürlus (2010).

9   For an insight into the installation, see www.zoebeloff.com/influencing/. For *Charming Augustine*, see www.zoebeloff.com/pages/augustine.html.

10 See also Beloff's *Shadow Land Or Light From the Other Side* 3D film on the medium Elizabeth D'Espérance (1855–1919) – a study in which Beloff extends her interest in the female bodies of modern media to the wider investigation of the virtual, and the ephemerality of the technical.

11 Sconce (2000: 31); Fahie (1884: 59); Thomas Commerford Martin, 'Tesla's Oscillator and Other Inventions', *Century Magazine* (New York), 49 (April 1895) in Tesla (1961: 27–9). Reading Nollet's (1749) *Recherches sur les causes particulières des phénomènes électriques* gives an insight into the enthusiasm concerning the Leyden jar at that time, and Nollet's continous experiments that had to do with the different material characteristics of bodies – organic and non-organic – in conveying, in communicating with each other, through the medium of electricity. Later, a similar enthusiasm surrounding Tesla's performances in his laboratory at Colorado Springs was reported in both wider public and specialist publications. The Tesla Coil was a spectacular demonstration of the powers of electricity – and the new worlds of different materialism emerging with that worldview, not without implications for how we approach and think about media technology: Samuel Cohen, 'Lightning Made to Order', *The Electrical Experimenter* (New York) 474 (16 November 1916), quoted from Tesla (1961: 93–4).

12 Du Prel's writings were part of his larger worldview that outlined a mystical overview of evolution that continuously developed new transcendental spheres of apperception. He continued to argue that biological development and such phenomena as somnambulism are interlinked, and the latter also had to do with the 'displacement of the threshold of sensibility', and acted as a signal of what he called the 'future biological form' (1899: xxv). Hence, we can see such mysticists as part of the larger redefinition of nature and the invisible world that suddenly had scientific backing through Maxwell and other key scientists, in relation to 'media' phenomena. New media and technologies, echoing in advance what Benjamin wrote of the photographic and cinematic as the scientific–surgeonlike cutting to non-human perceptions and depths, are for

du Prel (1889: 8) something we would now call posthuman: 'as there are parts of nature which remain invisible to us, being out of relation to our sense of sight – for instance, the microscopic world – so are there parts of nature not existing for us, owing to entire absence of relation to our organism'.

4 Media Theory and New Materialism

1   Instead of just part of discourses of artificial intelligence, many of these were more accurately understood as Augmented Intelligence, as Engelbart underlined. The focus was on a new ecosystem of sorts, in which humans and machines were synchronized through various equipments and input/output procedures. Pias (2002: 92–8) sees this culture of interface development as pedagogical fine-tuning of humans and the non-human algorithmic world. Engelbart's team was interested in gestural integration of computers and perception systems (new forms of computer displays) as well as cognitive handling and use of such systems, for example files. See Engelbart and English (1968). Also easily found on the web is the famous 1968 tele-presentation by Douglas Engelbart from the San Francisco Computer Conference, where he introduces key elements for future computing interaction, including the mouse and shared collaborative online work platforms. See, for example, www. dougengelbart.org (accessed 26 Nov. 2011). Bardini (2000) offers a good elaboration of Engelbart's work and the early development of a variety of sensory-motor interface systems for computer interaction beyond that of the hand: the knee, the back and the head were considered in various experiments (102, 112–14). See also Chun's (2011b) reading of Engelbart and HCI (human–computer interaction) in relation to neoliberalism.

2   As Eva Horn (2008: 7–8) notes, German media theory has established a lot of its agenda through a critique of a fixed definition of media – an extension of mediatic processes to such practices/materials as: 'Doors and mirrors, computers and gramophones, electricity and newspapers, television and telescopes, archives and automobiles, water and air, information and noise, numbers and calendars, images, writing, and voice' (2008: 7–8). For example, Siegert treats even such objects as mailboxes as media, or part of the media system, which both have an effect on the topology of a neighbourhood and, at the same time, turn spatially restricted openings of the mail slot into interfaces to an information network (Siegert 1999: 111–12). See Siegert (2008) for the idea of the media archaeology of the 1980s as Nietzschean 'gay science'.

3   Critiques of Kittler as a techno-determinist might be justified but are too often simplistically stated. Kittler is not that easily affiliated with McLuhan's theories – there might actually be much more 'social' in some of Kittler's ideas, and as Winthrop-Young (2011: 121) notes, 'To

label someone a technodeterminist is a bit like saying that he enjoys strangling cute puppies: the depraved wickedness of the action renders further discussion unnecessary.' Whereas there has been an emphasis on the media-determinist aspects of German theorists, for instance the notion of 'cultural technique' – as important to many theorists – has been neglected. See Siegert (2008).

5   Mapping Noise and Accidents

1   This is why Sigmund Freud himself was fond of archaeological metaphors, but also why Freud in his own way, as a contemporary of Benjamin, is another predecessor of media archaeology, as Thomas Elsaesser (2011) argues.

2   Another good example is the recent call for 'evil media studies' by Matthew Fuller and Andrew Goffey: a call to focus on deception, manipulation and trickery and to 'draw attention to a range and style of practices that are badly understood when explicitly or implicitly measured against the yardstick of autonomous rationality and the ideal of knowledge' (Fuller and Goffey 2009: 142).

3   In terms of aesthetics, it is possible to track back such ideas at least to Hermann von Helmholtz's influential studies and writings in the middle of the nineteenth century. Helmholtz played a crucial role in turning aesthetics from conscious meaning and judgment to nerves and affecting the body (see Hagen 2008: 93–5).

4   Walter H. Schottky (1886–1976) thematized the existence of shot noise and thermal noise in vacuum tubes, and soon his paper 'Über spontane Stromschwankungen in verschiedene elektrizitätsleitern' (1918) was exerting a strong influence on the research agenda.

5   See Cohen (2005) for a general introduction to the theme. Michel Serres's (2007) philosophical view on communication as parasitical by definition rests on such an understanding of physics. A communication relation from A to B can emerge only if it 'agrees' on a third excluded, the mediator of media. This is the parasite, the noise.

6   Expressions about secure communications like the one below from Daniel Schwenter (1585–1636) from the early 1600s are emblematic of the continuous desire for secured information channels – whether writing or signal-processing. This relates to the magnet-based sympathetic needle telegraphy perceived superior in terms of its security: 'Oh, I wish this mode of writing may become in use, a letter would travel safer and quicker, fearing no plots of robbers and retarding rivers' (Fahie 1884: 11).

7   France especially was occupied with the new paradigm of code writing, *cryptography*, after its defeat in the 1870 war with Prussia. The urge to find new patterns of computed communication methodology spurred novel inventions that were also automatized into special cipher devices

(Kahn 1967: 230–65). An apt example is the 'superphone' from 1922, which was to make possible uninterruptable communications for military use. See '"Superphone" to Assure Secrecy in Talking', *New York Times*, 25 January 1922. World War II saw cipher devices as key devices of communication – exemplary were the German Enigma machines for encrypting, and the decrypting machines of interception at Bletchley Park codebreaking centre (where Alan Turing worked as well). See Gere (2002: 40–3).

8   A good example of this issue is seen in Henry James's (1974 [1898]) short story about a young female telegraph operator who has access to the coded messages passing through the ether.

9   Of course, a lot of the attention went to natural phenomena that threatened communications. Despite the new ephemerality now surrounding communication, end devices and wires were the special focus of attention – their protection was imperative. This meant from not only people, criminals, but such things as storms and other dangers of nature, illuminating the fact that this ephemerality was cabled, wired and an increasing part of the lived environment. See, e.g., 'Protection of Telegraph Wires', *New York Times*, 30 August 1893.

6   Archive Dynamics: Software Culture and Digital Heritage

1   An edited (by Jussi Parikka) collection of Wolfgang Ernst writings is forthcoming from University of Minnesota Press in 2012, tentatively titled: 'Archives, Media and Diagrammatics of Cultural Memory'.

2   A warm thank you to Dr Robin Boast for discussions of and insights into modern archival and museum theory and debates, from the Dutch school to figures such as Jenkinson, Schellenberg and Bearman.

3   There is, however, a deeper issue in these questions. A big thank you to Dr Boast (private conversation) who points out that the relation of software and hardware goes deeper. Software is, of course, transportable as practices of emulation evidence. This does not lessen the question about software's materiality in any way. Furthermore, the idea that software would stay the same as long as the platform/hardware is the same is also mistaken. Every execution of software is a differentiation in the sense that software performs differently, even if the hardware is the same, as hardware is constantly reconfigured, and processing itself is dynamic. The temporality and execution of software is actually an internal condition for its operationality, and, as such, demonstrates the fragility of it as a cultural form. For an elaborate discussion of such themes, including why every computer process of reading is also rewriting, see Chun (2011b).

4   Gustav Deutsch's archivological film art-piece *Film ist* is a good example of this interest in old, almost disappeared and decaying film material found in various archives, and leaving the deteriorated materiality of the

film footage as part of his work is one way of demonstrating the duration involved in technical media. (On the complexity of archival temporality and cinematic materiality, see Doane 2002.)

5 The constantly slightly changing, fluctuating, disappearing nature of digital culture is addressed in the 'Onion News Network' joke (www.theonion.com/, accessed 8 July 2011) about an Internet archaeologist discovering the long-lost Friendster community (2002–) whose sudden disappearance from a population of 50 million users is tracked down only by online traces found through the 'media archaeologist's' browser. Or consider the media art-performance-type work of media remediation by 'archaeologists of the World Wide Web' (Cook 2007: 121) Jon Thomson and Alison Craighead (www.dot-store.com, accessed 26 Nov. 2011), which turned old web pages into vintage products further resold – a curious innovative twist to the archiving and remediating of 'Internet archaeology' through the consumer-oriented market discourse of online commercial space. Such projects of display bring to mind more closely the idea of the Internet as a curiosity cabinet of different rationality from the teleologically ordering Victorian museum, the aesthetics of curiosity in which borders of knowledge regimes are continuously mixed and blurring – collections of ephemera in constant movement and being organized through the algorhythmics of search (engines) rather than only through spatial storage (Henning 2007: 74, referring to Ernst).

6 This is well summarized by Gunther Reisinger, who directed a German research project on early net art (www.netpioneers.info, accessed 26 Nov. 2011) and flagged how, from mere art-historical and analytical debates concerning art on the net/net.art, we can move to more generally applicable points and practices of memory in the digital age: 'a more general elucidation of the situation of the media-art genre of Net art as a media-specific testing ground for the redevelopment and application of methods of restoring, archiving and re-presenting that are faithful to works and sources' (Reisinger 2009: 125). See also another pioneering project of curation and preservation, the Variable Media Network (www.variablemedia.net/, accessed 26 Nov. 2011) interested in art in ephemeral media. See also, as part of the emergence of repositories outside traditional institutions, Runme.org (http://runme.org/, accessed 26 Nov. 2011) as an open online database for software art.

7 A definition of 'born digital' from The Digital Preservation Coalition website (http://dpconline.org, accessed 26 Nov. 2011) is: 'Digital materials which are not intended to have an analogue equivalent, either as the originating source or as a result of conversion to analogue form. This term has been used in the handbook to differentiate them from 1) digital materials which have been created as a result of converting analogue originals; and 2) digital materials, which may have originated from a digital source but have been printed to paper, e.g. some electronic records.'

8 In addition to arts contexts, the question of archiving and excavating digital material is one that is crucial for post-World War II scientific

cultures, and hence histories of science and technology. For these cultures of innovation, where for the first time scientific research was inherently articulated through computational media, the materials left for 'future archaeologists' present practical problems. As flagged by Tim Lenoir (2007), such 'information archaeologies' point towards how a mapping of science is a mapping of the software and hardware platforms instrumental to the research. Of course, the development of so many aesthetic innovations in terms of HCI and screen technologies also rose from similar science-tech labs too.

9   As Kirschenbaum, Ovenden and Redwine (2010: 40) explain the term: 'The remarkable staying power of data stored in digital form is a function of the physical property of magnetic media known as *hysteresis*, or its capacity to retain a charge over time. Magnetic storage media have been the mainstay of the computer industry from early experiments with magnetic drums and ringlets in the 1940s, to magnetic tape, to the introduction of floppy disks and the current ubiquity of hard drives. Most storage media that an archivist is likely to encounter will be magnetic, though optical devices such as CD-ROMs and solid-state (flash) memory will also be present as part of collections.'

7   Media Archaeology: Creative Methodologies for Remediation

1   For an interview with Aleksander Kolkowski, see 'Sonic Alchemy' at www.jussiparikka.net/ (11 April 2011).

2   Also, Morten Riis's (http://mortenriis.dk/) Steam Engine Music performances, positioned directly in media archaeology, mobilize steampunk allusions.

3   ASCII is short for American Standard Code for Information Interchange and it was released in 1963 (with major revisions later) as a form of text encoding: it provides the information for how to encode digital binaries into text characters (as well as control characters).

4   Referring to Dieter Daniels, Arns talks about the 'unredeemed (technical) utopias of ... the historical avantgarde' (2008: 473) that are activated now as imagining futures of media cultures. Arnst insists that this differs from nostalgia in that it refers to pasts that never came to be and, as such, still act as dynamic potentials, forces of the new.

5   Thank you to Garnet Hertz for bringing this work to my attention. Zoe Beloff also talks of time-machines. In an interview I conducted in Spring 2011 (Beloff 2011), she referred to 'the nineteenth-century idea that machines of mechanical reproduction are really 'time-machines': cinema, a time-machine of movement, frame by frame awakening forgotten fantasies; stereo photography bringing about the artificial reconstruction of space and the phonograph resurrecting the voices of the dead'. However, the early use of the term 'time travel' to refer to media-archaeological art comes from Huhtamo (1995). His text

'Time-Travelling in the Gallery: An Archaeological Approach in Media Art' and other texts from that period used the idea extensively.

6　The full quote from Serres goes as follows: 'What things are contemporary? Consider a late-model car. It is a disparate aggregate of scientific and technical solutions dating from different periods. One can date it component by component: this part was invented at the turn of the century, another, ten years ago, and Carnot's cycle is almost two hundred years old. Not to mention that the wheel dates back to neolithic times. The ensemble is contemporary by assemblage, by its design, its finish, sometimes only by the slickness of the advertising surrounding it' (Serres and Latour 1995: 45).

7　See Geert Lovink's posting on the Net.time mailing list 15 December 1998, 'Net.times, not swatch time' (www.nettime.org, accessed 28 Nov. 2011).

8　Media theorists such as Sean Cubitt have increasingly tackled this dilemma. See, for instance, Sean Cubitt interviewed by Simon Mills, *Framed*, online at www.framejournal.net/interview/10/sean-cubitt (accessed 28 Nov. 2011).

9　For an early example of the discussions on computer art and the science–art collaboration, see Reichardt (1971). Reichardt was then affiliated to one of the most important UK institutions for these crossovers, the Institute of Contemporary Arts (ICA), and also the curator of 'Cybernetic Serendipity', the ground-breaking exhibition at ICA in 1968. For wider analytical discussions of art–science–technology histories, see Grau (2007a).

10　Such methodology was performed live on the Berlin Reboot radio station (14 Aug. 2011).

11　The historical reference point for the Sonic Archaeology project is the 1970s US National Security Agency paper 'TEMPEST: A Signal Problem', published in their *Cryptologic Spectrum* journal. It presented the problem of signal processing and its encryptability in the age of electronic communication from the point of view of national security, which taps into the Kittler-inspired interest in the military origins of media agendas and solutions, but also concretely into how any part of an electrical communication system emits through its switches, contacts, relays and other hardware components radio frequencies or acoustic energy (www.sonicarcheology.net/, accessed 28 Nov. 2011); approved for release by NSA on 27 Sept. 2007, FOIA Case#51633, 'TEMPEST: A Signal Problem. The Story of the discovery of various compromising radiation from communications and Comsec equipment', online at www.nsa.gov/public_info/_files/cryptologic_spectrum/tempest.pdf (accessed 28 Nov. 2011).

12　For a basic technical characterization, see the Wikipedia page for PAL: http://en.wikipedia.org/wiki/PAL (accessed 28 Nov. 2011).

13　For an introduction to her performance as part of Transmediale 2011 in Berlin, see www.transmediale.de/content/collapse-pal-rosa-menkman (accessed 28 Nov. 2011).

14   For a short project description, see *Neural*, www.neural.it/art/2008/11/
     tantalum_memorial_honoring_tho.phtml. The project was awarded the
     2009 Transmediale Award.
15   The Media-archaeological Fundus collections (Berlin Humboldt
     University Institute for Media Studies) include good Cold War-era
     examples of various toys and educational computers and circuit training
     devices.
16   Kolkowski interview 'Sonic Alchemy': http://jussiparikka.net, 11 April
     2011.

Bibliography

Abel, Richard & Altman, Rick, eds. (2001) *The Sounds of Early Cinema* (Bloomington: Indiana University Press).

Adams, Henry (1918/2000) *The Education of Henry Adams*, Project Gutenberg, www.gutenberg.org/ebooks/2044, accessed 27 Nov. 2011 (originally published by the Massachusetts Historical Society).

Alberts, Gerard (2010) 'Die Körperlichkeit des Rechnens oder Warum die Rechenautomaten Lautsprecher hatten'. Presentation, Humboldt University, Berlin, 8 Dec. 2010.

Alt, Casey (2011) 'How Object-Orientation Made Computers a Medium' in *Media Archaeology. Approaches, Applications, Implications*, ed. Erkki Huhtamo and Jussi Parikka (Berkeley, CA: University of California Press), 278–301.

Andriopoulos, Stefan (2002) 'Okkulte und technische Television' in *1929. Beiträge zue Archäologie der Medien*, ed. Stefan Andriopoulus and Bernhard J. Dotzler (Frankfurt am Main: Suhrkamp), 31–53.

Andriopoulos, Stefan (2005) 'Psychic Television' *Critical Inquiry* 31(3) (Spring), 618–37.

Armitage, John (2006) 'From Discourse Networks to Cultural Mathematics. An Interview with Friedrich A. Kittler' *Theory, Culture & Society* 23(7–8), 17–38.

Arns, Inke (2008) 'The Realization of Radio's Unrealized Potential. Media-Archaeological Focuses in Current Artistic Projects' in *Reinventing Radio. Aspects of Radio as Art*, ed. Heidi Grundmann, Elisabeth Zimmermann, Reinhard Braun, Dieter Daniels, Andreas Hirsch and Anne Thurmann-Jajes (Frankfurt am Main: Revolver), 471–92.

Bak, Arad and Sterling, Bruce (1999) 'Dead Media Project. An Interview with Bruce Sterling' *Ctheory* (16 March), www.ctheory.net.

Bal, Mieke (2002) *Travelling Concepts in the Humanities* (Toronto: Toronto University Press).

Bardini, Thierry (2000) *Bootstrapping: Douglas Engelbart, Co-Evolution, and the Origins of Personal Computing* (Stanford: Stanford University Press).

Bearman, David (2007) 'Addressing Selection and Digital Preservation as Systemic Problems' in *Preserving the Digital Heritage: Principles and Policies*, ed. Yola de Lusenet and Vincent Wintermans (Amsterdam: Netherlands National Commission for Unesco), 26–44.

Bellet, Daniel (1896) 'La télégraphie des dessins' *La Nature* 24(1), 26–7.

Beloff, Zoe (2002) 'An Ersatz of Life: The Dream Life of Technology' in *New Screen Media. Cinema/Art/Narrative*, ed. Martien Rieser and Andrea Zapp (London: BFI), 287–96.

Beloff, Zoe (2006) 'Towards Spectral Cinema' in *Book of Imaginary Media. Excavating the Dream of the Ultimate Communication Medium*, ed. Eric Kluitenberg (Amsterdam and Rotterdam: Debalie and NAi Publishers), 125–239.

Beloff, Zoe (2011) '"With Each Project I Find Myself Reimagining What Cinema Might Be"', an interview by Jussi Parikka, *Electronic Book Review* (November), www.electronicbookreview.com/thread/imagenarrative/numerous (accessed 28 Nov. 2011).

Bendt, Franz (1896) 'Die neue Berliner "Urania"' *Gartenlaube*. 38, 632–7.

Benjamin, Walter (1977) *Gesammelte Schriften*, ed. Rolf Tiedemann, Vol. I.1 (Frankfurt: Suhrkamp).

Benjamin, Walter (1992) 'Lichtenberg: A Cross Section', trans. Gerhard Schulte *Performing Arts Journal* 14(3), 37–56.

Benjamin, Walter (2008) *The Work of Art in the Age of Its Technological Reproducibility and Other Writings on Media*, ed. Michael W. Jennings, Brigid Doherty and Thomas Y. Levin (Cambridge, MA: The Belknap Press of Harvard University Press).

Bennett, Jane (2010) *Vibrant Matter. A Political Ecology of Things* (Durham: Duke University Press).

Blegvad, Peter (2006) 'On Imaginary Media' in *Book of Imaginary Media. Excavating the Dream of the Ultimate Communication Medium* on the attached DVD of Imaginary Media (Amsterdam and Rotterdam: Debalie and NAi Publishers).

Boast, Robin (2011) An interview by Jussi Parikka 11 Jan. 2011, in Cambridge. Online as part of the *Creative Technology Review* podcasts episode 11, http://createtalk.libsyn.com/, accessed 27 Nov. 2011.

Bolter, Jay David and Grusin, Richard (1999) *Remediation. Understanding New Media* (Cambridge, MA: The MIT Press).

Bosma, Josephine (2011) *Nettitudes. Let's Talk Net Art* (Rotterdam: NAi Publishers).

Bowser, Rachel A. and Croxall, Brian (2010) 'Introduction: Industrial Evolution' Steampunk special issue of *Neo-Victorian Studies* 3(1), http://neovictorianstudies.com/, accessed 8 Sept. 2011.

Braidotti, Rosi (2002) *Metamorphoses. Towards a Materialist Theory of Becoming* (Cambridge: Polity).

Braudel, Fernand (1980) *On History*, trans. Sarah Matthews (London: Weidenfeld and Nicolson).

Bredekamp, Horst (2003) 'A Neglected Tradition? Art History as Bildwissenschaft' *Critical Inquiry* 29 (Spring), 418–28.

Brewster, Sir David (1858) *The Kaleidoscope. Its History, Theory and Construction, with Its Application to the Fine and Useful Arts* (London: John Murray).

Brown, Bill (2010) 'Materiality' in *Critical Terms for Media Studies*, ed. W. J. T. Mitchell and Mark B. N. Hansen (Chicago and London: University of Chicago Press), 49–63.

Bukatman, Scott (1998) 'The Ultimate Trip: Special Effects and Kaleidoscopic Perception' *Iris* 25, 75–97.

Burke, Peter (2004) *What Is Cultural History?* (Cambridge: Polity).

Bush, Vannevar (2006) 'Memex Revisited' in *New Media, Old Media. A History and Theory Reader*, ed. Wendy Hui Kyong Chun and Thomas Keenan (New York: Routledge), 85–95.

Cameron, Fiona and Kenderdine, Sarah, eds. (2007) *Theorizing Digital Culture Heritage. A Critical Discourse* (Cambridge, MA: The MIT Press).

Campanelli, Vito (2010) *Web Aesthetics. How Digital Media Affect Culture and Society* (Rotterdam: NAi Publishers / Institute of Network Cultures).

Cartwright, Lisa (1995) *Screening the Body: Tracing Medicine's Visual Culture* (Minneapolis: University of Minnesota Press).

Ceram, C. W. (1965) *Archaeology of the Cinema* (London: Thames and Hudson).

Christie, Ian (2007) '"Toys, Instruments, Machines". Why the Hardware Matters' in *Multimedia Histories. From the Magic Lantern to the Internet*, ed. James Lyons and John Plunkett (Exeter: University of Exeter Press), 3–17.

Chun, Wendy Hui Kyong (2004) 'On Software, or the Persistence of Visual Knowledge' *Grey Room* 18 (Winter), 26–51.

Chun, Wendy Hui Kyong (2006a) *Control and Freedom. Power and Paranoia in the Age of Fiber Optics* (Cambridge, MA: The MIT Press).

Chun, Wendy Hui Kyong (2011a) 'The Enduring Ephemeral or The Future Is a Memory' in *Media Archaeology. Approaches, Applications, Implications*, ed. Erkki Huhtamo and Jussi Parikka (Berkeley, CA: University of California Press), 184–203.

Chun, Wendy Hui Kyong (2011b) *Programmed Visions. Software and Memory* (Cambridge, MA: The MIT Press).

Chun, Wendy Hui Kyong and Keenan, Thomas, eds. (2006) *New Media, Old Media. A History and Theory Reader* (New York and London: Routledge).

Cohen, Leon (2005) 'The History of Noise on the 100th Anniversary of Its Birth' *IEEE Signal Processing Magazine* (November), 33–5.

Cook, Sarah (2007) 'Online Activity and Offline Community: Cultural Institutions and New Media Art' in *Theorizing Digital Culture Heritage. A Critical Discourse*, ed. Fiona Cameron and Sarah Kenderdine (Cambridge, MA: The MIT Press), 113–30.

Cramer, Florian (2010) 'A Kind Rewind, The Rebirth of Cassette Tape Music' *Neural* 35, 17–19.

Crary, Jonathan (1990) *Techniques of the Observer. On Vision and Modernity in the Nineteenth Century* (Cambridge, MA: The MIT Press).

Crary, Jonathan (1999) *Suspensions of Perception. Attention, Spectacle, and Modern Culture* (Cambridge, MA: The MIT Press).

Crookes, William (1892) 'Some Possibilities of Electricity' *Fortnightly Review* 51 (February), 173–81.

Cubitt, Sean (2004) *The Cinema Effect* (Cambridge, MA: The MIT Press).

Cubitt, Sean (2010) 'Making Space' *Senses of Cinema* 57, www.sensesofcinema.com, accessed 27 Nov. 2011.

Cubitt, Sean, Hassan, Robert and Volkmer, Ingrid (2011) 'Does Cloud Computing Have a Silver Lining?' *Media, Culture & Society* 33(1), 149–58.

Daniels, Dieter (2002) *Kunst als Sendung. Von der Telegraphie zum Internet* (Munich: C. H. Beck).

DeLanda, Manuel (2000) *A Thousand Years of Non-Linear History* (New York: Zone).

Deleuze, Gilles (2006) *Foucault*, trans. Seán Hand (London: Continuum).

Deleuze, Gilles and Guattari, Félix (2004) *A Thousand Plateaus*, trans. Brian Massumi (London: Continuum).

DeMarinis, Paul (2010) *Buried in Noise*, ed. Ingrid Beirer, Sabine Himmelsbach and Carsten Seiffarth (Heidelberg and Berlin: Kehrer).

DeMarinis, Paul (2011) 'Erased Dots and Rotten Dashes, or How to Wire Your Head for a Preservation' in *Media Archaeology. Approaches, Applications, Implications*, ed. Erkki Huhtamo and Jussi Parikka (Berkeley, CA: University of California Press), 211–38.

Derrida, Jacques (1996) *Archive Fever. A Freudian Impression*, trans. Eric Prenowitz (Chicago: University of Chicago Press).

Didi-Huberman, Georges and Ebeling, Knut (2007) *Das Archiv brennt* (Berlin: Kadmos).

Doane, Mary Ann (2002) *The Emergence of Cinematic Time. Modernity, Contingency, The Archive* (Cambridge, MA: Harvard University Press).

Dolar, Mladen (2006) *A Voice and Nothing More* (Cambridge, MA: The MIT Press).

Douglas, Susan J. (1989) *Inventing American Broadcasting, 1899–1922* (Baltimore, MD: Johns Hopkins University Press).

Druckrey, Timothy (2006) Foreword in Siegfried Zielinski, *Deep Time of the Media* (Cambridge, MA: The MIT Press), vii–xi.

Dulac, Nicolas and Gaudreault, André (2006) 'Circularity and Repetition at the Heart of the Attraction: Optical Toys and the Emergence of New Cultural Series' in *The Cinema of Attractions Reloaded*, ed. Wanda Strauven (Amsterdam: Amsterdam University Press), 227–44.

Elsaesser, Thomas (2004) 'The New Film History as Media Archaeology' *CINéMAS*, 14(2–3), 71–117.

Elsaesser, Thomas (2006) 'Early Film History and Multi-Media: An Archaeology of Possible Futures?' in *New Media, Old Media. A History and Theory Reader*, ed. Wendy Hui Kyong Chun and Thomas Keenan (New York: Routledge), 13–25.

Elsaesser, Thomas (2008) 'Afterword: Digital Cinema and the Apparatus: Archaeologies, Epistemologies, Ontologies' in *Cinema and Technology.*

Cultures, Theories, Practices, ed. Bruce Bennett, Marc Furstenau and Adrian Mackenzie (Basingstoke: Palgrave Macmillan), 226–40.

Elsaesser, Thomas (2011) 'Freud and the Technical Media. The Enduring Magic of the *Wunderblock*' in *Media Archaeology. Approaches, Applications, Implications*, ed. Erkki Huhtamo and Jussi Parikka (Berkeley, CA: University of California Press), 95–115.

Elsaesser, Thomas and Hagener, Malte (2010) *Film Theory. An Introduction Through the Senses* (New York and London: Routledge).

Engelbart, Douglas C. and English, William K. (1968) 'A Research Center for Augmenting Human Intellect', *AFIPS '68 (Fall, Part I): Proceedings of the December 9–11, 1968, Fall Joint Computer Conference, Part I*, 395–410.

Enns, Anthony (2008) 'Psychic Radio: Sound Technologies, Ether Bodies and Spiritual Vibrations' *The Senses and Society* 3(2) (July), 137–52.

Ernst, Wolfgang (2000) *M.edium F.oucault. Weimarer Vorlesungen Über Archive, Archäologie, Monumente und Medien* (Weimar: VDG).

Ernst, Wolfgang (2002) 'Between Real Time and Memory on Demand: Reflections on/of Television' *South Atlantic Quarterly* 101(3) (Summer), 625–37.

Ernst, Wolfgang (2003) 'Telling versus Counting? A Media Archaelogical Point of View' *Intermédialités* 2 (Autumn), 31–44.

Ernst, Wolfgang (2005) 'Let There Be Irony: Cultural History and Media Archaeology in Parallel Lines' *Art History* 28(5) (November), 582–603.

Ernst, Wolfgang (2006) 'Dis/continuities: Does the Archive Become Metaphorical in Multi-Media Space?' in *New Media, Old Media. A History and Theory Reader*, ed. Wendy Hui Kyong Chun and Thomas Keenan (New York and London: Routledge), 105–23.

Ernst, Wolfgang (2008) 'Distory. 100 Years of Electron Tubes, Media-Archaeologically Interpreted vis-á-vis 100 Years of Radio' in *Re-inventing Radio. Aspects of Radio as Art*, ed. Heidi Grundmann, Elisabeth Zimmermann, Reinhard Braun, Dieter Daniels, Andreas Hirsch and Anne Thurmann-Jajes (Frankfurt am Main: Revolver), 415–30.

Ernst, Wolfgang (2009a) 'Die Frage nach dem Zeitkritischen' in *Zeitkritische Medien*, ed. Axel Volmar (Berlin: Kadmos), 27–42.

Ernst, Wolfgang (2009b) 'Underway to the Dual System: Classical Archives and/or Digital Memory' in *Netpioneers 1.0*, ed. Dieter Daniels and Gunther Reisinger (Berlin: Sternberg Press), 81–99.

Ernst, Wolfgang (2010) 'Cultural Archive versus Technomathematical Storage' in *The Archive in Motion*, ed. Eivind Røssaak (Oslo: Novus Press), 53–73.

Ernst, Wolfgang (2011) 'Media Archaeography: Method and Machine versus History and Narrative of Media' in *Media Archaeology. Approaches, Applications, Implications*, ed. Erkki Huhtamo and Jussi Parikka (Berkeley, CA: University of California Press), 239–55.

Fahie, John Joseph (1884) *A History of Electric Telegraphy, to the Year 1837* (London: E. & F. N. Spon).

Fahie, John Joseph (1899) *A History of Wireless Telegraphy, 1838–1899: Including Some Bare-Wire Proposals for Subaqueous Telegraphs* (Edinburgh and London: William Blackwood and Sons).

Flichy, Patrice (1997) *Une histoire de la communication moderne: éspace public et vie privée* (Paris: La Découverte).

Foucault, Michel (1995) *Discipline and Punish. The Birth of the Prison*, trans. Alan Sheridan (New York: Vintage Books).

Foucault, Michel (1998) 'Nietzsche, Genealogy, History' in *Aesthetics. Essential Works of Foucault 1954*–1984, Vol. II, ed. James D. Faubion (London: Penguin).

Foucault, Michel (2002) *The Archaeology of Knowledge* (London and New York: Routledge).

Franklin, Seb (2009) 'On Game Art, Circuit Bending and Speedrunning as Counter-Practice: "Hard" and "Soft" Nonexistence' *Ctheory* (6 Feb.), www.ctheory.net/.

Friedberg, Anne (1993) *Window Shopping. Cinema and the Postmodern* (Berkeley, CA: University of California Press).

Friedberg, Anne (2006) *The Virtual Window. From Alberti to Microsoft* (Cambridge, MA: The MIT Press).

Fuller, Matthew (2005) *Media Ecologies. Materialist Energies in Art and Technoculture* (Cambridge, MA: The MIT Press).

Fuller, Matthew and Goffey, Andrew (2009) 'Evil Media Studies' in *The Spam Book: On Porn, Viruses and Other Anomalous Objects from the Dark Side of Digital Culture*, ed. Jussi Parikka and Tony Sampson (Cresskill: Hampton Press), 141–59.

Gabrys, Jennifer (2011) *Digital Rubbish. A Natural History of Electronics* (Ann Arbor: University of Michigan Press).

Galloway, Alexander R. (2004) *Protocol. How Control Exists After Decentralization* (Cambridge, MA: The MIT Press).

Galloway, Alexander R. (2009) 'The Unworkable Interface' *New Literary History* 39, 931–51.

Galloway, Alexander R. and Thacker, Eugene (2007) *The Exploit: A Theory of Networks* (Minneapolis: University of Minnesota Press).

Gane, Nicholas (2005) 'Radical Post-humanism: Friedrich Kittler and the Primacy of Technology' *Theory, Culture & Society* 22(3), 25–41.

Gane, Nicholas and Beer, David (2008) *New Media: The Key Concepts* (Oxford: Berg).

Gaudreault, André (2006) 'From "Primitive Cinema" to "Kine-Attractography"' in *The Cinema of Attractions Reloaded*, ed. Wanda Strauven (Amsterdam: Amsterdam University Press), 85–104.

Gere, Charlie (2002) *Digital Culture* (London: Reaktion).

Gitelman, Lisa (2006) *Always Already New. Media, History, and the Data of Culture* (Cambridge, MA: The MIT Press).

Gitelman, Lisa and Pingree, Geoffrey B., eds. (2003) *New Media, 1740–1915* (Cambridge, MA: The MIT Press).

Grau, Oliver (2003) *Virtual Art. From Illusion to Immersion*, trans. Gloria Custance (Cambridge, MA: The MIT Press).

Grau, Oliver, ed. (2007a) *MediaArtHistories* (Cambridge, MA: The MIT Press).

Grau, Oliver (2007b) 'Remember the Phantasmagoria! Illusion Politics of the Eighteenth Century and its Multimedial Afterlife' in *MediaArtHistories*, ed. Oliver Grau (Cambridge, MA: The MIT Press), 137–61.

Griffin, Matthew, Herrmann, Susanne and Kittler, Friedrich A. (1996) 'Technologies of Writing. Interview with Friedrich A. Kittler' *New Literary History* 27(4) (Autumn), 731–42.

Grusin, Richard (2010) *Premediation* (Basingstoke: Palgrave MacMillan).

Guattari, Félix (2000) *The Three Ecologies*, trans. Ian Pindar and Paul Sutton (London and New Brunswick, NJ: The Athlone Press).

Guins, Raiford (2009) *Edited Clean Version: Technology and the Culture of Control* (Minneapolis: University of Minnesota Press.)

Gunning, Tom (1990) 'The Cinema of Attractions. Early Film, Its Spectator and the Avant-Garde' in *Early Cinema. Space, Frame, Narrative*, ed. Thomas Elsaesser with Adam Barker (London: Bfi Publishing), 56–62.

Gunning, Tom (1995) 'An Aesthetic of Astonishment: Early Film and the (In) Credulous Spectator', in *Viewing Positions. Ways of Seeing Film*, ed. Linda Williams (New Brunswick, NJ: Rutgers University Press), 114–33.

Hagen, Wolfgang (2005) *Das Radio. Zur Geschichte und Theorie des Hörfunks – Deutschland/USA* (Minich: Wilhelm Fink).

Hagen, Wolfgang (2008) 'Busoni's Invention: Phantasmagoria and Errancies in Times of Medial Transition' in *Artists as Inventors, Inventors as Artists*, ed. Dieter Daniels and Barbara U. Schmidt (Ostfildern: Hantje Cantz), 86–107.

Hall, Gary and Birchall, Clare, eds. (2006) *New Cultural Studies. Adventures in Theory* (Edinburgh: Edinburgh University Press).

Hansen, Mark B. N. (2006) *Bodies in Code: Interfaces with Digital Media* (New York: Routledge).

Hartley, R. V. L. (1928) 'Transmission of Information' *Bell Systems Technical Journal* 7 (July), 535–63.

Harwood, Graham (2008) 'Pixel' in *Software Studies. A Lexicon*, ed. Matthew Fuller (Cambridge, MA: The MIT Press), 213–17.

Hayles, N. Katherine (1999) *How We Became Posthuman: Virtual Bodies in Cybernetics, Literature, and Informatics* (Chicago: University of Chicago Press).

Hayles, N. Katherine (2008) 'Traumas of Code' in *Critical Digital Studies. A Reader*, ed. Arthur Kroker and Marilouise Kroker (Toronto: University of Toronto Press), 25–44.

Helmholtz, Hermann von (1867) *Handbuch der physiologischen Optik* (Leipzig: L. Voss).

Henning, Michelle (2006) *Museums, Media and Cultural Theory* (Maidenhead: Open University Press).

Henning, Michelle (2007) 'The Return of Curiosity: The World Wide Web as Curiosity Museum' in *Multimedia Histories. From the Magic Lantern to the Internet*, ed. James Lyons and John Plunkett (Exeter: University of Exeter Press), 72–84.

Hertz, Garnet (2009) 'Methodologies of Reuse in the Media Arts: Exploring Black Boxes, Tactics and Archaeologies'. Ph.D. thesis, Visual Studies, University of California, Irvine.

Hertz, Garnet and Parikka, Jussi (2012, forthcoming) 'Zombie Media: Circuit Bending Media Archaeology into an Art Method' *Leonardo*.

Horn, Eva (2008) 'Editor's Introduction: There Are No Media' *Grey Room* 29 (Winter), 6–13.

Howse, Martin (2008) 'The Aether and Its Double' in *Spectrotopia. Illuminating Investigations in the Electromagnetic Spectrum* (Riga: MPLab and RIXC), 158–63.

Huhtamo, Erkki (1992) 'Ennen Broadcastingia' *Lähikuva* 1.

Huhtamo, Erkki (1995) 'Time-Travelling in the Gallery: An Archaeological Approach in Media Art' in *Immersed in Technology. Art and Virtual Environments*, ed. Mary Anne Moser with Douglas McLeod (Cambridge, MA: The MIT Press, 1996), 232–68.

Huhtamo, Erkki (1997) 'From Kaleidoscomaniac to Cybernerd: Notes Toward an Archaeology of Media' *Leonardo* 30(3), 221–4.

Huhtamo, Erkki (2004) 'Elements of Screenology: Toward an Archaeology of the Screen' *ICONICS: International Studies of the Modern Image* 7, 31–82.

Huhtamo, Erkki (2005) 'Slots of Fun, Slots of Trouble: An Archaeology of Arcade Gaming' in *Handbook of Computer Game Studies*, ed. Joost Raessens and Jeffrey H. Goldstein (Cambridge, MA: The MIT Press), 3–21.

Huhtamo, Erkki (2006) 'The Pleasures of the Peephole: An Archaeological Exploration of Peep Media' in *Book of Imaginary Media*, ed. Eric Kluitenberg (Amsterdam and Rotterdam: Debalie and NAi Publishers), 75–141.

Huhtamo, Erkki (2007) 'Twin-Touch-Test-Redux: Media Archaeological Approach to Art, Interactivity, and Tactility' in *Media Art Histories*, ed. Oliver Grau (Cambridge, MA: The MIT Press), 71–101.

Huhtamo, Erkki (2010) 'Thinkering with Media: On the Art of Paul DeMarinis' in Paul DeMarinis, *Buried in Noise* (Heidelberg and Berlin: Kehrer), 33–9.

Huhtamo, Erkki (2011) 'Dismantling the Fairy Engine: Media Archaeology as Topos Study' in *Media Archaeology. Approaches, Applications, Implications*, ed. Erkki Huhtamo and Jussi Parikka (Berkeley, CA: University of California Press), 27–47.

Huhtamo, Erkki (2012, forthcoming) *Illusions in Motion: Media Archaeology of the Moving Panorama and Related Spectacles* (Cambridge, MA: The MIT Press).

Huhtamo, Erkki and Parikka, Jussi (2011) 'Introduction: An Archaeology of Media Archaeology' in *Media Archaeology. Approaches, Applications, Implications*, ed. Erkki Huhtamo and Jussi Parikka (Berkeley, CA: University of California Press), 1–21.

James, Henry (1974/1898) 'In The Cage,' in *In the Cage and Other Stories* (1898; repr., London: Penguin Books, 1974).

Jameson, Fredric (1989) 'Nostalgia for the Present' *South Atlantic Quarterly* 88(2), 517–37.

Johnston, John (2008) *The Allure of Machinic Life: Cybernetics, Artificial Life, and the New AI* (Cambridge, MA: The MIT Press).

Kahn, David (1967) *The Codebreakers: The Story of Secret Writing* (New York: Macmillan).

Kahn, Douglas (1999) *Noise Water Meat. A History of Sound in the Arts* (Cambridge, MA: The MIT Press).

Kahn, Douglas (2010) 'Some Artworks by Paul DeMarinis' in *Buried in Noise: Paul DeMarinis*, ed. Ingrid Beirer, Carsten Seiffarth and Sabine Himmelsbach (Heidelberg: Kehrer Verlag), 47–57.

Kapp, Ernst (1877) *Grundlinien einer Philosophie der Technik: Zur Entstehungsgeschichte der Cultur aus neuen Gesichtspunkten* (Braunschweig: Druck und verlag von George Westermann).

Kasprzak, Michelle (2005) 'Back to the Future: Ars Electronica at 25' *Mute Magazine*, 9 February, http://www.metamute.org, accessed 27 Nov. 2011.

Kern, Stephen (2003) *The Culture of Time and Space* (Cambridge, MA: Harvard University Press).

Kirschenbaum, Matthew G. (2008) *Mechanisms. New Media and the Forensic Imagination* (Cambridge, MA: The MIT Press).

Kirschenbaum, Matthew G., Ovenden, Richard and Redwine, Gabriela (2010) *Digital Forensics and Born-Digital Content in Cultural Heritage Collections*, Council on Library and Information Resources (CLIR) 149, www.clir.org Washington.

Kittler, Friedrich A. (1990) *Discourse Networks 1800/1900*, trans. Michael Metteer, with Chris Cullens (Stanford, CA: Stanford University Press).

Kittler, Friedrich A. (1995) 'There is No Software' *Ctheory* (18 Oct.), www.ctheory.net.

Kittler, Friedrich A. (1996) 'The History of Communication Media', *Ctheory* (30 July), www.ctheory.net.

Kittler, Friedrich A. (1997) *Literature, Media, Information Systems*, ed. and intro. John Johnston (Amsterdam: G+B Arts).

Kittler, Friedrich A. (1999) *Gramophone, Film, Typewriter*, trans. Geoffrey Winthrop-Young and Michael Wutz (Stanford, CA: Stanford University Press).

Kittler, Friedrich A. (2001) 'Computer Graphics: A Semi-Technical Introduction', trans. Sara Ogger *Grey Room* 2(Winter), 30–45.

Kittler, Friedrich A. (2009) 'Towards an Ontology of Media' *Theory, Culture & Society* 26(2–3), 23–31.

Kittler, Friedrich A. (2010) *Optical Media*, trans. Anthony Enns (Cambridge: Polity).

Klein, Norman (2003) *The Vatican to Vegas. A History of Special Effects* (New York: The New Press).

Kluitenberg, Eric, ed. (2006a) *Book of Imaginary Media. Excavating the Dream of the Ultimate Communication Medium* (Amsterdam and Rotterdam: Debalie and NAi Publishers).

Kluitenberg, Eric (2006b) 'Second Introduction to an Archaeology of Imaginary Media' in *Book of Imaginary Media. Excavating the Dream of the Ultimate Communication Medium* (Amsterdam and Rotterdam: Debalie and NAi Publishers), 7–26.

Kluitenberg, Eric (2011) 'On the Archaeology of Imaginary Media' in *Media Archaeology. Approaches, Applications, Implications*, ed. Erkki Huhtamo and Jussi Parikka (Berkeley, CA: University of California Press), 48–69.

Kusahara, Machiko (2011) 'The "Baby Talkie", Domestic Media and the Japanese Modern' in *Media Archaeology. Approaches, Applications, Implications*, ed. Erkki Huhtamo and Jussi Parikka (Berkeley, CA: University of California Press), 123–47.

Lazzarato, Maurizio (2008) 'Art, Work and Politics in Disciplinary Societies and Societies of Security' *Radical Philosophy* 149 (May/June), 26–32.

Lenoir, Timothy (2007) 'Making Studies in New Media Critical' in *MediaArtHistories*, ed. Oliver Grau (Cambridge, MA: The MIT Press), 355–80.

Levin, Thomas Y. (2003) '"Tones from out of Nowhere": Rudolf Pfenninger and the Archaeology of Synthetic Sound' *Grey Room* 12 (Summer), 32–79.

Lichty, Patrick (2008) 'Reconfiguring Curation: Noninstitutional New Media Curating and the Politics of Cultural Production' in *New Media in the White Cube and Beyond. Curatorial Models for Digital Art*, ed. Christiane Paul (Berkeley: University of California Press), 163–87.

Lightning Flashes and Electric Dashes: A Volume of Choice Telegraphic Literature, Humor, Fun, Wit and Wisdom (1877) (New York: W. J. Johnston).

Lovink, Geert (2003) *My First Recession: Critical Internet Culture in Transition* (Rotterdam: V2_NAi Publishers).

Lovink, Geert (2008) 'Whereabouts of German Media Theory' in *Zero Comments* (New York: Routledge), 83–98.

Lovink, Geert and Ernst, Wolfgang (2003) 'Archive Rumblings. Interview with German Media Theorist Wolfgang Ernst'. Originally posted on Nettime mailing list, online at http://laudanum.net/geert/files/1060043851/, accessed 27 Nov. 2011.

Ludovico, Alessandro (1998) 'Bruce Sterling: The Dead Media Interview' *Neural* (September), www.neural.it/english/brucesterlingdeadmedia.htm, accessed 27 Nov. 2011.

Lyons, James and Plunkett, John, eds. (2007) *Multimedia Histories. From the Magic Lantern to the Internet* (Exeter: University of Exeter Press).

Mackenzie, Adrian (2008) 'Codecs' in *Software Studies. A Lexicon*, ed. Matthew Fuller (Cambridge, MA: The MIT Press), 48–55.

Mackenzie, Adrian (2010) *Wirelessness: Radical Empiricism in Network Cultures* (Cambridge, MA: The MIT Press).

Maines, Rachel P. (1999) *The Technology of Orgasm: 'Hysteria', the Vibrator, and Women's Sexual Satisfaction* (Baltimore, MD: Johns Hopkins University Press).

Mannoni, Laurent (2000) *The Great Art of Light and Shadow. Archaeology of the Cinema*, trans. Richard Crangle (Exeter: University of Exeter Press).

Manovich, Lev (2001) *The Language of New Media* (Cambridge, MA: The MIT Press).

Mareschal, G. (1892) 'Le théatrophone' *La Nature* 20(2), 55–8.

Marks, Laura U. (2010) *Enfoldment and Infinity. An Islamic Genealogy of New Media Art* (Cambridge, MA: The MIT Press).

Marvin, Carolyn (1988) *When Old Technologies Were New. Thinking about Electric Communication in the Late Nineteenth Century* (Oxford: Oxford University Press).

Mason, Catherine (2008) *A Computer in the Art Room. The Origins of British Computer Art 1950–1980* (Shrewsbury: Quiller Press).

Mattelart, Armand (2001) *The Information Society: An Introduction*, trans. Susan G. Taponier and James A. Cohen (Thousand Oaks, CA: Sage).

Merewether, Charles, ed. (2006) *The Archive. Documents of Contemporary Art*. (London and Cambridge, MA: Whitechapel and MIT Press).

Michaud, Philippe-Alain (2007) *Aby Warburg and the Image in Motion*, trans. Sophie Hawkes (Cambridge, MA: The MIT Press).

Mindell, David A. (2002) *Between Human and Machine. Feedback, Control, and Computing before Cybernetics* (Baltimore, MD, and London: Johns Hopkins University Press).

Miyazaki, Shintaro (2011, forthcoming) 'AlgoRHYTHMS Everywhere – A Heuristic Approach to Everyday Technologies' in *Pluralizing Rhythm: Music, Arts, Politics*, ed. Jan Hein Hoogstad and Birgitte Stougaard (Amsterdam and New York: Rodopi).

Montfort, Nick and Bogost, Ian (2009) *Racing The Beam. The Atari Video Computer System* (Cambridge, MA: The MIT Press).

Mulvey, Laura (1975) 'Visual Pleasure and Narrative Cinema' *Screen* 16(3): 6–18.

Musser, Charles (2006a) 'A Cinema of Contemplation, A Cinema of Discernment: Spectatorship, Intertextuality and Attractions in the 1890s' in *The Cinema of Attractions Reloaded*, ed. Wanda Strauven (Amsterdam: Amsterdam University Press), 159–79.

Musser, Charles (2006b) 'Rethinking Early Cinema: Cinema of Attractions and Narrativity' in *The Cinema of Attractions Reloaded*, ed. Wanda Strauven (Amsterdam: Amsterdam University Press), 389–416.

Nadarajan, Gunalan (2007) 'Islamic Automation: A Reading of al-Jazari's *The Book of Knowledge of Ingenious Mechanical Devices* (1206)' in *MediaArtHistories*, ed. Oliver Grau (Cambridge, MA: The MIT Press), 163–78.

Nollet, Jean Antoine (1749) *Recherches sur les causes particulières des phénomènes électriques* (Paris : Chez les frères Guérin).

Nyquist, Harry (1924) 'Certain Factors Affecting Telegraph Speed' *Bell Systems Technical Journal* 3 (July), 324–46.

Otis, Laura (2001) *Networking: Communicating With Bodies and Machines in the Nineteenth Century* (Ann Arbor: University of Michigan Press).

Parikka, Jussi (2007) *Digital Contagions. A Media Archaeology of Computer Viruses* (New York: Peter Lang).

Parikka, Jussi (2010) *Insect Media. An Archaeology of Animals and Technology* (Minneapolis: University of Minnesota Press).

Parikka, Jussi (2011a) 'Media Ecologies and Imaginary Media: Transversal Expansions, Contractions and Foldings' *Fibreculture* 17, http://seventeen.fibreculturejournal.org/, accessed 27 Nov. 2011.

Parikka, Jussi (2011b) 'Operative Media Archaeology: Wolfgang Ernst's Materialist Media Diagrammatics' *Theory, Culture & Society* 28(5), 52–74.

Parikka, Jussi and Hertz, Garnet (2010) 'Archaeologies of Media Art. Ctheory Interview with Jussi Parikka' *CTheory* (April), www.ctheory.net.

Parikka, Jussi and Suominen, Jaakko (2006) 'Victorian Snakes? Towards a Cultural History of Mobile Games and the Experience of Movement' *Game Studies* 6 (December), http://gamestudies.org/0601/articles/parikka_suominen, accessed 27 Nov. 2011.

Paul, Christiane (2009) 'Context and Archive: Presenting and Preserving Net Art' in *Net Pioneers 1.0*, ed. Dieter Daniels and Gunter Reisinger (Berlin: Sternberg Press), 101–20.

Peters, John Durham (1999) *Speaking Into the Air. A History of the Idea of Communication* (Chicago and London: University of Chicago Press).

Pias, Claus (2002) *Computer Spiel Welten* (Munich: Diaphanes).

Pias, Claus (2011) 'The Game Player's Duty: The User as the Gestalt of the Ports' in *Media Archaeology. Approaches, Applications, Implications*, ed. Erkki Huhtamo and Jussi Parikka (Berkeley, CA: University of California Press), 164–83.

Prel, Carl du (1889) *The Philosophy of Mysticism*, Vol I, trans. C. C. Massey (London: George Redway).

Prel, Carl du (1899) *Die Magie als Naturwissenschaft. Erster Teil* (Jena: Kostenoble).

Protevi, John (2009) *Political Affect: Connecting the Social and the Somatic* (Minneapolis: University of Minnesota Press).

Rabinovitz, Lauren (2004) 'More than the Movies. A History of the Somatic Visual Culture through Hale's Tours, Imax and Motion Simulation Rides' in *Memory Bytes*, ed. Lauren Rabinovitz and Abraham Geil (Durham: Duke University Press), 99–125.

Rabinovitz, Lauren and Geil, Abraham, eds. (2004) *Memory Bytes. History, Technology, and Digital Culture* (Durham: Duke University Press).

Reichardt, Jasia (1971) *The Computer in Art* (London: Studio Vista).

Reisinger, Gunther (2009) 'Digital Source Criticism: Net Art as a Methodological Case Study' in *Net Pioneers 1.0*, ed. Dieter Daniels and Gunter Reisinger (Berlin: Sternberg Press), 123–44.

Riskin, Jennifer (2003) 'The Defecating Duck, Or, The Ambigious Origins of Artificial Life' *Critical Inquiry* 20(4) (Summer), 599–633.

Roch, Axel (2010) *Claude E. Shannon: Spielzeug, Leben und die geheime Geschichte seiner Theorie der Information* (Berlin: gegenstalt).

Ross, Seamus and Gow, Ann (1999) *Digital Archaeology: Rescuing Neglected and Damaged Data Resources*, a JISC/NPO Study within the Electronic Libraries (eLib) Programme on the Preservation of Electronic Materials, February, www.ukoln.ac.uk/services/elib/, accessed 27 Nov. 2011.

Røssaak, Eivind, ed. (2010a) *The Archive in Motion. New Conceptions of the Archive in Contemporary Thought and New Media Practices* (Oslo: Novus Press).

Røssaak, Eivind (2010b) 'The Archive in Motion: An Introduction' in *The Archive in Motion*, ed. Eivind Røssaak (Oslo: Novus Press), 11–26.

Roussel, Raymond (2008 [1914]) *Locus Solus*, trans. Rupert Copeland Cunningham (Surrey: Oneworld Classics).

Schivelbusch, Wolfgang (1986) *The Railway Journey. The Industrialisation of Time and Space in the 19th Century*, 2nd edn (Berkeley, CA: University of California Press).

Schmidgen, Henning (2002) 'Of Frogs and Men: The Origins of Psychophysiological Time Experiments, 1850–1865' *Endeavour* 26(4), 142–8.

Schreber, Daniel-Paul (1903/55) *Memoirs of My Nervous Illness*, trans. Ida Macalpine and Richard A. Hunter (London: W. M. Dawson & Sons).

Schrenck-Notzing, Baron von (1923) *Phenomena of Materialisation. A Contribution to the Investigation of Mediumistic Teleplastics*, trans. E. E. Fournier D'Albe (London: Kegan Paul).

Sconce, Jeffrey (2000) *Haunted Media. Electronic Presence from Telegraphy to Television* (Durham and London: Duke University Press).

Sconce, Jeffrey (2011) 'On the Origins of the Origins of the Influencing Machine' in *Media Archaeology. Approaches, Applications, Implications*, ed. Erkki Huhtamo and Jussi Parikka (Berkeley, CA: University of California Press), 70–94.

Serres, Michel (2007 [1982]) *The Parasite*, trans. Lawrence R. Schehr (Minneapolis: University of Minnesota Press).

Serres, Michel and Latour, Bruno (1995) *Conversations on Science, Culture, and Time*, trans. Roxanne Lapidus (Ann Arbor: University of Michigan Press).

Shannon, Claude E. and Weaver, Warren (1949) *The Mathematical Theory of Communication* (Urbana, IL: University of Illinois Press).

Shaviro, Steven (1998) 'Future Past: *Zoe Beloff's* Beyond', *ARTBYTE*, 1(3).

Siegert, Bernhard (1999) *Relays. Literature as an Epoch of the Postal System*, trans. Kevin Repp (Stanford, CA: Stanford University Press).

Siegert, Bernhard (2003) *Passage des Digitalen. Zeichenpraktiken der neuzeitlichen Wissenschaften 1500 –1900* (Berlin: Brinkmann & Bose).

Siegert, Bernhard (2008) 'Cacography or Communication? Cultural Techniques in German Media Studies', trans. Geoffrey Winthrop-Young *Grey Room* 29 (Winter), 26–47.

Sly, A. J. (1976) *A Short History of Computing*, 2nd edn (St Albans: The Advisory Unit for Computer Based Education).

Spieker, Sven (2008) *The Big Archive: Art from Bureaucracy* (Cambridge, MA: The MIT Press).

Stafford, Barbara Maria and Terpak, Frances (2001) *Devices of Wonder. From the World in a Box to Images on a Screen* (Los Angeles: Getty Research Institute Publications).

Standage, Tom (1999) *The Victorian Internet* (London: Phoenix).

Sterling, Bruce (1994) *The Hacker Crackdown: Law and Disorder on the Electronic Frontier* (London: Penguin Books).

Sternberger, Dolf (1977) *Panorama of the 19th Century*, trans. Joachim Neugroschel (New York: Mole Editions).

Sterne, Jonathan (2003) *The Audible Past: Cultural Origins of Sound Reproduction* (Durham: Duke University Press).

Sterne, Jonathan (2009) 'The Times of Communication History'. Presented at 'Connections: The Future of Media Studies', University of Virginia, 4 April.

Stiegler, Bernard (2010) *For a New Critique of Political Economy*, trans. Daniel Ross (Cambridge: Polity).

Story, Alfred T. (1904) *The Story of Wireless Telegraphy* (London: George Newnes, Ltd).

Strauven, Wanda (2006) 'Introduction to an Attractive Concept' in *The Cinema of Attractions Reloaded*, ed. Wanda Strauven (Amsterdam: Amsterdam University Press, 2008), 11–27.

Strauven, Wanda, ed. (2008) *The Cinema of Attractions Reloaded* (Amsterdam: Amsterdam University Press).

Strauven, Wanda (2009) 'Futurist Images For Your Ear: Or, How to Listen to Visual Poetry, Painting, and Silent Cinema' *New Review of Film and Television Studies* 7(3) (September), 275–92.

Strauven, Wanda (2011) 'The Observer's Dilemma. To Touch or Not to Touch' in *Media Archaeology. Approaches, Applications, Implications*, ed. Erkki Huhtamo and Jussi Parikka (Berkeley, CA: University of California Press), 148–63.

Strauven, Wanda (2012, forthcoming) 'Media Archaeology: Where Film History, Media Art and New Media (Can) Meet' in *Preserving and Exhibiting Media Art: Challenges and Perspectives*, ed. Julia Noordegraaf, Cosetta Saba, Barbara Le Maître and Vinzenz Hediger (Amsterdam: Amsterdam University Press).

Suominen, Jaakko (2008) 'The Past as the Future? Nostalgia and Retrogaming in Digital Culture' *Fibreculture* 11, http://journal.fibreculture.org/issue11/issue11_suominen.html.

Sutherland, Ivan (1965) 'The Ultimate Display' *Proceedings of IFIP Congress*, 506–8.

Sutherland, Ivan (1968) 'A Head-Mounted Three Dimensional Display' *AFIPS '68 (Fall, Part I): Proceedings of the December 9–11, 1968, Fall Joint Computer Conference, Part I*, 757–64.

Swade, Doron (1998) 'Preserving Software in an Object-Centred Culture' in *History and Electronic Artefacts*, ed. Edward Higgs (Oxford: Clarendon Press), 195–206.

Tarde, Gabriel (1890) *Les lois de l'imitation* (Paris: F. Alcan).

Terranova, Tiziana (2004) *Network Culture. Politics for the Information Age* (London: Pluto Press).

Tesla, Nikola (1961) *Tribute to Nikola Tesla. Presented in Articles, Letters, Documents* (Beograd: Nikola Tesla Museum).

Thibodeau, Kenneth (2002) 'Overview of Technological Approaches to Digital Preservation and Challenges in Coming Years' in *The State of*

Digital Preservation: An International Perspective. Conference Proceedings, Council on Library and Information Resources 107, www.clir.org/pubs/reports/pub107/thibodeau.html, accessed 27 Nov. 2011.

Thompson, Emily (2004) *The Soundscape of Modernity. Architectural Acoustics and the Culture of Listening in America, 1900–1933* (Cambridge, MA: The MIT Press).

Tomas, David (2004) *Beyond the Image Machine. A History of Visual Technologies* (London: Continuum).

Tuller, W. G. (1952) 'Use of Computing Machinery in Applications of Information Theory' in *Proceedings of the 1952 ACM National Meeting (Pittsburgh)* (New York: ACM Press), 111–12.

Turner, Fred (2010) 'The Pygmy Camelan as Technology of Consciousness' in Paul DeMarinis, *Buried in Noise* (Heidelberg and Berlin: Kehrer), 23–7.

Uricchio, William (2004) 'Historicizing Media in Transition' in *Rethinking Media Change: The Aesthetics of Transition*, ed. David Thorburn and Henry Jenkins (Cambridge, MA: The MIT Press), 23–38.

Uricchio, William (2009a) 'The Future of a Medium Once Known as Television' in *The Youtube Reader*, ed. Pelle Snickars and Patrick Vonderau (Stockholm: National Library of Sweden), 24–39.

Uricchio, William (2009b) 'Moving Beyond the Artefact: Lessons from Participatory Culture' in *Digital Material. Tracing New Media in Everyday Life and Technology*, ed. Marianne van den Boomen, Sybille Lammes and Ann-Sophie Lehmann (Amsterdam: Amsterdam University Press), 135–46.

Väliaho, Pasi (2010) *Mapping the Moving Image. Gesture, Thought and Cinema Circa 1900* (Amsterdam: Amsterdam University Press).

Virilio, Paul (2004) 'The Museum of Accidents' in *The Paul Virilio Reader*, ed. Steve Redhead (New York: Columbia University Press), 255–62.

Vismann, Cornelia (2008) *Files. Law and Media Technology*, trans. Geoffrey Winthrop-Young (Stanford, CA: Stanford University Press).

Volmar, Axel, ed. (2009) *Zeitkritische Medien* (Berlin: Kadmos).

Volmar, Axel (2010) 'Listening to the Body Electric. Electrophysiology and the Telephone in the Late 19th Century' *The Virtual Laboratory*, online essay at http://vlp.mpiwg-berlin.mpg.de/references?id=art76, accessed 27 Nov. 2011.

Wardrip-Fruin, Noah (2009) *Expressive Processing. Digital Fictions, Computer Games, and Software Studies* (Cambridge, MA: The MIT Press).

Wardrip-Fruin, Noah (2011) 'Digital Media Archaeology: Interpreting Computational Processes' in *Media Archaeology. Approaches, Applications, Implications*, ed. Erkki Huhtamo and Jussi Parikka (Berkeley, CA: University of California Press), 302–22.

Weaver, Warren (1949) 'Recent Contributions to the Mathematical Theory of Communication' in Claude E. Shannon and Warren Weaver, *Mathematical Theory of Communication* (Urbana, IL: University of Illinois Press), 94–117.

Wiener, Norbert (1948) *Cybernetics, or Control and Communication in the Animal and the Machine* (Cambridge, MA: The MIT Press).

Williams, Raymond (2003 [1974]) *Television. Technology and Cultural Form* (London and New York: Routledge Classics).

Wilson, Elizabeth A. (2004) *Psychosomatic: Feminism and the Neurological Body* (Durham and London: Duke University Press).

Winston, Brian (1998) *Media Technology and Society: A History from the Telegraph to the Internet* (London: Routledge).

Winthrop-Young, Geoffrey (2000) 'Silicon Sociology, or, Two Kings on Hegel's Throne? Kittler, Luhmann, and the Posthuman Merger of German Media Theory' *Yale Journal of Criticism* 13(2), 391–420.

Winthrop-Young, Geoffrey (2002) 'Drill and Distraction in the Yellow Submarine: On the Dominance of War in Friedrich Kittler's Media Theory' *Critical Inquiry* 28(4) (Summer), 825–54.

Winthrop-Young, Geoffrey (2005) *Friedrich Kittler zur Einführung* (Hamburg: Junius).

Winthrop-Young, Geoffrey (2006) 'Cultural Studies and German Media Theory', in *New Cultural Studies: Adventures in Theory,* ed. Gary Hall and Clare Birchall (Edinburgh: Edinburgh University Press).

Winthrop-Young, Geoffrey (2011) *Kittler and the Media* (Cambridge: Polity).

Winthrop-Young, Geoffrey and Wutz, Michael (1999) 'Translators' Introduction: Friedrich Kittler and Media Discourse Analysis' in Friedrich A. Kittler, *Gramophone, Film, Typewriter* (Stanford, CA: Stanford University Press), xi–xxxviii.

Zielinski, Siegfried (1999) *Audiovisions. Cinema and Television as Entr'actes in History*, trans. Gloria Custance (Amsterdam: Amsterdam University Press).

Zielinski, Siegfried (2006a) *Deep Time of the Media. Toward an Archaeology of Hearing and Seeing by Technical Means*, trans. Gloria Custance (Cambridge, MA: The MIT Press).

Zielinski, Siegfried (2006b) 'Modelling Media for Ignatius Loyola. A Case Study on Athanasius Kircher's World of Apparatus between the Imaginary and the Real' in *Book of Imaginary Media. Excavating the Dream of the Ultimate Communication Medium*, ed. Eric Kluitenberg (Amsterdam and Rotterdam: Debalie and NAi Publishers), 29–55.

Zielinski, Siegfried and Fürlus, Eckhard, eds. (2010) *Variantology 4. On Deep Time Relations of Arts, Sciences and Technologies in the Arabic-Islamic World and Beyond* (Cologne: Walther König).

Zittrain, Jonathan (2008) *The Future of the Internet. And How to Stop It* (London: Penguin Books).

Žižek, Slavoj (1992) *Looking Awry. An Introduction to Jacques Lacan through Popular Culture* (Cambridge, MA: The MIT Press).

Index

Note: Page numbers in italics indicate illustrations.

3-D, 10, 53, 169 n.3, 173 n.10
8-bit, 3, 139

A Parallel Image (Sengmüller),
    41–2, 140
abandonware, 3
Adams, Henry, 44, 59, 63
affect, 3, 16, 20, 23, 25, 28, 29–34, 37,
    39, 53, 71, 73, 91, 122, 144, 163–4,
    170 n.7, 175 n.3
Alberti, Leon Battista, 71
Alberts, Gerard, 94
Aldini, Giovanni, 56
Algorhythmics, *see* Institute for
    Algorhythmics
aliens (extraterrestials), 55–6, 61,
    109
Alt, Casey, 38
alternative histories, 7, 12–14, 43,
    139, 144, 157, 167
American Society for Psychical
    Research, the, 58
an-archaeology of media (Zielinski),
    49
Angliss, Sarah, 12, 137, 140
anthropology, 7, 21, 30, 170 n.8
Arcangel, Cory, 141
Archaeological Media Lab, 169 n.8
archaeology of knowledge, 6, 13,
    47–8, 130, 132
archive, 5–6, 9, 15–17, 20–1, 33, 44,
    47–8, 52, 65, 83, 87–8, 95, 101,

109–12, 113–34, 140, 145, 152,
    159–60, 162, 166, 167, 169 n.8,
    169 n.4, 174 n.2, 176 n.4, 177 n.5,
    177 n.6, 177 n.8, 178 n.9
    Internet, 120
    operational, 129–33
    peer-to-peer (P2P), 121
Ars Electronic festival, 116, 137
Art of the Overhead Projector, 12,
    139
Atari VCS, 87
attention, 7, 32–3, 37
    economy, 24
attractions (Gunning), 9, 23, 25, 33,
    35, 38

Babbage, Charles, 37, 43
Badiou, Alan, 84
Baird, John Logie, 42
Bal, Mieke, 15
Barad, Karen, 84
Bann, Stephen, 82
Baudrillard, Jean, 84
Baudry, Jean-Louis, 9, 27
Bell Labs, 96–7
Beloff, Zoe, 12, 28, 52–5, 61, 62, 107,
    137, 139, 141, 144, 157, 173 n.10,
    178 n.5
Benjamin, Walter, 5–7, 20, 21, 24,
    51–2, 76, 83, 90–1, 153–4, 166,
    170 n.7, 172 n.7, 173 n.12, 175
    n.1

Bentham, Jeremy, 27
Berardi, Franco 'Bifo', 73
Berlin, 49, 53, 66–7, 75, 86, 112, 130,
    133, 136, 137, 140, 141, 151, 160,
    169 n.9
Berners-Lee, Sir Tim, 128
Beyond (Beloff), 52–3
biopolitics, 22, 31, 73, 117, 144
Birds (film), 57–8
Birmingham School of Cultural
    Studies, 75, 85
Blegvad, Peter, 49
Boast, Robin, 129, 176 n.2 and n.3
Boddy, William, 11
body, the, 13, 22, 24–35, 51, 53–7, 61,
    63–4, 70–8, 84, 92–3, 96, 99, 163,
    170 n.7, 170 n.10, 170 n.11, 175
    n.3
Bogost, Ian, *see* Platform Studies
Bolter, Jay David, *see* remediation
Bolzmann, Ludwig, 97, 99–100
Bosma, Josephine, 165
Braidotti, Rosi, 84, 161
brain, the, 23, 58, 59, 60, 69, 73, 74
Braudel, Fernand, 90, 145–6, 164
Burch, Noël, 13
Burckhardt, Jacob, 8
Bush, Vannevar, 119

Cage, John, 93, 109
camera obscura, 9, 32, 170 n.8
capitalism, 2, 7, 13, 24–5, 32, 37, 51,
    90, 107, 115, 147
    cognitive, 59, 73, 133
cartography, 15, 37, 109, 112,
    161–2
cathode ray tube, 58, 130, 133
Centre for Cultural Techniques
    (Humboldt University Berlin),
    75
Ceram, C. W., 8
Chappe, Claude, 104
Charming Augustine (Beloff), 53
Chun, Wendy Hui Kyong, 17, 86,
    119, 121, 123, 130, 162, 174 n.1
cinema, 7–10, 13, 19–39, 47, 52–3,
    64–5, 68–9, 71–5, 136, 139, 154,

169 n.3, 169 n.4, 170 n.7, 170
    n.11, 172 n.5, 173 n.12, 176 n.4,
    178 n.5
circuit bending, 2, 3, 14, 83, 140,
    147–9
Clausius, Rudolf, 100
Clock of the Long Now (Brand), 165
cloud computing, 134, 151, 160, 166
Codecs, 36, 80–1, 116
Collapse of PAL, The, see Menkman
Comolli, Jean-Louis, 9, 35
computer games, *see* games
computer viruses, *see* software,
    malicious
Conceiving Ada (Hershman
    Leeson), 138
Concept lab, 14, 169 n. 8
conditions of existence, 6, 18, 99,
    157, 166
Coney Island, 25
Cook, Sarah, 122–3
Cosic, Vuk, 139
counter-history, *see* genealogy
Crary, Jonathan, 7, 31–3, 34, 37–8,
    74, 76
Crookes, William, 58
cryptography, 96, 100, 102, 104, 175
    n.7, 197 n.11
Cubitt, Sean, 36, 161, 179 n.8
cultural memory, *see* memory
cultural techniques, 35, 75, 111, 174
    n.3
Curtius, Ernst Robert, 11
cybernetics, 98, 101, 109, 111, 156,
cyberwar, *see* war

Daguerreotype, 9, 44
database, 36, 52, 83, 114, 115, 159
Dead Media, 3, 15, 91, 140, 146,
    147–50, 153, 165
    Dead Media Lab, *see* Hertz
Debord, Guy, 31
DeCerteau, Michel, 27
Delanda, Manuel, 84, 164
Deleuze, Gilles, 32, 48, 73, 84, 85, 86,
    132, 161–2
Della Porta, Giambattista, 49, 52

DeMarinis, Paul, 8, 12, 41, 49, 92–3, 120, 136, 139–44, 148, 151, 154–5, 157, 162, 169 n.3,

Derrida, Jacques, 66, 133

descent (Foucault), 6, 22, 36, 80–1, 83, 89

Deutsch, Gustav, 21, 140, 176 n.4

Difference Engine (machine), 37, 43, 117

Difference Engine, The (novel), 1, 139

digital humanities, 15, 88, 115, 126, 127, 134

Diorama, 10, 27

discourse network (Kittler), 34, 57, 61, 68–74, 76, 78, 79, 81, 88, 111

DIY-culture, 1–2, 15, 147, 148

DJ Spooky (Paul D. Miller), 145

Donkey Kong, 3

Douglas, Susan J., 11

Druckrey, Timothy, 162, 166

Duchamp, Marcel, 109, 145, 148, 150, 159

Early Media Goes to Movies (DeMarinis), 169 n.3

Edison, Thomas-Alva, 24, 37, 49, 56, 140, 157, 170 n.11, 171 n.3

Edison Effect, The (DeMarinis), 140

Edison Manufacturing Company, *see* Edison

Electric Voice Phenomena (EVP), 61

electricity, 11, 42, 44, 56, 58, 61, 154, 173 n.11, 174 n.2

electromagnetism, 15, 22, 44–5, 53, 58, 60–2, 105, 140, 151, 152

electronic waste (e-waste), 147–9, 160, 164, 166

Electrophone, the, 45

Elsaesser, Thomas, 6, 10, 134, 16, 19, 21–3, 32, 33, 35, 162, 164, 175 n.1

Embroidered Text Message (Ginger Anyhow), 147

Engelbart, Douglas, 76, 128, 174 n1.

epistemological perversions, *see* S/M-histories

Ernst, Wolfgang, 15, 17, 63, 67, 82–3, 86–8, 110–12, 113, 116, 120, 123–7, 130–3, 137, 162, 163–4, 176 n.1

on diagrammatics, 132–3

Errata Erratum, see DJ Spooky

Eva C (medium), *54*, 172 n.5

evil media studies (Fuller and Goffey), 175 n.2

Exploding Camera (Maire), 165

Facebook, *4*, 36, 63, 114, 115

factory system, the, 27, 65

Fahrenheit 451 (Truffaut), 121

Fechner, Gustav, 74

Film ist, see Deutsch

Film Studies, 2, 9, 15, 16, 19, 33, 39, 160

Fitz, Matthias, 140–1

floppy disks, 3, 126, 178 n.9

Fludd, Robert, 52

forensics, (computer), 68, 86, 88, 126–9, 154, 162

Foucault, Michel, 5–6, 10, 13, 17, 18, 22, 27, 32, 34, 45, 47–8, 66, 68, 70, 73, 81, 83, 85–7, 89, 113, 132

Fourier, Joseph, 34–5, 99, 125

Fox-Talbot, Henry, 36

Frankfurt School, the, 66–7

Freud, Sigmund, 72, 74, 175 n.1

Friedberg, Anne, 6–7, 19, 25–8

Fujihata, Masaki, 12, 165

Gabrys, Jennifer, 165–7

Gadamer, Hans-Georg, 78

Galloway, Alexander, 79, 123, 156, 169 n.1

Galvani, Luigi, 56

games, 1, 3, 20, 24, 28, 35, 38, 76–7, 122, 141, 143, 145

Gansing, Kristoffer and Hilfling, Linda 12, 139

Gastev, Aleksej, 52

Gates, Bill, 91, 155

Gaudreault, André, 23, 28

gay science, media archaeology as, 161, 174 n.2
gender, 7, 9, 22, 26, 52, 53–5, 107, 139, 144, 158, 161, 163
genealogy, 6, 13, 16, 22–3, 28, 34, 35, 36, 38, 55, 68, 73, 78, 81, 83, 91, 110, 130, 162, 168 n.6
German media theory, 15–16, 63, 66, 73, 77, 78, 82, 87, 163, 174 n.2
Giedion, Siegfried, 6, 7–8, 52
Gilbreth, Frank, 76
Gitelman, Lisa, 163
Godard, Jean-Luc, 21, 169 n.3
Gödel, Kurt, 97
Google, 115, 119
Gould, Stephen Jay, 51
gramophone, *see* sound recording
Grosz, Elizabeth, 84
Grusin, Richard, 30, 137, 157, 170 n.7
Guins, Raiford, 86–7
Gunning, Tom, 6, 9, 11, 19, 24, 34, 38
gut, the, 25–6, 33
Gutenberg, 64, 71

hackers, hacking, 1, 2, 83, 103, 106, 139, 140, 148
Hansen, Mark, 115
Hansen, Mark B. N., 30
Haraway, Donna, 84
hard drives, 88, 119, 126, 133, 134, 151, 178 n.9
hardware 1, 15, 36, 38, 63–6, 70, 76, 80–1, 85, 87–9, 117, 119, 127, 129–33, 140, 150, 169 n.4, 176 n.3, 177 n.8, 179 n.11
    hacking, 2, 83, 140, 148–9, 152
Hayles, Katherine N., 101
Helmholtz, Hermann von, 32, 74–5, 93, 99, 175 n.3
Henning, Michelle, 118
Hertz, Garnet, 12, 137, 146–9, 157, 166, 178 n.5
Hilbert, David, 97
Hoberman, Perry, 137
Horologium Sapientiae (Suso), 49
Howell, Brendan, 12, 137
Howse, Martin, 12, 84, 137, 151

Huhtamo, Erkki, 6, 11–12, 25, 28, 55, 67, 91, 113, 134, 136–7, 141, 157, 162, 164, 169 n.4, 170 n.6, 178 n.5
Human–Computer Interfacing (HCI), *see* interface
Humboldt-University, *see* Berlin
hysteresis, 178 n. 9

I Love You (exhibition), 110–11
The Ideoplastic Materializations of Eva C, The (Beloff), *see* Eva C
imaginary media, 16–17, 39, 41–62, 63, 86, 109, 137, 139, 149, 171 n.3
immersion, 11, 13, 24, 28
Influencing Machine, The, 53, 56, 60
The Influencing Machine of Miss Natalija A., 53
Innis, Harold, 68
inscription, 22, 57, 68, 69, 73, 88, 94, 115, 118, 126–8, 132, 134, 151, 157
Institute for Algorhythmics, 83, 140, 151, 169 n.9
interface 20, 28, 30, 38, 39, 45, 76, 80–2, 85, 86, 125, 169 n.1, 174 n.1, 174 n.2
Irigaray, Luce, 27
ISEA festival, 137

James, Henry, 176 n.8
James, William, 74
Jefferson, Thomas, 121
Jesuits, 49, 51, 71
Jodi, 111
Johnston, John, 100
Jünger, Ernst, 76

Kahle, Brewster, 120
Kahn, Douglas, 94, 111–12, 144, 149
Kapp, Ernst, 60, 170 n.8
Kasprzak, Michelle, 116
Kay, Alan, 38, 76
kinaesthesia, 28, 30, 33, 170 n.11
Kircher, Athanasius, 49, 51, 52
Kirschenbaum, Matthew G., 17, 85–8, 126–8, 162, 178 n.9

Kittler, Friedrich, 6–8, 15, 17, 27, 34–8, 55, 56–7, 60–1, 63, 66–89, 93, 95–6, 111–12, 126, 150, 152, 162–4, 170 n.9, 171 n. 3, 174 n. 3, 179 n.11
Kluitenberg, Eric, 45–9, 61
Koch, Robert, 21
Kolkowski, Aleksander, 12, 137, 157
Koss, Mildred, 130
Kracauer, Siegfried, 24, 170 n.7

Lacan, Jacques, 26, 45–7, 53, 57, 62, 66, 72, 85
Laclos, Pierre Choderlos de, 103
Laokoon (Lessing), 82
Larcher, David, 136
Latour, Bruno, 84, 164
Lazzarato, Maurizio, 73, 145
Le vingtième siècle (Robida), *50*
Leblanc, Maurice, 41
Leroi-Gourhan, André, 30
Lichty, Patrick, 128
Licklider, J. C. R., 76
Lifewriter, The (Mignonneau and Sommerer), 145, 165
Lightning Flashes and Electric Dashes, 108
Link, David, 12, 137, *138*, 140, 157
Listening Post, The, 115–17
Locus Solus (Roussel), 61, 171 n.3
Lovink, Geert, 156, 179 n.7
LSD, 71
Lubell, Bernie, 12, 137, 139, 151, 157
Lumière brothers, 25

Mackay, Donald, 101
Mackenzie, Adrian, 84
magic lantern, 9, 28, 130
magnetic tape, 3, 126, 127, 178 n.9
Maire, Julien, 12, 140, 141, 145, 165
Manning, Erin, 84
Mannoni, Laurent, 6, 9
Manovich, Lev, 6, 8, 36, 83, 114, 126
Marey, Étienne-Jules, 30, 169 n.3
Marx, Karl, 37, 104
Massumi, Brian, 84

materiality, 3, 13, 16, 34, 43, 47, 55, 63, 66, 72, 75, 76, 79, 81, 84–8, 111, 123, 126–7, 131, 134, 150, 155, 163–4, 176n3, 176n4
Mathematical Theory of Communication, the (Shannon and Weaver), 69, 95, *96*, 98, 100–1
mathematics, 23, 34–7, 51, 62, 67, 71, 74, 77–84, 95–100, 123, 125, 131
McLuhan, Marshall, 6, 20, 59, 64, 68, 69, 74, 152, 169 n.1, 170 n.8, 174 n. 3
Media Archaeological Fundus (Humboldt University, Berlin), *65*, 130, *131*, 134, 169 n.8
Media Arts, 2, 5, 14, 15, 30, 61, 66, 83, 116, 121, 123–4, 136–58, 164, 168 n.5, 177 n.5, 177 n.6
    history, 14, 123, 136
media education, 156–7
Mediashed (Southend-on-Sea), 149
medium-specificity, 54, 63, 73, 84–9, 94, 99, 115, 122–3, 128
memory, 2, 5, 7, 15, 17, 19, 68, 73, 80, 81, 87–8, 92, 110, 111, 115–17, 119–22, 125, 134, 145, 147, 148, 160, 177 n.6, 178 n.9
Menkman, Rosa, 12, 112, 137, 140, 151–3
Mesmer, Franz Anton, 60
Messenger, The (DeMarinis), 41, 139
Metz, Christian, 9
Metzger, Gustav, 111
microresearch lab, 61, 84, 140
military, *see* war
Miyazaki, Shintaro, 12, 137
mobility, 26–8, 159, 168 n.6
Modified Toy Orchestra, The, 3
Moholy-Nagy, László, 8, 94
money, 37, 84
monstration, 23
Montfort, Nick (*see also* Platform Studies), 87, 126
Morel's Panorama (Fujihata), 165
Morse, Samuel, 104
Münsterberg, Hugo, 73–5

museums, 7, 91, 110–11, 115, 116–19, 128, 129, 130, 133, 159–60, 166, 176 n. 2, 177 n.5
Music Room, The (DeMarinis), 143
mutoscope, 9, 28, 170 n.6

Nechvatal, Joseph, 111
Nelson, Theodor, 128
nerves, 23, 56–7, 60, 74–5, 175 n.3
neuromarketing, 32
new cultural history, 13, 19
New Film History, 5, 9–10, 16, 19–20, 23, 29, 43, 38, 39, 164, 169n4
new materialism (*see also* materiality), 39, 60, 63–89
new media studies, 84–8
New Urania (Berlin), 171 n.3
Nietzsche, Friedrich, 22, 72, 161, 174 n.2
Nipkow disc, the, 42
Nollet, Jean-Antoine, 56, 173 n.11

obsolescence, 1, 3, 117, 118, 139, 141, 145–50, 153, 157, 159, 160, 166–7
Oram, Daphne, 157
oscilloscope, 49, 130

Pac Man, 3
Paik, Nam June, 123, 136
PAL (Phase Alternating Line) signal, 152–3
Panofsky, Erwin, 8, 21
panorama, 7, 9, 10, 27, 165, 169 n.3, 169 n.5
Parisi, Luciana, 84
Paul, Christiane, 124
Paul, Robert W., 24
PDP 1 computer, 38
Peters, John Durham, 58, 61
Phantasmagoria (Robertson), 9, 59
phenakistoscope, 9, 28, 76
phonography, *see* sound recording
photography, 7, 9, 21, 36, 37, 57, 102, 117, 127, 134, 172 n.5, 173 n. 12, 178 n. 5
physiology, 30, 34, 74–5, 170 n.9
   neurophysiology, 57

political, 84
Pias, Claus, 17, 63, 76–7, 88, 174 n.1
pixel, 35–6, 41–2, 71, 80, 127, 139
planned obsolescence, *see* obsolescence
Platform Studies, 68, 86–7, 162
postal system, the, 78–9, 103
posthuman, 68, 70, 75, 77–9, 84, 85, 173 n.12
praxinoscope, 9, 130
pre-cinematic, *see* Cinema
Prel, Carl Du, 59–60, 173 n.12
Price, Katy, 157
processuality, 17, 82–3, 87, 116–17, 121, 128–9, 131, 133–4
Protevi, John, 84
protocols, 36, 70, 79, 86–7, 93, 110, 121, 123, 127–8, 140, 150–1, 154, 163
Psychopathia medialis, 12, 43, 51
psychotechnics, 34, 73–4
Pygmy Gamelan, The (DeMarinis), 143
Pynchon, Thomas, 69

quantification, 34–6, 82, 171 n. 14
Quicktime, 28, 52

radiosity, 36
raytracing, 36
Redundant Technology Initiative, 149
remediation, 3, 63, 80, 118, 120, 134, 136–7, 139, 140, 144, 158, 169 n.1, 177 n.5
remixing, 14, 15, 123, 134, 144–5, 150, 167
RFID, 20, 121, 159
Richards, Catherine, 12, 137
Riis, Morten, 137, 178 n.2
Riskin, Jennifer, 65
Ritter, Johann Wilhelm, 52
Robida, Albert, *50*
Roch, Axel, 96, 100
Rodchenko, Alexander, 8
Rome to Tripoli (DeMarinis), 142
Ronell, Avital, 11

Røssaak, Eivind, 120
Roussel, Raymond, 61, 171 n.3
Rube films, 24
Rubin, Ben, 115–16
Russolo, Luigi, 94, 109

S/M-histories, 14, 32
schizophrenia, 51, 55, 57, 69
Schmidgen, Henning, 75
Schreber, Daniel Paul, 56–7, 69–70
Schrenck-Notzing, Baron von, 172
    n.5
Science Museum, The (London), 43,
    116–17, 129, 140, 157, 159
Sconce, Jeffrey, 55–7, 107
security, 96, 99–101, 104–5, 175 n.6
semiconductor, 154–5
Sengmüller, Gehbhard, 12, 41–3, 61,
    140, 165
Serres, Michel, 101, 146–7, 175 n.5,
    179 n.6
Shannon, Claude, 68–9, 77–8,
    95–101, 110, 163
Shaw, G. B., 76
Shulgin, Alexei, 139
Siegert, Bernhard, 17, 63, 78–9, 88,
    160, 174 n.2
signal, 41–3, 56, 59, 61, 67, 69–70, 75,
    77, 88, 95–9, 101–2, 112, 131–2,
    150–4, 179 n.11
  ping, 102
Simondon, Gilbert, 30
Skadden, Elizabeth, 12
Slow Scan Television (Sengmüller),
    165
Smalltalk (Alan Kay), 38
Society for Psychical Research, the,
    58
software, 1, 2, 5, 15, 16, 17, 20, 65, 70,
    76–7, 79–81, 84–9, 111–12, 159,
    165, 176 n.3, 177 n.8
  and archival culture, 113–35
  and visual culture, 33–9, 86–7
  art, 111, 116, 122, 125, 140, 149,
    152, 156, 177 n.6
  malicious, 56, 91, 96, 107, 110–11
  studies, 17, 68, 87–8, 128, 132, 162

Sony Walkman, 3
sound, 3, 19–20, 24, 35–6, 57, 60,
    65, 67, 70, 72, 81, 86, 88, 92–4,
    109, 110–12, 116–17, 132, 137,
    139–40, 142–3, 151, 153, 155,
    157, 169 n.3, 171 n.3
sound recording, 22, 56–7, 59–60, 69,
    71, 83, 92–3, 111, 125, 130, 140,
    145, 174 n.2, 178 n.5
Spacewar! (game), 38
spectacle, 10, 11, 24, *26*, 31–5, 38, 56,
    170 n.7
spectator, 9, 10, 20, 24, 27, 31–3, 43,
    93
Spieker, Sven, 109–10, 140
Spigel, Lynn, 11
Standage, Tom, 37
standardization, 36–7, 39, 78–9, 102,
    143
Star Trek, 49
steam punk, 1–2, 44, 139, 168n2,
    178n2
stereoscope, 9, 10, *29*, 53, 130
Sterling, Brucem 3, 91, 139, 140,
    147
Stern, Daniel, 30
Sternberger, Dolf, 7–8
Sterne, Jonathan, 164
Stiegler, Bernard, 73
Story Teller, The (Jennings), 145–6
Strachey, Christopher, 140
Strauven, Wanda, 19–20, 164, 168
    n.5
Super-8, 3
Super Mario, see games
surveillance, 14, 36, *50*
Suso, Heinrich, 49
Sutherland, Ivan, 76
Swade, Doron, 117–18
synaesthesia, 28, 38

Tantalum Memorial (Harwood,
    Wright, Yokokoji), 154
Tarde, Gabriel, 171 n.3
Tausk, Victor, *see* Influencing
    Machine, The
Technics 1200 turntable, 3

technological determinism, 69, 72, 81, 174 n.3
technological obsolescence, *see* obsolescence
Telefon Hirmondo, 45
Telegraph, the, 11, 17, 37, 41, 44, 55, 58, 60, 63, 77, 96, 98–9, 102–10, 112, 154, 170 n.8, 175 n.6, 176 n.8
telephone, the 7, 11, 42, 45, 77, 96, 107, 109, 153, 154
Terranova, Tiziana, 73
Tesla, Nikola, 56, 171 n.3, 173 n.11
Tetris, 3
Thacker, Eugene, 156
Theatrophone, the, 45,
Ticchi, Cecilia, 11
time 3, 15, 21, 28, 42, 47, 49, 50–2, 60–1, 74–5, 79–83, 90, 91, 92, 101, 102, 111, 116–18, 120, 124, 129, 137, 138, 147–9, 151–2, 160, 164–7
    and degeneration, 119–20
    and dust, 166
    as pleated, 146–7
    cyclical, 11, 67, 91
    deep time (Zielinski), 12, 36, 43, 51, 147, 165
    machines, 49, 144–7, 178 n.5
    multirhythmic, 90–1, 145–6
    real-time, 28, 39, 49, 123
    non-linear, 10, 18, 45, 67, 83, 137, 146, 155, 164
    Queer, 165
    time-critical, 82–3, 88, 116–17, 124, 130–2, 134, 165
    time-based, 82, 111, 116, 118
    time and motion studies, 30–1, 75
Tomkins, Silvan, 30
transdisciplinary, 1, 10, 14, 18, 47, 134, 160–1
Transmediale festival, 41, 137, 140
travelling theory, 15, 160, 172 n.8
Turing, Alan M., 37, 77, 145, 175 n.7
Twain, Mark, 56

typewriter, 37, 45, 69–70, 72, 74, 77, 80, 114, 145

Uricchio, William, 121, 137

Valie Export, 136
valves, 130
    as transmedia, 154
Vasulka, Steina and Woody, 136
Vaucanson duck, 65
Vertov, Dziga, 8
Victorian culture, 1, 118, 177n5
Victorian Internet, the, 37, 107
VinylVideo (Sengmüller)
Virno, Paolo, 73
virtual reality, 11, 24, 27
Vismann, Cornelia, 17, 113–14
von Foerster, Heinz, 101
Von Neumann, John, 81, 119, 126
    computer architecture, 81

war, 76–7, 96, 104, 109, 100, 112, 165, 168n.6, 175 n.7, 180 n.15
Warburg, Aby, 6, 8
Wardrip-Fruin, Noah, 87, 128
Weaver, Warren, 95–8, 110, 163
Wedel, Michael, 19
Weibel, Peter, 136
Where Where There There Where (Beloff, 53)
Wiener, Norbert, 100–1
Wikipedia, 121
Williams, Linda, 170 n.6
Williams, Raymond, 46, 133,
Wilson, Elizabeth, 170 n.10
Windows, 26–7, 71
Windows 3.1 (OS), 139
Winthrop-Young, Geoffrey, 66–7, 85, 93, 96, 174 n.3
wireless, 36, 55, 83, 84, 105–6, 142, 151, 154
Wölfflin, Heinrich, 21
World War II, 2, 20, 37, 76, 77, 80, 94, 95–6, 100, 129, 152, 175 n.7, 177 n.8
Wundt, Wilhelm, 74
Wutz, Michael, 93

X-rays, 44, 60
Xerox Palo Alto labs, 76

Zielinski, Siegfried 6, 11–12, 27, 43, 49–54, 62, 91, 136–7, 147, 156–7, 162, 164–5, 172 n.8

Zittrain, Jonathan, 81
Žižek, Slavoj, 57–8, 60, 85
Zoetrope, 28
zombie, 3, 5, 60, 61
    media 3, 147–50